Cont

MW00627927

Forward

If you're very lucky in life, you find yourself working at a job that also happens to be fun for you. As a lover of North Carolina history, particularly that of the coastal part of the state, I have the best job in the world. I get to travel to historic sites and reenactments, spend time plundering through the treasure troves that most people call libraries, and tell stories about it for a living. Those stories first appeared in book form two years ago, in *The Coastal Chronicles Volume I* (Dram Tree Books, 0-9723240-0-3). The tales in it were all true and factually accurate, but written like a storyteller or fiction writer would. There was a reason for that.

When someone says they don't like history, nine times out of ten I've found that what they're really saying is that they don't like the dry names and dates they got out of their sixth grade history book. What I've tried to do in *Coastal Chronicles* is present those stories in a way that is historically accurate and at the same time entertaining, too. If you can put a human face on history, then you have something that people can relate to. To do that, the stories in *Coastal Chronicles* are written as a storyteller or fiction writer might tell them, while maintaining as best we can the accuracy of the facts we impart. Having said that, it should also be noted that I am not a professional historian - just an enthusiastic amateur who finds the stories of our past fascinating. I try very hard to insure the accuracy of our stories, but I'm certain that errors do sometimes occur. I apologize in advance to all those avid history fans who might read this book and find fault with specific points where I've erred.

In the meantime, here is the new collection of stories that make up *Coastal Chronicles*. I hope you find them entertaining as well as informative.

Jack E. Fryar, Jr.
August 10, 2004

Royal Governor Josiah Martin, whose intrigues led to the battle at Moores Creek.

An Ounce of Prevention

By Jack E. Fryar, Jr.

Richard Caswell slowly made his way across the one hundred yards of open ground separating his militia's position on a slight rise east of Moores Creek from the naked girders of the bridge spanning the black waters to the west. The ground in front of him was littered with the enemy's dead and dying. They were Highlanders from the Cross Creek and Bladen County areas of North Carolina who had taken up the King's banner in the civil war pitting American colonials against their British motherland, and neighbors who sided with England over the issue of independence.

In February of 1776, Highland Scots from the interior of the colony had received the blessings of the famed Flora McDonald at Cross Creek and begun a march to the sea at Wilmington where they would join with British army regulars to crush the budding rebellion in North Carolina. The large force of kilted Scots played a cat and mouse game with patriot militia over the ninety miles from the trading village on the northeast Cape Fear River, until reaching a small bridge spanning a murky creek on property belonging to the Widow Moore in what is today's Pender County. The loyalists were only thirty miles from their destination where the river meets the sea. Richard Caswell and Alexander Lillington lay in wait for the Highlander enemy, and in a fierce but brief battle, the militia routed the Scots and shattered England's plans to take North Carolina out of the fight. The patriots won the field at a cost of just one dead, but for the Highlanders who had departed Cross Creek weeks earlier in such high spirits, the death toll was much higher. The number of Scots wounded and taken prisoner was even higher still. England's ambitious plan for keeping North Carolina firmly in the Crown's orbit was swallowed by the sharp bark of the cannons known as "Old Mother Covington and her Daughter," and with it, any chance of local support from British sympathizers in the Cape Fear region. It would stay that way for the next four years.

Now Caswell surveyed the aftermath of the battle as his militia surged across the creek to give pursuit to the retreating Scots. He found it strange that a people who had a strong history of opposition to English rule in their own motherland would side with King George III and his representative, Governor Josiah Martin, over the issue of independence in America. He stopped and knelt by the body of a fallen Highlander, his tartan kilt sopping up blood from the gut wound a piece of grape shot had slashed across his abdomen, and was strangely saddened. Caswell wondered if there might have been a way to prevent what had happened that morning in the swirling dawn mists by the otherwise inconsequential creek. Remembering how the Highlanders had charged into the face of an overwhelming concentration of fire, Caswell couldn't help but admire their courage and be saddened that such fine soldiers had chosen to be foes in the growing struggle. Had there been a way to prevent the Battle of Moores Creek?

Perhaps there was.

Mostly large planters along the coast headed revolutionary efforts in North Carolina in 1776. There, wealthy men with vast holdings stood to gain the most from independence, as opposed to the Scots and men called Regulators further inland, who for the most part were small subsistence farmers. Bad feelings were especially prevalent between the Regulators and the coastal gentry, the latter having played a significant roll in putting down the Regulator revolt years earlier. Despite the bad blood, however, if local committees of safety in Wilmington and other coastal areas had been more vigilant in their control over British sympathizers, it is entirely possible that the Battle of Moores Creek could have been averted.

By late 1775, Royal Governor Josiah Martin was in such fear for his safety that he had withdrawn the seat of government from New Bern to the sloop-of-war *HMS Cruizer*, a British warship lying in the Cape Fear River. Local patriot leaders, through the Wilmington and Brunswick Committees of Safety, had been charged with maintaining a quarantine of the hapless governor. The object was to prevent Martin from fomenting opposition to Whig control over local government and engaging in military action against forces rebelling against the king. Apparently, the local committees of safety did a poor job of it, because Martin managed to maintain robust communications with parties in the interior of the colony loyal to King George. Samuel Johnston wrote that same year "The Committees below have been too remiss."

Johnston was right. Despite knowing that Martin had conceived a plan to raise loyal troops from among Tories in the inland precincts, and that local loyalists were facilitating this plan by carrying messages between Martin and North

Both Declaration of Independence signer William Hooper (left) and Major General Robert Howe (right) seved on Cape Fear committees of safety.
(photos courtesy Library of Congress)

Carolinians siding with the crown upriver, no serious steps were taken to eliminate the message traffic. As late as February 1776, just weeks before the fateful clash at Moores Creek, known loyalists were still being allowed virtually unchecked freedom of movement in Wilmington.

Why didn't the committees take stronger action? The signs were all there that Martin and backcountry loyalists were plotting to take action against the Whigs. In June of 1775, Highland leaders came through Wilmington on their way to Fort Johnston to petition the governor for arms and ammunition. In July of the same year, Cross Creek loyalist James Hepburn was brought before the Wilmington Committee of Safety after being charged with spreading a rumor that the British had hired 50,000 Russians to squash the still infant rebellion. Hepburn had visited Martin aboard his floating headquarters and was said, along with others, to have offered his services to the governor and asked permission to raise irregular forces from among his neighbors around Cross Creek. The committee was also concerned over information they had received that Hepburn had applied to the Cumberland County committee to raise a company of militia to be used against the Whigs from among his heavily loyalist neighbors. The Wilmington committee ended up drafting a resolution that labeled Hepburn "inimical to the liberties of his country and the common cause of America." A month after the resolution, Hepburn petitioned the committee to restore him to their good graces, but it seems to have been just a ploy, because Hepburn was one of the leaders of the loyalist uprising that led to the Battle of Moores Creek.

By the summer of 1775, the Wilmington and New Bern committees had managed to intercept a number of communiques between Martin, British General Thomas Gage in Boston, and loyalists residing up the Northeast Cape Fear River in the backcountry. As August came around, the committees knew for sure there was something afoot, writing in their minutes that "...we have learned from undoubted authority, that Governor Martin intends going into the backcountry, to collect a number of men, for the purpose of disturbing the internal peace of this province..."

Following the lead of the New Bern committee, Wilmington patriot leaders issued a decree forbidding communication with Martin without permission. But saying it didn't make it so. In late July of 1775, Samuel Johnston sent a message from Edenton to the Wilmington committee with a warning that British officers were heading south from New Bern. The plan was for the New Bern committee to take them into custody, but Johnston advised that if they should elude capture, that the Wilmington patriots should scoop them up. Johnston said in the message, "They pretend they are on a visit to some of their countrymen on your river but I think there is reason to suspect their errand of a base nature...I doubt not the prudence of the Gentlemen with you will have suggested the necessity of securing the Highlanders and that proper measures have been adopted for that purpose."

Apparently not. Despite the warnings, Major Donald MacDonald and Captain Donald McLeod went into the backcountry without ever setting foot in Wilmington and carried out their mission of raising loyalist troops. They remained there until the march to Wilmington began in February of 1776.

Martin's communications weren't only with Tories upriver. In Wilmington, the governor maintained contact with loyalists Alex McLean, Samuel Campbell, Robert Hogg, William McTier, and John Slingsby. McLean's part in the plan was to act as an intelligence source for the uprising, coordinating between the backcountry Highlanders and the British regulars that were supposed to be sent from Ireland. Samuel Campbell and his brother, William, along with Campbell's business partner Robert Hogg, surreptitiously provided supplies to the two British sloops-of-war *Cruizer* and *Scorpion*, which Martin had drafted into the role of seat of government. McTier carried messages to the governor.

Of all the Wilmington residents depended on by Martin, Alex McLean was the man he depended on most. McLean had arrived in the port city a year before the Battle of Moores Creek Bridge and married a local girl. McLean was a half-pay British officer, and when Martin fled New Bern in June to take up residence at Fort Johnston, McLean willingly assisted him. McLean was vocal in his denunciations of the local patriots, so much so that the Wilmington committee on one occasion gave him thirty days to recant some of his remarks or leave the province. Even that proved to be extraordinarily lenient, as other committees of safety issuing similar ultimatums only allowed twenty-four hours for the accused to recant. Elizabeth Catherine DeRossett, of one of Wilmington's most prominent loyalist families, took notice of McLean's outspoken attitudes in a letter to John Burgwin in England, writing that the vociferous officer spoke "such things as are disagreeable to the people" and that his friends wished he would leave. He did leave for a visit to the backcountry, but within months was once again in hot water with the local Whigs.

The governor's secretary, Archibald Nelson, and loyalist planter Alexander Schaw provided another example of how local Tories came and went as they pleased in the summer of 1775, traveling back and forth between Martin's offices on the *Cruizer* and coastal plantations owned by Tories and Whigs alike. Nominally cautious, the mere fact that they were welcome in the great houses of other coastal planters indicates they were getting aid in some form from other Cape Fear crown sympathizers. Aid came not just from loyalist residents, either. It seems that friendships in many cases carried more weight than political leanings with many locals. In one instance, loyalist Alex Schaw was ashore visiting his sister, Janet, prior to his departure for England with a report on the situation in the Cape Fear intended for Lord Dartmouth, the Colonial Secretary. Knowing of Schaw's plans, local rebels guarded the roads in hopes of capturing Schaw and preventing the report from being delivered. Despite their diligence, however, friends of Alex Schaw helped him avoid the patrols and return safely to the *Scorpion*, which immediately set sail for England.

On August 8, 1775, Governor Martin issued what came to be known as his "Fiery Declaration," in which he pretty much laid down the law to the rebels and warned of dire consequences for those who opposed King George's rule in the colony. Unfortunately for Archibald Nielson, local Whigs recognized the handwriting on the proclamation as being his, and "about a dozen of the greatest brutes" the rebels had went to John Rutherford's Point Pleasant plantation to take Nielson into custody. Rutherford, a friend of Nielson, was known to afford the governor's secretary with lodging on occasion as the sloop *Cruizer* was becoming full to the gunnels with loyalists seeking refuge from their rebellious neighbors. Unfortunately, the group got drunk on the way to Point Pleasant and lost their way, winding up at a neighboring plantation. Although this plantation owner sided with the rebels, he offered no help beyond a few more open bottles. It didn't take much more drink for the committeemen to become so drunk they were unable to continue their search, so they went home, asking the plantation owner to locate Nielson in the morning. Instead, the planter dispatched a rider to Point Pleasant with the warning that committeemen were looking for Nielson and would probably kill him if they managed to find him. Nielson beat a hasty retreat back to the ship.

But his narrow miss with the Wilmington Committee of Safety did little to curb Nielson's activities. Through friends ashore with whom he was in communication, Nielson was able to provide money to Janet Schaw and others to finance their trips back to England. Despite prohibitions from the committee to the contrary, Nielson's friends openly came aboard the *Cruizer* with enough gold and silver to fill Miss Schaw's dressing box.

Meanwhile another shipload of several hundred Highlanders was landed at the Cape Fear. Poor and bewildered at their new home, Martin took the opportunity to administer loyalty oaths to them before they could fall under the influence of the Whigs. Loans were made to them from the Tory Highlanders of the Cross Creek area, to solidify their obligation to the crown supporters. Once they were settled in the backcountry among their clansmen, the rebels would have little influence over them. Local Whigs knew this, yet no attempt was made to win over these newcomers.

All the while, Alex McLean was proving to be a thorn in the side of local Whigs, carrying communications between Martin and the Highlander leaders in the backcountry. He proved to be Governor Martin's best envoy, despite the suspicions he was under by the Wilmington Committee of Safety. It is inconceivable that the local patriots did nothing to curb his efforts, yet that remained the case. By January of 1776, McLean had been in the backcountry so long that Martin became worried that something had happened to his courier. He recruited a new man to the job from among some Brunswick County residents who claimed to be tired of the overbearing attitudes of the rebels in power. It turns out the man he recruited was a plant sent by the Whigs to infiltrate Martin's operations. Afraid that the Whigs now knew the names of his agents in the backcountry, Martin was forced to issue the call to arms before the arrival of the regular army troops enroute from Ireland.

There were numerous instances in 1775 and 1776 when due diligence on the part of the Wilmington Committee of Safety might have prevented the bloodshed that occurred at Moores Creek. Had the committee enforced its restrictions on communication with Governor Martin aboard the *Cruizer*, carrying out the plan to raise loyalist troops in the backcountry might have met with little if any success. If penalties had been enforced against local merchants and others who provided material support to the Tories, perhaps others would have been less inclined to offer a helping hand. If, following the New Bern example, local Tories had been disarmed in 1775, there certainly would have been fewer musket barrels to face in 1776 when the uprising finally did break out. If the committee had simply paid attention to the warning signs cropping up all around them, steps may have been taken to avert the clash to come in modern Pender County.

The signs were there. In January 1776, loyalist Dr. Joseph Fallon posted a paper at the Wilmington courthouse at front and Market Streets criticizing the Wilmington Committee of Safety, warning that "The Public will shortly avenge itself on the injury offered to it in my person." Tory William McTier was arrested for trying to reach Martin's ship by boat along with three other men. He claimed to have the committee's permission, but that was not the case. Even knowing this, McTier was still released. Then there is the material support given the loyalist Highlanders. After the Battle of Moores Creek, militiamen recovered 350 guns, 1500 rifles, and a huge sum of money that could only have come from the coffers and stores of Wilmington merchants loyal to England. The evidence is lent veracity by the fact that several of Wilmington's merchants were among the Tory dead in the aftermath of Moores Creek.

So why didn't the committee do more? Part of the answer is the political climate at the time. The white population of the town in 1776 was around 250, with roughly sixty to one hundred being adult males. Of these, forty were merchants, and of that forty another half were unsympathetic to the rebel cause. In fact, only six of Wilmington's merchants appear to have stayed true to the struggle for independence throughout the war. Despite the fact that better known planters like Cornelius Harnett and John Ashe were ardent supporters of the revolution, an equal if not larger number of the mercantile class stood firmly against it. The list is not restricted to just merchants, either. Doctors, lawyers, planters, and Crown officials - all lent their support to the mother country in the struggle. Some of these men even served on the Wilmington Committee of Safety at different times, further obstructing the committee's ability to carry out its edicts.

Even though the Wilmington Committee of Safety was hampered by less than zealous enforcement of its own edicts and the presence of a sizable portion of the voting population that sided with the Crown, it still managed to force Governor Martin to call out the Highlanders before all the elements of the British plan were in place. Because of this the Highlanders were defeated at great cost, and British efforts in North Carolina were stymied for another four years - all because of a minutes-long battle at an inconsequential bridge over a small creek in Pender County. But had the Wilmington Committee of Safety been a little more diligent, perhaps the fight wouldn't have occurred at all.

Highlanders who made it across Moores Creek Bridge were met with a hail of musket and grape shot.

The Battle at Widow Moore's Creek
By Jack E. Fryar, Jr.

Under the cabbage patch, sir?" The manservant looked at Royal Governor Josiah Martin as if he had been nipping at the excellent claret that usually sat in a crystal decanter in the drawing room of Tryon Palace, the palatial residence of Great Britain's chief administrator in colonial North Carolina, and defacto seat of English rule.

"You heard me," snapped the young governor. "Bury as much of the gunpowder we have in the cellar as you can, then bury what's left under the cabbage patch. There's too much to carry with us, and we cannot allow the rebels to get their hands on it. Lord knows they've been troublesome enough as it is."

In 1775, Josiah Martin was a man tired of looking over his shoulder. As royal governor in North Carolina, he was a young, headstrong firebrand who vigorously supported the right of King George III to rule his American subjects as he saw fit, but unfortunately, the people who lived in the colony were becoming harder and harder to control. Already local rebels had formed committees of safety to usurp Crown control of the colonies, and local militia were being mustered with the openly stated purpose of opposing any British efforts to wrest that control back from the more and more vocal rebels. Martin had seen the Crown's authority erode to the point that he himself had been put under open surveillance by the rebels, and now feared for his very life. The time had come to abandon the luxurious confines of Tryon Palace, which was ill suited to provide much of a defense against rebel troops, for the greater safety of Fort Johnston, at the mouth of the Cape Fear River.

After dismounting the palace's cannon and dispersing the powder reserves, Martin slipped away in the night.

At Fort Johnston, the governor's heart sank a little further. Located on the spit of land that is now modern Southport, where the river meets the Atlantic at Old Inlet, the installation was not much to inspire confidence. Garrisoned by only a few token troops to act as caretakers, Martin was immediately aware that the fort would not provide any big stumbling block to enemy troops who wanted to take it. And enemy troops were on their way.

When Martin occupied the fort and began petitioning General Thomas Gage in New York for men and funds to strengthen the decrepit installationt, the Wilmington Committee of Safety became alarmed and decided to take steps to nip Martin's plans in the bud. On July 15, 1775, Colonel Robert Howe, John Ashe and Cornelius Harnett led a body of militia and minutemen in a march on Fort Johnston. Having sent word ahead that they were coming, Gov. Martin put the forewarning to good use. He dismounted the fort's cannon and moved all its supplies of powder and shot on board the *HMS Cruizer*, on station in the Cape Fear River. The incensed representative of the Crown watched Howe and Harnett's rebel forces burn the installation to the ground from the decks of the British sloop-of-war three days later.

Alexander Schaw

Irate at the way Wilmington area Whigs had openly flouted royal authority, Martin began to form a scheme to take back control of the colony. Feeling that he was the obvious choice to lead any military campaign against the rebels, Martin concocted a plan whereby loyalists from the interior regions of the colony would join with British regulars sent either from New England by General Gage or from Britain and begin a march into the interior to eradicate the rebel forces. Initially, the plan called for arming 3,000 recently immigrated Scotch Highlanders from the interior counties, who would make the trek to the sea to link up with Gage's redcoats landed at Wilmington. Martin figured that with his core force of 3,000 Highlanders to offer protection, at least two thirds of the colony's estimated 30,000 fighting men would rally to the King's standard. To pull it off, Martin requested 10,000 stands of arms, six brass six-pounder cannon, and everything else necessary to supply an army on the move.

Martin sent the audacious plan to General Gage in New York for his consideration. He also dispatched Alexander Schaw, a loyalist planter from the Wilmington area, to England to make the pitch before Lord Dartmouth. In London, Martin's plan was seen to have merit. The perception of affairs in North Carolina led war planners in England to believe that most of the insurrectionist sentiments were seated along the coast, where wealthy planters like the Moores were the ones chafing at British rule and instigating the bulk of the troubles. When some members of the cabinet argued that Charleston, S.C. would make a better target, Alexander Schaw reasoned that a strike at the Cape Fear would provide a base of operations for an attack on the South Carolina port city and at the same time open up the Carolina backcountry to an occupying British army that could close the back door on any rebel retreat from the coast. Striking first at Wilmington would only delay a move on Charleston by a small bit, and would pay dividends that would make it well worthwhile. Martin's plans were approved.

Lord George Germain, Dartmouth's successor, authorized seven regiments under the command of Lord Charles Cornwallis to be sent from Ireland to the Cape Fear in ships provided by Admiral Sir Peter Parker. There, they would link up with a contingent sent from Boston by General Howe, who had replaced General Gage. Once joined with Martin's loyalist forces from the North Carolina interior, the army would commence offensive operations.

Martin got word of his plan's endorsement on January 3, 1776, and a week later raised the call for men to rally to the King's cause. Tory militia leaders in Anson, Cumberland, Chatham, Guilford, Mecklenburg, Rowan, Surry and Bute Counties were authorized to begin commissioning officers and raising troops. The loyalists were to join together at Cross Creek and be at Brunswick on the Cape Fear no later than February 15.

The Highlanders of the Cross Creek area were the key to Martin's plan. The canny governor had for some time been requiring the newly arrived Scots to pledge loyalty to the Crown before granting them land in the interior. The object was to get their loyalty before they could make friends and ties with rebellious factions in their new home. Now he was counting on those oaths to bind the Scots to the royal standard.

Despite the activity of local Whigs through their committees of safety, or perhaps because of it, there were a goodly number of people in the Cape Fear region who stood ready to side with the British. Brunswick residents visited Martin aboard the *Cruizer* in significant numbers to complain of their rebel neighbors' high-handedness. These people added to Martin's confidence by asserting that thousands of troops were standing by, ready to rally to the loyalist cause once the Highland regiments were raised and had marched to the coast. Feeling ready, Martin sent word to inland loyalist leaders with the final details of his plan. But trouble reared its head when the messenger entrusted with the orders turned out to be a rebel spy, who turned the dispatches over to Whig authorities.

Martin immediately dispatched Alexander McLean to get word to the waiting Highlanders at Cross Creek. His job was to make a concrete determination of how many men the Scots had been able to raise and start them for the coast. McLean found that while the Highlanders around Cross Creek could muster 3,000 men, there was only one stand of weapons to arm them with. Optimistically, if nonetheless misleading, McLean reported to the governor that everyone there was in high spirits and by his estimation numbered the army at 6,000. One thousand of that number was detailed off to guard loyalist families and property left behind by the soldiers at Cross Creek. The rest were ready to march to Wilmington. On January 10, Martin authorized McLean to bring the clans together.

Meeting at Cross Creek, the Highlander leadership wasn't all gung ho for Martin's plan. The older, more settled Scots were much less enthusiastic over the governor's scheme than the younger, more recent immigrants. Some of the Highlanders urged caution, suggesting they wait until at least March before mobilizing unless Parker's fleet showed up first. But the hotheads in the group demanded immediate action. The older Scots yielded to the youngsters' wishes, but not without misgivings.

Brigadier General Donald MacDonald was appointed leader of the expedition, with Lieutenant Colonel Donald McLeod as his second in command. The two had arrived in the Cross Creek area earlier to recruit Highlanders for the British army, and had been drafted into service by Martin to assist in his plans. The call went out to take up arms in the King's service. Martin's plan was ready for execution.

Militiamen under Alexander Lillington and Richard Caswell dealt the loyalist Highlanders a crippling blow in the Moores Creek fight.

Calling for men to rally around the flag is one thing. Getting them to actually do it is something else, as the two British officers were soon to discover. In many places, Tories who might have answered the call to arms were in no position to do so, having been run from their homes by rebels. Many of them were living scattered in the woods and swamps, unable to answer the call. Quick action by patriot militia against some of the loyalist troops who did attempt to march to Cross Creek stopped others from reaching the gathering point. Finally 500 men managed to meet McLeod to be escorted in, but rumors that a force of patriot militia was headed towards them had them all fleeing back into the woodlands before McLeod could stop them.

Still, the offer of 200 acres of land to any Highlander who joined the King's ranks was an inducement that appealed strongly to many of the Scots, and Cross Creek was a beehive of activity by February 12. Over the next several days, more stragglers trickled in to join the force, and by the middle of the month, MacDonald was able to muster 1,400 men.

All of the preparations going on at Cross Creek had not escaped the notice of area patriots. Ever since 1775 they had been keeping an eye on Martin, and were aware of his plans. Sister colonies Virginia and South Carolina sent aid in the form of gunpowder and lead for shot. Militia and minutemen were mustering at points all through the North Carolina interior. Along the coast Colonels James Moore and Robert Howe mobilized the Continental Line units they were raising to march against the Highlanders. To the Tories, it was Moore who posed the most serious threat. Those familiar with both men knew James Moore to be the sharper military mind of the pair. In addition to the men they raised, Wilmington's militia, commanded by Col. Alexander Lillington, rallied to the occasion as well. According to historian Hugh Rankin, these men weren't poster boys for the ideal 18th century soldier. Raggedly dressed and consuming almost as much rum as they did powder and shot, they were a motley crew. Nevertheless, they had a lethality about them that didn't go unnoticed. As one observer said:

"I must really laugh while I recollect their figures: 2,000 men in shirts and trousers, preceded by a very ill-beat drum and a fiddler, who was also in his shirt with a long sword and a cue at his hair, who played with all his might. They indeed made a most unmartial appearance. But the worst figure there can shoot from behind a bush and kill even a General Wolfe."

In New Bern, Richard Caswell's militia and minutemen also turned out to meet the Highlander threat. Armed with light artillery, Caswell's force was augmented by troops from Dobbs, Johnston, Pitt and Craven Counties.

When word reached Wilmington that the loyalists were on the move, the town's citizens began a hasty fortification of the city. An abatis was thrown up around the town upon hearing that *HMS Cruizer* was headed upriver to shell the port. Martial law was decreed, and all who refused to take an oath supporting the rebel cause were forced to work building the town's defenses. Guns were mounted, fire rafts prepared, stores removed to safety, and women and children evacuated to the country out of range of the warship's guns. The precautions were wise, because shortly the *Cruizer's* sails were spotted by lookouts posted to give the warning.

The primary mission of the sloop-of-war was to lend aid to the loyalist forces upriver. They were thwarted in that regard by a floating boom stretched across the river that prevented them from getting past the town. A landing party made for shore to attempt removal of the boom, but armed townsmen were waiting for them and forced them back to the ship after a brief skirmish. The *Cruizer* gave up and retired back downriver to Brunswick, accompanied by Wilmington rebels who followed them from shore, taking pot shots at the ship for miles.

By February 15, Col. Moore had arrived at Rockfish Creek, just seven miles from Cross Creek. At the bridge there, he decided to set up in a defensive position to contain the Highlander column until help could arrive. Emplacing his five artillery pieces, he waited. Four days later, his force had swelled to 1,100, versus MacDonald's estimated 1,500. The night before, on the eighteenth, the Highlanders had marched out of Cross Creek and camped for the night a scant four miles from Moore's position.

Although preparations were made for battle on the morning of the nineteenth, MacDonald's primary mission was to get his men to the coast to link up with Cornwallis' regulars. Much to the chagrin of the young firebrands among his force, he chose to avoid contact with Moore if he could. He sent a message to Moore, saying the usual things about the rebels being outnumbered, etc., and advising them to surrender. Moore demurred, playing for time so that more troops could make it to his side. MacDonald suspected as much, and a council of war was called with an eye towards engaging the Whigs the next morning. Upon hearing this news, two companies of Anson County Tories promptly slipped out of camp and went home.

The loss of the Anson men was disturbing to MacDonald. When word came that Caswell and 600 men were on their way to join Moore, the commander of the Highlanders decided to forego battle and make immediately for Brunswick. Farquard Campbell suggested crossing the Cape Fear at Campbellton, then using Negro Head Point Road to make the journey to the coast. That way they would bypass Moore's militia all together.

With the famed Flora MacDonald waving them on, Donald MacDonald and his men hit the road on February 20 in high spirits. Moore was left holding a position no one threatened until intelligence reached him that the Scots had slipped away. Looking at a map, Moore figured out where MacDonald was headed and quickly sent a messenger to Col. Caswell with orders to take Corbett's Ferry on the Black River. Another force was sent to close the backdoor by occupying Cross Creek. Meanwhile Lillington was ordered to try a link-up with Caswell; barring that, he and his men were to march on Moores Creek Bridge and set up a defensive position there.

Upon reaching Corbett's Ferry, scouts reported to MacDonald that Caswell was entrenched on the far side with a considerable force. Once at the bridge, dispatch riders had sent word throughout the area to destroy as many of the river and creek crossings as possible to deny them to the Highlanders. For the moment, MacDonald was stymied, until some cavalry scouts found a sunken barge a few miles away that could be refloated to provide a means of fording the waterway. Leaving behind a skeleton force to distract Caswell, MacDonald slipped away to raise the barge and get his army across Black River.

Back at the ferry, Caswell's men were entertained with a loud demonstration of bagpipes and drums, while the handful of decoys thrashed through the underbrush to create the illusion that the Scots were still opposite the Whig force. By the time Caswell figured out he had been duped it was already February 26, and MacDonald had managed to get his army across the river and send his mounted units to scout ahead. The cavalry captured a small supply train intended for Caswell, and it was from the captured mule drivers that MacDonald learned of the reinforcements being sent to link up with the New Bern militia officer's men at Corbett's Ferry. Feeling pretty good at the trick they had played on Caswell, the Scots turned to the south and made for the coast.

James Moore read Caswell's dispatch with a frown. If MacDonald had given Caswell the slip, then there was nothing to stop him from reaching Wilmington unless Moore acted fast. Moore immediately ordered Caswell to march hell for leather to Moores Creek Bridge to try to block the Highlanders there. If he couldn't beat them to the winding creek in modern Pender County, then he was to fall in on their rear and harass them as best he could until Moore could bring the various elements of his force together for a showdown. Meanwhile, Moore loaded his command onto boats and barges and floated sixty miles down river from Elizabethtown to Dollison's Landing, where he made camp for the night. As sunlight gave way to stars, Moore was worried that the patriot troops would not be able to catch MacDonald in time. That night his fears were assuaged when word came that Caswell had made the link with Lillington at Moores Creek.

When you stand on the ridge just east of the bridge at Moores Creek, you can look around and see that it is ground tailor-made for a defensive action. The hill where Lillington and Caswell dug their earthworks is several feet higher than the winding trail that leads up to it from the bridge. From the ridge west is thick swamp that would slow down both mounted troops and infantry equally well. The creek itself is five to eight feet deep, and winds like a black snake throughout the muddy swampland that surrounds it. The only place to cross the creek is over the bridge built on a sandbar roughly 150 yards from where the Whig militia and minutemen chose to dig in. The narrow constraints imposed by the swamp, deep creek, and single bridge create a kill zone out of an infantry officer's dreams, as the terrain forces an approaching enemy to funnel his advance through a single, easily defended

The Scots marched south from Cross Creek, to where they were to link up with British regulars at the mouth of the Cape Fear River. The journey was cut short by the clash with militia at a little creek in modern Pender County.

point at which the defenders can concentrate their fire with maximum efficiency. This was the ground Caswell and Lillington chose to meet the Highlanders on.

When Caswell's 800 men joined up with Lillington's 150 Wilmington minutemen, Caswell immediately began constructing an earthwork on the west side of the bridge, stationing part of his force there. Another position was built just east of the bridge, between the creek and Lillington's position at the top of the rise. Their cannons, Old Mother Covington and her daughter, were positioned to either side of the trail leading up the rise so that their cones of fire would overlap, doubling the effectiveness of their shot. The patriots were ready.

Though MacDonald tried his best to reach the bridge first, scouts reported to him that he had lost the race when they got within six miles of the creek. By now MacDonald, feeling his years, had fallen ill. To ascertain the defenses facing them, he sent James Hepburn with a flag of truce into Caswell's camp under the ruse of offering the rebels a chance to surrender. As expected, Caswell and Lillington refused, but the primary mission of scouting out the bridge's defenses was accomplished. Hepburn reported to MacDonald that Caswell's men were positioned with their backs to the creek, making an inviting target for the Highlanders. MacDonald called a council of war in which he expressed a reluctance to attack, citing the larger numbers of colonials facing him and a scarcity of arms among his own ranks. But others in the group voted to take the bull by the horns and make the assault. MacDonald yielded to their sentiments.

Bedridden now, MacDonald placed Donald McLeod in command of the Highlanders for the dawn attack. At one o'clock in the morning, McLeod and his men began covering the six miles to the bridge. After delays caused by unfamiliar terrain, the Scots were in place by an hour before sun up. Under the murky shadows of the pine and cypress trees, it was difficult to pinpoint where the bridge was. McLeod formed his troops from three columns to one long line of battle, with the claymore-bearing Highlanders who would serve as shock troops at the center. Stealthily, they crept into the camp Caswell had occupied on the west side of the creek - only to find that the wily militia officer had withdrawn to the east side of the bridge. Caswell had left his fires burning to create a deception of his own.

McLeod ordered that the signal to attack would be the cry, "King George and Broadswords!" followed by three cheers. As the men waited for the signal, an advance patrol led by Alexander McLean stumbled on the bridge in the dark and saw the figures of men on the other side. When challenged, McLean said he was a friend. The silhouettes on the other bank asked, "A friend to who?" McLean replied, "To the King." The shapes suddenly disappeared as they went to ground seeking cover. McLean issued his own challenge in Gaelic, and got no reply. Deciding he

Militiamen from all of the central and southeastern coastal North Carolina counties contributed men to the force sent to stop the Highlanders.

had met the enemy, he ordered his patrol to open fire across the creek from the west bank.

Meanwhile, McLeod heard the firing from up ahead. The need for action got the best of him, and the signal, "King George and Broadswords!" followed by three cheers rang out into the lightening gloom. Bagpipes began squealing through the mist rising off the creek, and drums beat a tattoo that signified the advance of a marching army. Upon reaching McLean, McLeod encountered his second surprise of the morning. When Caswell fell back in the night to the east side of the creek, he ordered the planks pulled up from roughly half the bridge. Now the only way across the black water was across two thin girders that had been made even more treacherous by being coated with soft soap and tallow.

The hesitation was only momentary. With the bulk of his army pressing from behind, McLeod gingerly ventured out onto one of the slippery girders. Across from him Farquard Campbell took the other. By driving their sword points into the wood they were able to slowly make their way across to the east bank, followed by their Highlander soldiers, still bellowing their war cries.

From the rise to the east, Lillington and his men watched the crossing. Flitting through the trees on the other bank they could make out the colorful kilts of the Highlander army. As McLeod and Campbell reached the near side of the creek, desperate gunners, who had for some moments been trying to ignite the primer on their two cannon, were shoved aside by Caswell, who supposedly finally got the guns to fire by discharging his pistols into the touch holes. Old Mother Covington and her more diminutive though still deadly daughter squelched the shrill sounds of the bagpipes with their own roar of defiance. Musket balls fired in volley sped down-slope to join the grape shot from the cannon in one murderous greeting to the newcomers on the east bank. The two Highlander leaders went down immediately. On the bridge, where there had been men a moment before, there was only the empty skeleton of a span, the Scots swept from the girders and into the icy waters where many of them drowned. McLeod gamely tried to rally his men despite his wounds, but was quickly riddled with more balls that put an end to him. After the battle, Whig militiamen would count nine bullets and thirty-four pieces of swan shot in him.

On the west bank of the creek, Highlanders took cover and began a sporadic return fire. Though the Scots seemed up for the fight, the Regulators and other loyalists turned tail and headed for the safety of their camp. Sometimes traveling three to a horse they fled, and it wasn't long before the remaining Highlanders followed suit. Gleeful rebels jumped up and began a pursuit, although slowed by stopping to loot the bodies of the fallen Scots. As the patriots looked around, the Whig soldiers were amazed by the lightness of the butcher's bill. Only two men were wounded, and of those only Anson County's John Grady would die, four days later, from wounds sustained at the Battle of Moores Creek. Loyalist losses were put at between thirty and seventy, though more were believed to have drowned in the creek or succumbed to their wounds during their retreat.

Several hours later Col. Moore arrived at Caswell's camp and began sending patrols to pursue the Highlanders fleeing back towards their homes. The loyalist retreat was so hasty that no one thought to collect the hapless Donald MacDonald from his sick bed back at camp. The first he knew of the disaster that had befallen his command was when Whig militiamen took him prisoner in his own tent.

Moores Creek Bridge today, the centerpiece of Moores Creek National Battlefield, in Currie, N.C.

Meanwhile the loyalists were running helter-skelter back towards Cross Creek, unaware that James Martin's force was already there and waiting for them. Upon learning that the rebels held their sanctuary on the Northeast Cape Fear, the loyalist army disbanded, with everyone trying to find their own way back to their homes in the interior. The plan was to stay together as far as Smith's Ferry, twenty-five miles from Cross Creek, before disbanding so as to provide at least some mutual protection from the pursuing Whigs. The loyalists got as far as Black Mingo Creek before rebel troops surrounded them and forced them to surrender.

At Smith's Ferry, the captured Highlanders and other loyalists were turned over to Col. Nicholas Long's 500 troops for safekeeping. Their arms and munitions were confiscated, as was their rolling stock. Nearly 850 regular soldiers were immediately paroled and sent home after giving oaths not to take up arms against the patriots in the future. At least thirty officers were transported to the jail in Halifax to await disposition later. Among them were Donald MacDonald and Allen MacDonald, Flora's husband. Not only did the Whigs scoop up much needed supplies from the captured soldiers, but in Cross Creek a search found 350 gun and shot bags, 150 dirks and swords, 1,500 rifles, two medicine chests fresh from England, and 15,000 pounds in sterling and gold coins were also added to patriot coffers.

Back aboard the *Cruizer*, Gov. Martin refused to call a spade a spade. He continued to write letters to England describing the fight at Moores Creek as a minor setback and urging Crown war planners to try his plan again, though conceding that perhaps next time they should wait until British regulars were actually on the ground in North Carolina before raising the royal standard. He even tried to extort supplies from Wilmington by threatening the town with the sloop's cannons, but Wilmingtonians didn't go for it. The addition of Col. Moore's regulars to the town's defenses only reinforced their resolve.

With the defeat of the Highlanders, Americans scored their first victory in the war for independence, and kept loyalists at bay for another four years until 1781.

Though Alexander Lillington and Richard Caswell usually get the lion's share of the glory for the victory at Moores Creek, it was Col. James Moore who really won the fight by out-maneuvering the Highlanders and forcing them to give battle at a time and place of his choosing, and on ground beneficial to the Whig forces. The fight itself lasted only minutes, but the effects of it were a hundred times greater than its duration. As the sun peeked through the trees on February 27, 1776 to reflect off the claymores and kilts of the loyalist Highlanders, patriot forces struck a blow that would keep British troops out of North Carolina for another four years. More importantly, the victory by the Whigs so cowed the loyalists of the region that they failed to challenge rebel authority in the colony on any large scale until Major James Craig's redcoats occupied Wilmington in 1781. The short but furious fight at a little creek in Pender County bought Cape Fear patriots the time they needed to consolidate their hold on North Carolina, and prevented Washington's struggling Continentals from having to wage a war on two fronts.

photo courtesy N.C. Dept. of Archives & History

Major James Reilly, CSA

False Starts & Firing First

By Jack E. Fryar, Jr.

While the firing on Fort Sumter is generally considered by most people to be the event which signaled the start of the Civil War, it could be argued that the Citadel cadets who took aim at the Stars and Stripes fluttering above Sumter's ramparts were a bit tardy when compared with their brethren in the Cape Fear region. When the first cannonball arced across the channel to open the fighting in America's most bloody war, men from the Cape Fear had already taken steps to confront Mr. Lincoln's Union army up to four months earlier.

By December of 1860, South Carolina had seceded from the Union and begun a military build-up aimed at defending the city of Charleston from the expected federal fleet and the Union army garrison occupying Fort Sumter. North Carolina was much slower to withdraw from the Union than its more southern sister states. In fact, as the new year dawned in January 1861, most public sentiment in the state probably still favored reconciliation with the north, and the people of the interior showed a marked reluctance to follow in the footsteps of their neighbors to the south. That was true everywhere except along the coast, where the planter class was wholeheartedly with the rebellious South Carolinians. For them, the question of war and succession was not a matter of if, but when. As the situation in Charleston grew closer and closer to open belligerence, people in Wilmington decided steps had to be taken locally.

At the time, there were two federal forts guarding access to the Cape Fear River - Fort Johnston at Smithville (now Southport) and Fort Caswell three miles away on modern Oak Island. Caswell was the stronger of the two, a masonry fort with redoubts constructed as part of the coastal defense program undertaken by Congress in the wake of the War of 1812. Fort Fisher wasn't even a gleam in William Lamb's eye at the time, and Federal Point on the east side of the Cape Fear was guarded by only one gun battery.

At the beginning of 1861, only a sergeant manned each of the forts, but if Yankee troops should occupy Johnston and Caswell it could have made things very difficult for Confederates later. A Union presence at the mouth of the Cape Fear would prohibit Confederate activities far upriver, not just in Wilmington. With their command of the approaches to Old Inlet, access to the state's principal inland waterway would be denied to supplies coming into the fledgling country and provide a base from which to stage Union operations into the interior. Whether it was an oversight on the part of the federals or an attempt by the Lincoln administration to not do anything that might precipitate secession by North Carolina, no move had been made to beef up the garrisons at the two forts. Pro-secessionist residents of Wilmington and Brunswick County decided to act before the lanky new president could correct the oversight.

On January 10, the Wilmington Committee of Safety dispatched Major John Hedrick with such men as he could gather to occupy Forts Johnston and Caswell. Armed with such personal weaponry as they could find, the irregular troops loaded into boats and began the journey down the river. By three o'clock in the afternoon, Hedrick landed his force in Smithville and proceeded to Fort Johnston, where Ordinance Sergeant James Reilly promptly turned over the installation to the armed men. Reilly probably didn't hesitate too much to surrender his command, as once hostilities broke out he sided with the South and was commissioned a captain in the Confederate Army. Later, he would command a gun battery bearing his name at Fort Fisher.

With Fort Johnston in their possession, the men of Hedrick's command then marched three miles west to Fort Caswell, on the other side of the bay. Here, the loyalties of the sergeant in charge of the fort, a man named Walker, were in no doubt. Though he, too, surrendered immediately in the face of Hedrick's armed band, he tried several times in the days that followed to contact his Union superiors and let them know what had happened. He was eventually placed under close confinement to prevent him from reporting.

It may not have been much of an occupying force, and the level of military experience of the group may have been debatable, but Hedrick's men did begin manning the ramparts in the bitter cold of that January with a diligence that did them credit. Though the force was small, they counted on reinforcements from the militias of Wilmington and Brunswick Counties should the expected Yankee warships arrive once word reached Washington, D.C. of what they had done. That confidence in their brethren was borne out when a ship was sighted approaching the harbor. Suspecting it to be a Union ship, the alarm was sounded and soon boatloads of Cape Fear men began filtering into the forts from both sides of the river. The ship turned out to be friendly, but the readiness with which support showed up was heartening to Hedrick's little troop.

Meanwhile in Raleigh, the governor was concerned that the actions of the Cape Fear irregulars might be seen as imprudent. As the state was still technically a part of the Union, and the state legislature still hoped to avoid the break South Carolina had made, it was determined that the forts must be returned to federal control, at least until such time as North Carolina did break away to join its southern sisters. An emissary from the state militia was sent down the Cape Fear bearing a letter from the governor ordering the return of the forts to the Union. After a long journey to the coast, calm winds forced the courier to hike the last four miles to Fort Caswell after dark. The order was delivered to Major Hedrick, who asked for a day to consider the situation.

On January 14, 1861, the forts were returned to their Union Army caretakers - though not without reluctance. Four months later, when the first cannon barked out its challenge to the Union garrison at Fort Sumter, North Carolina quickly joined its sister states in secession. The same governor who had earlier ordered the return of Forts Caswell and Johnston to the bluecoats then quickly ordered Hedrick and other militia companies on the lower Cape Fear to re-occupy the installations. As the conflict progressed, those militia companies and irregulars would be absorbed into the Confederate Army and would not only garrison the two installations guarding Old Inlet, but also begin work on what would eventually become the largest and toughest fort in the Confederacy, Fort Fisher.

While the notoriety of having fired the first shots of the Civil War goes to Charleston, S.C., it is worth noting that four months prior to that, the men of Wilmington took up arms and took hostile action against a foe that would plague them for the next four years.

Fort Johnston, at the mouth of the Cape Fear River in Southport, along with Oak Island's Fort Caswell, were seized by Southern sympathizers months before the firing on Ft. Sumter.

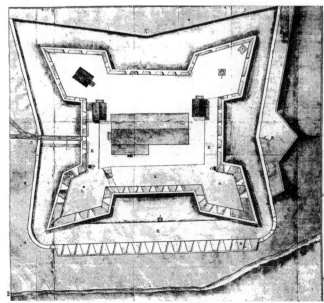

Famed Scottish heroine Flora MacDonald did not fare well during her time in America. Her husband was part of the Highlander force defeated by Caswell and Lillington at Moores Creek in 1776.

Flora MacDonald

By Jack E. Fryar, Jr.

I have hazarded my life for the House of Stuart and for the House of Hanover and I do not see that I am a great gainer by either." The statement came through clenched teeth as the ship's surgeon tightened the bandages worn by the Scotswoman wounded in the brief sea battle. Flora MacDonald had, indeed, risked life and limb in support of two branches of royalty, and all she had to show for it was a bleeding wound, a husband in a prisoner of war camp, two children serving in King George III's army, and a far from certain future.

Born in 1722, Flora MacDonald was a native of Uist Island in the Hebrides whose mother remarried to a Hugh MacDonald when her father died. Educated by kinsmen both there, at the Isle of Skye, and in Edinburgh, by the time Flora returned she was a polished young lady able to hold her own among the aristocracy of her native Scotland and the English who were her country's overlords. It was a skill that would come into play on behalf of the Stuart household two years later.

By 1746 Charles Edward Stuart, the "Bonnie Prince Charlie" of the Stuart clan, was gathering an army to contest his right to the throne of England. The Hanoverian dynasty that was then ruling England took exception to Stuart's pretensions, and began gathering an army of their own to crush the infant rebellion. Many Scots joined with Charles Edward out of loyalty to the Stuart clan, but not all of Scotland rallied around the Stuart tartan. Nevertheless, a substantial army threw their lot in with the Bonnie Prince, and that made for a showdown at the Battle of Culloden in April of 1746.

Luck didn't ride on Charles Edward's shoulder that day, and the Duke of Cumberland, representing England's ruling House of Hanover, soundly trounced the upstart Scots. While Scottish blood soaked into the field at Culloden, supporters of the pretender to the throne whisked Charles Edward away from the ever-advancing ranks of Cumberland's army. Prince Charles made it as far as the Isle of Skye before the net finally closed him in, and capture became all but inevitable - except for the intervention of Flora MacDonald and her family.

Donning woman's clothes, the fugitive prince assumed the identity of Betty Burke, an Irish spinning maid traveling with Flora MacDonald on passports secured by Flora's stepfather. The two of them carefully made their way out of the dragnet surrounding Skye and after a dangerous journey during which both the Prince and Flora fought back fears of discovery, they reached the home of Lady Margaret MacDonald. But upon arrival they discovered English officers dining at MacDonald's table. Flora realized just how precarious their position was. Anything even slightly out of the ordinary would no doubt arouse the suspicions of Cumberland's soldiers. In an instant she made a decision, and boldly joined the dinner party. Accounts say that Flora was so enchanting and relaxed that the English soldiers never once suspected the plain looking Irish maid with her was none other than the most hunted man in Scotland. The next day, Charles Stuart boarded a boat for France and slipped out of reach of his hunters.

Flora was arrested when the story of Bonnie Prince Charlie's escape became known to the English, and eventually locked away in the notorious Tower of London. During that time her celebrity grew beyond the borders of Scotland and eventually garnered admirers among the English as well. Released in 1747 as part of the Act of Indemnity, Flora remained in London campaigning for the release of the Scottish prisoners still under lock and key in British prisons. By 1750, Flora MacDonald was once again breathing the fresh air of Scotland, and getting married in the process. The heir to the very same home that had played host to Flora and "Betty Burke", Allan MacDonald, took her for his wife in November of that same year.

Economic conditions after Culloden caused an emigration by many Scots to the new lands in America. North Carolina became the landing place of many of the Scottish newcomers, and Allan and Flora MacDonald were among them. Sailing from Campbelltown, Argyll, the MacDonalds arrived in Wilmington, North Carolina in 1774. Her fame had preceded her, and the citizens of Wilmington were delighted to throw a grand ball in her honor. The MacDonalds - especially Flora - became an instant hit among the wealthy landowners of the Cape Fear and among the Scottish immigrants who were flooding into the colony by the boatload. Traveling further inland, the MacDonalds stayed for a while at Cross Creek (modern Fayetteville) before finally settling down on a piece of land they dubbed Killiegray in Anson County.

By now the fifty-two year old Flora must have been ready to put down roots. It had been more than twenty years since her efforts to save a fugitive prince had brought her notoriety and fame. Since then she had born seven children and crossed an ocean to a new and virtually untamed world. To get there she and her family had been required to swear an oath of loyalty to the ruling House of Hanover. Now Flora wanted to have a bit of peace in her life. Unfortunately for her, it was not to be.

Even as the MacDonalds touched shore and accepted the accolades of the people of Wilmington, war with England was on the horizon. More and more the American colonies were chaffing at the yoke of British rule. Nine years earlier the people of Wilmington expressed their displeasure with their treatment by the British government by lining the banks of the Cape Fear River with their rifles and muskets to prevent the landing of the

Charles Stuart, The "Bonnie" Prince
(photo courtesy Library of Congress)

hated stamp papers during the Stamp Act Defiance of 1765. Local rebels had begun to form shadow governments to enforce embargoes on British goods. Congress was openly discussing the possibility of armed revolt. As Allan and Flora built their Anson County home, war was already on the way, and it would once again sweep the MacDonald clan along with it.

Aboard the British warship *HMS Cruizer*, anchored close by Fort Johnston at the mouth of the Cape Fear River, Royal Governor Josiah Martin was formulating a plan to crush the infant rebellion in his colony. It called for the raising of Highlander troops from the interior counties who would march to Brunswick and join with British regulars sent from Ireland. The combined force would then sweep away the belligerent rebels and secure the South for the Crown. To affect the plan, Martin chose General Donald MacDonald to raise a force from among the Scottish immigrants living in the counties surrounding Cross Creek. Thanks to what the Scots had come to call the "Bloody Oath" they were forced to swear before being granted lands by the English government in the interior, Martin felt they were the group most likely to prove loyal to the British cause. Martin related as much to the Earl of Dartmouth in a November 1775 letter. In it he mentions a Captain Alex MacLeod, formerly of the British Royal Marines, as a candidate to command a battalion of Highlanders. He also goes on to mention MacLeod's father-in-law, a man Martin wished to commission as a major of the Highland Corps, Allan MacDonald.

Allan was sought after not only by the English, but also by the Whigs. The Wilmington Committee of Safety resolved to write MacDonald to find out for themselves whether the stories they were hearing were true. The rebels wanted Allan MacDonald to use his - and his wife's - influence to prevent the Highlanders from rallying to the English banner. Since first landing at Wilmington, the rebels had sought Allan MacDonald's backing for their cause, but the MacDonalds just wanted to settle down. The days when they championed political causes were behind them, they hoped. But while the Wilmington rebels conceded that they would not get the MacDonalds on their side in the coming conflict, at least they might be able to stop them from joining the British, either.

With her husband and son-in-law now holding a King's commission, Flora dutifully threw her not inconsiderable influence behind Martin's plan. Loyalist meetings among the Highlanders saw her assuming the role of cheerleader and advocate for the cause of the English king. A campaign was planned for early 1776, and once again the MacDonald clan went down the road to war.

By February 1776, Flora stood by the road waving good-bye to her husband, her sons Alexander and James, and the more than 1000 Highlanders who had taken up arms in support of the King's banner. Though Allan and her son-in-law, Alex MacLeod, had purchased clothing and weapons for many of the volunteers who came to the rally point empty handed, there were still a great many men marching off to face the enemy without arms. Many of the men marching off to war were doing so at her urging. Flora might have felt a little guilty about that had her own men folk not been among them.

In Wilmington, Col. James Moore of the Continental Line knew of the governor's plan to raise a Highland regiment. When word reached him that the Scots were on the march, he immediately called his men to arms and set out to head them off before they could make their link-up with the British regulars expected any day at Brunswick. The Wilmington militia under Alexander Lillington, and the New Bern militia under Richard Caswell were called out, too. Donald MacDonald and Col. Moore maneuvered across the countryside between Cross Creek and Wilmington for almost a month before the two forces finally came together at the Widow Moore's Creek in modern Pender County.

On February 27, 1776, the two sides clashed in an engagement that lasted less than five minutes, but which shattered the loyalist Highlanders and sent them fleeing back the way they had come. Caswell and Lillington's militias took off in pursuit, capturing many of the fleeing Scots and Regulators in the process. Among them were Allan MacDonald, Flora's son Alexander, her sister's husband and two of his brothers. Alexander MacLeod avoided capture by laying low in the woods until he could safely make his way back home. Allan was imprisoned in Halifax for a short time until being marched to a prisoner of war camp in Pennsylvania.

Back at home, things were uneasy for Flora. A simmering resentment at the part she had played in sending so many Highlander husbands, fathers, sons and brothers off to a war that had ended in disaster was evident in the way Flora was treated after Moores Creek. To make matters worse, local Whigs demanded that Flora make an oath of allegiance to North Carolina in 1777, and when she refused the family plantation was confiscated. The same thing happened to her daughter, Anne. With a husband in a POW camp, her adulation among her neighbors suddenly turned to resentment, and no roof over her head that she could call her own, uneasiness turned to bleakness for Flora and her family. The only thing to do was leave North Carolina, and in 1778, under a flag of truce arranged by Major Alexander McLeod, the MacDonald family set sail for New York.

It is seven hundred miles from Moores Creek to Philadelphia, and Allan MacDonald walked the whole way. After several years as a prisoner, he was exchanged and met up with his wife and family in New York. Later that year Allan was assigned to the British forces at Halifax, Nova Scotia. Ever the dutiful wife, Flora went with him, and suffered a horrendous twelve months fighting the bitter cold and a homesickness that threatened to break her in two at times. It had been five years since she had seen her youngest children. Flora wanted to go home.

When the rebels had burned Killiegray, Flora and her family had been left destitute, save for the silver tea service presented to her by admirers while she was imprisoned in the Tower of London. The service had become a cherished heirloom of the family, but Flora willingly sold it in 1779 to buy passage back to London for herself and her daughter on a British warship bound for England. Bad luck would not leave Flora alone, though. During the crossing the British ship was drawn into battle with a French vessel and Flora was wounded in the attack. Upon arriving in London she learned that her son, Alexander, had died at sea on his way home to convalesce after wounds he received at Moores Creek. Two years later another son, Ranald, died at sea while serving as a Royal Marine. But at long last Flora MacDonald was reunited with her youngest offspring. Traveling back to Scotland, she lived with her brother until she could be reunited with her husband.

After the American Revolution ended in 1783 and his regiment disbanded, Allan MacDonald tried to develop 3000 acres he had received for his war services but failed because of a lack of funds. Six years after Flora had made the trip, he too returned to London to be reunited with his family. Hopes of being compensated for his losses in the war were dashed when his claim for reparations netted him only 440 pounds out of the 1,341 MacDonald valued his losses at.

Allan and Flora, sons Charles and James, daughters Anne and Fanny returned to the Isle of Skye. Living quietly for their remaining years, Flora MacDonald passed away in 1790. Allan followed her two years later. Flora's burial shrouds were the sheets slept on by the infamous "Betty Burke" so long ago, when Flora's cool confidence had saved the life of a prince. The sheets were the only things she had kept with her all through the years. They were the one heirloom that had traveled the world with her, only to once again arrive back where the grand adventure that was her life had started.

*The northeast corner of
Fort Fisher, where the sea and
land faces met. It is also the
place where, in the attack of
January 1865, the
U.S. Marine Corp was repulsed
by the withering fire of
Col. William Lamb's
Confederate defenders.*

photo courtesy Fort Fisher State Historic Site

The Repulse of the Sea Soldiers

By Jack E. Fryar, Jr.

Captain Lucien L. Dawson, USMC, peered through the evening twilight of January 14, 1865 at the earthen fortification in the distance that was the almost mythical Fort Fisher. On the southern tip of what was once called Federal Point, where the Cape Fear River empties itself into the Atlantic Ocean, the Confederates under the direction of Col. William Lamb and Gen. W.H.C. Whiting had constructed a behemoth that rivaled the great European fort at Sebastopol, and which was by far the strongest fortification in the Confederacy. Two weeks earlier the Union fleet and army sent to reduce the sandy monster that guarded Wilmington, North Carolina had been sent packing in an embarrassing defeat on Christmas Day, 1864. Now a more determined federal force was back to do the job right.

Doing the job right was not going to be an easy task, but it was one that had to be done. Wilmington was the last link to the outside world for Gen. Robert E. Lee's Army of Northern Virginia. The arms, ammunition, food, medicine and other supplies which came in aboard the daring little blockade runners who braved the U.S. Navy cordon off the Cape Fear were the lifeblood of a Confederacy finding itself increasingly on the ropes in the five year old war. Lee bluntly observed that his army could not survive should Wilmington fall, and Union war planners such as Secretary of the Navy Gideon Welles readily agreed with Lee's assessment.

Welles had been pushing for the men and materials to reduce the city since 1862, but other priorities had kept the Union from granting his wishes until December of 1864. Then the Christmas Day assault on Fort Fisher had ended in defeat. A split command structure and grandstanding on the part of Union General Benjamin Butler resulted in such a bungled operation that Lamb's garrison had taunted the retreating Yankee fleet with the music of "Dixie" as they sailed back over the horizon for points north. An angry Gen. Ulysses S. Grant had determined that Fort Fisher would fall, and then dispatched the men and materials to see that it did. Rear Admiral David Porter would once again lead the naval contingent of the operation, but the inept Benjamin Butler would be replaced by the quietly competent Alfred Terry in the rematch planned for January 1865.

Captain Lucien Dawson, USMC

Admiral Porter found General Terry to be a vastly preferable commander to Butler, and was sure that he could work with the new army boss to successfully reduce Fort Fisher. Nevertheless, he didn't intend to let the army garner all the accolades for bringing the Confederate Goliath to its knees, either. Porter determined to land a contingent made up of sailors and Marines to make an assault upon the northeast corner of the fort while Terry's infantry advanced against the land face to the west, on the river side of the peninsula. While Terry advanced, using the low ground around the Wilmington Road to provide some shelter for his men, Porter's sailors and Marines would attack the fort from the ocean side, advancing to the point where the land and sea faces met. Once there, Marine sharpshooters would keep enemy gunners at bay while the sailors, armed with cutlasses and pistols, "boarded the fort" and eliminated rebel opposition.

Terry's concerns lay in the rebel guns that filled the traverses on Fort Fisher's land face. When the Union general met with Porter on January 14, he made it clear that he would not order an advance against the fort while any of the big guns lining the earthen walls were still operable. Porter promised to destroy the guns, and immediately directed his naval gunners to concentrate fire upon the land face where the ground action was scheduled to take place.

All through the night shot screamed through the air, forcing Fort Fisher's defenders to hunker down in their bombproofs while Yankee steel methodically destroyed all of the guns on the land face except one. The wooden palisade fence in front of the fort's earthen wall was shattered by shot hurled by the navy's guns so that it began to resemble a mouth full of missing teeth. Attempts by the Confederates to send 1,000 reinforcements to Lamb's aid by river were frustrated by the Cape Fear's sandy river bottom which grabbed hold of the steamers transporting the men and held them fast. With the sun came an increased pounding by Union gunners. By 11:00 am the entire Yankee fleet was raining shells down on Lamb and his men. All the land face guns were knocked out. The traverses were tattered ghosts of what they had been before the attack began. Up the beach, out of range of rebel guns that no longer existed, the Yankee landing force continued to form up.

Porter's plan called for his sailors and Marines to begin landing at 10am on January 15th, and while the first contingent did come ashore around 10:15am, others didn't make the movement until up to two hours later. Ship captains preoccupied with the naval bombardment of the fort in many cases simply forgot about the landing party, despite repeated signal flags from Porter's *USS Malvern* flagship to "Arm and away all boats." Once ashore two miles north of the fort, the sailors and Marines

photo courtesy Library of Congress

USS Malvern, Admiral David Porter's flagship

were to form two separate elements. Navy Lieutenant S.W. Preston was to take a party armed with shovels and commence digging rifle pits as close to the fort as possible. As the dirt was excavated, it would be piled to offer protection for the men who manned the pits. Once one line of pits were dug, sailors and Marines would fill them while the sappers advanced and began another line, until they were close enough to the fort that the sailors could storm the walls with their cutlasses and revolvers. The Marines would use their rifles to pick off rebel defenders while the sailors streamed over the mounds to invest the fort. Porter's plan called for the attack to go off simultaneously with Terry's infantry attack against the western side of the fort. Both commanders agreed on 2:00pm as the time to make their move.

As his boat grounded on the white beach, Captain Dawson surveyed the formation of sailors and Marines. The plan called for the Marines to form the first of four lines that would advance against the fort, while the navy contingent would form up three more organized to correspond to the positions their ships held in the line of battle. While Dawson would take charge of all the Marines, command of the entire force fell to Porter's fleet captain, Lieutenant Commander Kidder R. Breese. Dawson was familiar with the old adage that no plan survives first contact with the enemy, but what he was seeing now was a gaggle that bore little resemblance to the admiral's plan even before the first Confederate shot had been fired at it.

The disorganized landing of the various ship's contingents that were to make up the naval force led to confusion on the beach. While men from the same ship generally were kept together, their officers ended up all over the place. One line of the attack force was stretched out as much as a half mile closer to the fort than its sister columns. And while men from each ship knew each other, the men they were lined up with from other ship's companies were total strangers. The sailors were untrained in how to use the cutlasses and pistols they found themselves armed with, and totally ignorant of the drill steps required to maneuver a body of men in a land attack.

photo courtesy
Library of Congress

LtCmdr Kidder Breese, USN

The naval force milled around the beach like a bunch of raw recruits. The sight horrified Dawson and his Marines, as well as Terry's army commanders across the peninsula. Brevet Brigadier General Newton M. Curtis was one of the appalled army officers, and when a navy courier was sent to coordinate the attack, he told him so.

"Your men are too compactly formed. Your front is too narrow for the depth of your column. To go into action as you are now formed places you under a great disadvantage," he advised. "You should hold your main body until your advanced line gets a foothold on the fort. If you go forward as you are, you will be fearfully punished, and the only good you will do us will be to receive fire which otherwise would come to our lines."

The courier bristled at what he construed to be an army slur against the navy. He brusquely informed Curtis that the "Navy would do its part and merit approval whether the army gave it or not."

Meanwhile Col. Lamb and his men had noticed the activity on the beach. Seeing the landing force forming, Lamb ordered his men to their positions to prepare for the coming attack. Six hundred yards away, Lieutenant Preston's diggers were hurriedly excavating the first line of rifle pits. LtCmdr Breese ordered the Marine guard from the *USS Wabash* forward to assist and cover them. With rifles useless from 600 yards, there was nothing for the Marines to do but to become diggers themselves, all the while hoping that the Rebs would not be able to direct any cannon fire at their exposed position. While Porter's men and the Marines dug, another naval party advanced to a point two hundred yards from Fort Fisher's palisade and began digging yet another trench. The *Wabash's* Marines were ordered to advance to cover them.

Advance they did. Dodging rebel grape and canister shot, the Marines closed the distance between themselves and the frantically digging sailors. Two Napoleon field pieces at Fort Fisher's central sally port dropped two of the Marines, and Corporal Andrew Tomlin braved the fire to carry one of the injured to safety. It was an act that would earn him one of the many Medals of Honor awarded for heroism during the fight for Fort Fisher. As he did so, Marine marksmen focused their fire on the crews serving the two Napoleons. Their sharp, accurate fire killed several of the gunners and drove off the rest.

photo courtesy
Library of Congress

Bvt. BrigGen Newton Curtis, USA

Sergeant Richard Binder, of the *USS Ticonderoga's* Marine Guard, was one of a second party of sea soldiers sent forward to cover the digging sailors. Breese had asked for volunteers to go forward initially, but there weren't too many takers. With rifle fire, grape shot and canister making a hell of the ground between the landing force and the fort, and the white sand mined with electronically detonated torpedoes, no one relished the idea of crossing the fire-swept beach - even with the .52 caliber Spencer Repeating Rifles the *Ticonderoga's* Marines were armed with.

"Volunteers were not plentiful," Binder wrote later, "indeed for a time not a single one offered his services for the undertaking. Then Lieutenant Williams offered the whole guard of which I was sergeant as sharpshooters."

Binder's Marines crawled all the way to their positions in the face of withering fire from the fort. Once there, they found themselves stranded because of the heavy rate of rebel fire. "...no one would venture to go to the rear, nor did anyone from behind come out to us," he wrote. "...to show your hat above cover meant almost instantly to get it knocked off by a bullet." Despite the rebel fire, the Marines managed to put up an accurate fire of their own, aided by the rapid firing Spencers. Binder and his men kept their fire until running out of ammo, at which time they were out of the fight. But while the Marines were out of bullets, the same didn't apply to the Confederates who were facing them. The Marines became experts at digging while trying to burrow their way underneath the rebel gunfire.

All told, by the time 2:00pm rolled around, there were 2,261 sailors and Marines on the beach to carry out Porter's assault on Fort Fisher's northeast bastion. Captain Dawson hastily organized his 350 remaining Marines into units, and then wheeled to face the fort and begin the advance down the beach. After marching a half mile, LtCmdr. Breese stopped to see if the army was advancing to their right along the river side. Then the navy officer made a mistake and extended his men in a battle line in front of the fort, a maneuver that brought his force into plain sight of Lamb and his men. Not only was the move a direct deviation from Porter's orders to keep the formation with the smallest front possible until the attack commenced, but also it put Dawson's Marines at the rear of the line. Breese hurriedly sent orders for Dawson to bring his men up to the front, not allowing the exasperated Marine commander to establish chains of command, equalize his force, post guides, or any of the other things that must be done to make an assault successful. Dawson brought his Marines up despite not being able to properly form his men.

As they reached the first line of trenches, the Marines executed a side step to allow the assaulting sailors to pass through their ranks. The palisade stood a mile away, and the naval and Marine contingent was ready to attack. Breese and Dawson kept looking for a sign that Terry's infantry to the west were advancing, but no sign of the attack came. Lamb's gunners leisurely bracketed the naval formation on the beach a mile away and began to drop shells uncomfortably close. One exploded to

photo courtesy Library of Congress

The poorly armed Marines and sailors landed north of the fort.

the front and suddenly there were several bloody holes in the front line of sailors. The seamen began to get jittery standing in the open waiting on the army to attack, and Breese knew he had to move soon or lose control of his men.

Breese tried and failed to get a commitment to attack from the army, and decided to move his men down to the beach, where they could find shelter in the dunes from Lamb's artillery while waiting for Terry's tardy attack on the river side. Dawson was dumbstruck at the command. Admiral Porter's orders had expressly forbidden any advance closer to the fort until the army began their attack to the west. But after determining that those were, indeed, Breese's orders, the Marine officer complied.

Now the sailors joined Dawson and his Marines, and the entire force was pinned down below the high water mark of the beach. Not only were the rebels picking men off from the fort, but incoming shells from the federal fleet kept bursting above the beach and raining hot shrapnel down on the landing force's heads. Dawson surveyed his new position and wondered what kind of liquor Breese had been drinking. The "splendid cover" the naval commander had referred to was nowhere to be seen, and to the front of the cowering sailors and Marines lay 600 yards of open sand. Dawson realized that from this new position the only place his men could cover the sailors' assault was from the palisade wall itself. It was here he would take his men when the attack finally came.

The signal to attack came at 3:05pm, more than an hour late. The *USS Malvern's* steam whistle sounded the signal after seeing the flag from Terry's signalman, and the entire fleet shifted its fire away from the land face and began pounding the sea face. On the beach, LtCmdr. Breese sprang to his feet along with his men, who formed into a column 1,600 strong. Unsheathing his cutlass, Breese bellowed "Charge!" and the entire force began their run to the fort.

Dawson spared a quick glance to see if Terry's men were in the fight, and was dismayed to see they weren't. Porter's orders had been to begin the naval assault only in conjunction with the army attack, but Breese had jumped the gun and ordered his assault before the army had even formed up. Still, after having to be on the receiving end of the rebels' fire for so long, the Marines were anxious for the chance to give some back. With a lusty cheer they followed Dawson's lead and joined the sailors in the mad dash for the relative safety of the cover provided by the palisade. Still the army wasn't in the fight, and Dawson knew he and his men could expect to bear the brunt of the Confederates' punishment.

The punishment came quickly. In the fort, Col. Lamb had seen the assault force on the beach and ordered the one remaining gun from the land face to be shifted around to face the threat. He also ordered the two long-range guns at Mound Battery to be ready to take the attackers under fire. When Breese's men charged beyond the safety afforded by the sloping beach, the Confederate gunners were ready. Lamb ordered the gun crews of the destroyed cannons to fight as infantry, and the two abandoned Napoleons that had caused Sgt. Binder's Marines so much grief earlier were wheeled about to rake the attackers with canister. The remaining heavy cannons added their grapeshot to the mix with violent roars. Still the sailors and Marines advanced.

Dawson's Marines were hurrying to catch up to the head of the column of sailors advancing to the Marines' left. The enemy continued to rake the field with a withering fire, and the long distance to the fort began to affect the charging men as tired lungs and legs began to bog down in the sugary sand. The Marines managed to cover a hundred yards before the fastest of the sailors made it to the palisade and vanished around a corner. A moment later Dawson heard a roar of musketry and saw the survivors of that first contingent to breach the defenses head back toward the beach at a flat out run. Seeing the hasty retreat, those following immediately bolted for the nearest cover at the palisades.

The rest of the charging sailors saw what was happening, and quickly took cover behind a smallish sand dune a hundred yards from the fort. Soon there were one thousand sailors trying to make themselves very small behind the dune's ever-smaller rise, while another mixed bag of sailors and Marines huddled at the palisade. On the beach, LtCmdr. Breese was still trying to get the rest of the column on its feet and advancing. The party at the palisade realized they were in deep trouble if something didn't happen soon. With Breese unable to issue orders from where he was, some of the men decided to try and press the attack through one of the holes blown in the wooden wall of the palisade. The sixty attackers went into the breach gamely enough, but Lamb's men stopped them cold.

"The fire from the fort was terrific, and we had only pistols to reply," wrote one Union navy officer trapped at the palisade. "It was a mere slaughterhouse, and, after taking in the utter impossibility of any further effort, Jack sensibly concluded that the next best and most seaman-like thing he could do would be to get out of that, and, suiting the action to the word, the whole of the force that could do so scudded away down the beach like ships before the wind, as fast as their legs could carry them."

The sailors panicked, fleeing down the beach while leaving their dead and dying to litter the ground before the fort. Disbelieving navy officers couldn't fathom the defeat. Desperate for an excuse to explain the failure that had left so many of their men dead and wounded, they turned to the Marine Corp. After the battle, navy officials chastised the Marines for not giving the assaulting sailors the cover fire they needed. The accusers failed to acknowledge that the assault party was poorly trained and armed, and disorganized to the point of bedlam. Three times the naval officer commanding the assault force, LtCmdr. Breese, went against Admiral Porter's orders in his panic once the sailors and Marines came under Confederate fire. Poorly coordinated movements between the army and the navy also contributed to the piecemeal attack that allowed Lamb's gunners to administer such a deadly fire on the navy and Marines.

But the attack did serve one purpose, as warned by Brigadier General Curtis earlier. It focused the attention of the Fort's defenders on the action at the northeast bastion, allowing Terry's infantry to breach Fort Fisher's defenses at Shepherd's Battery. Once into the fort, the Yankees would not be ejected again.

Despite the fact that much of the blame for what happened to the combined navy and Marine assault force at Fort Fisher was the fault of poor planning and preparation by Admiral Porter, as well as poor choices on the ground by LtCmdr Breese, it is the Marines who have come down through history bearing the blame for a defeat that they had little control over. Still, after all is said and done, Fort Fisher remains as the one beach the sea soldiers failed to take in the more than 225 year history of the United States Marine Corp.

The only known portrait of Col. James Moore, courtesy of his descendant, Mr. Roger Moore.

Cape Fear's Ablest Soldier

By Jack E. Fryar, Jr.

James Moore stared intently at the map showing southeastern North Carolina, his brow screwed down in concentration. Word had reached Wilmington that the loyalist Highlanders were on the march in support of Royal Governor Josiah Martin's plan to secure the south for Great Britain. As a result Moore, who along with Robert Howe had been selected as colonels of the North Carolina regiments of the fledgling Continental Army, had assembled his men and marched towards Cross Creek, where MacDonald's force of Scots and Regulators had last been seen. The campaign would be the toughest test yet of what was generally becoming recognized as one of the best military minds to ever come out of the Cape Fear region.

Born in 1737 to the elder Maurice Moore, James Moore was a member of the planter aristocracy of the lower Cape Fear region of North Carolina. His bloodline included "King" Roger Moore, the founder of Orton Plantation in 1725, and a host of other prominent leaders of the colony, including brother Maurice, a judge and leader in the rebellion against British rule in America. His sister Rebecca was married to John Ashe, another soldier and prominent member of the gentry committed to American independence. His grandfather and namesake had been governor of South Carolina. James Moore lived at the family's Rocky Point plantation above Wilmington, land that had been in his family since his father had first brought the Moore clan up from South Carolina after the Tuscarora War in the early 1700's.

James Moore exhibited an interest in the martial arts early, being appointed captain of the militia contingent manning Fort Johnston, at the mouth of the Cape Fear River, in what is modern Southport, in 1758. He was just twenty-one at the time. British Royal Governor Arthur Dobbs later recalled giving Moore command of a company of soldiers, describing him as "...a young gentleman of one of the best families of the province, and who for one year commanded in Fort Johnston, who was expert in military discipline and well beloved in the province." Moore's early military experience included an expedition to give aid to the people of South Carolina during an uprising there.

After the French and Indian War, James Moore parleyed his status as a respected soldier of a leading family into terms in the provincial House of Commons. From 1764 to 1771, then again for a single year in 1773, Moore made an impact in local government by serving on a variety of committees overseeing the administration of Great Britain's North Carolina colony. But Moore's military uniform was not packed away in mothballs during his time as a civilian representative to the House of Commons.

When the British parliament passed the hated Stamp Act in 1765, James Moore joined the other residents of Wilmington and Brunswick in what may have been the first open, armed act of rebellion against British rule in America. Trying to recoup the costs of the French and Indian War, as well as offset the expense of keeping large numbers of troops in America, parliament levied a tax on a wide range of documents issued in the colonies, including items as diverse as newspapers and land deeds. Outrage over the action was swift and vocal. In Wilmington, a mob of protesters burned Lord Bute, the king's advisor who had been the tax's most ardent advocate in parliament, in effigy. They even went so far as to force the man selected by the King to serve as Stamp Master, Dr. William Houston of Duplin County, to make an oath that he would not enforce the act. When the sloop of war *H.M.S. Diligence* arrived in the Cape Fear River with the first load of stamps, the captain of the ship was dismayed to see literally hundreds of locals lining the riverfront with muskets and rifles to prevent the landing of the hated symbols of what locals perceived as London's overbearing treatment of its colonies. Later, Moore led a force of 150 men in an unprecedented march on the home of Royal Governor William Tryon. Moore and his men were after the royal comptroller of the province, a Colonel William Pennington. When the governor refused to deliver the comptroller, Moore's men prepared to take him by force. Bloodshed was averted when Pennington surrendered after resigning his position to save face for the governor. Before it was over, Moore and his confederates extracted oaths from all of the King's representatives except Governor Tryon not to enforce the Stamp Act. The act was repealed shortly after.

Moore's role in the Stamp Act Defiance obviously didn't result in long-term bad feelings between him and Governor Tryon. In 1768, dissatisfaction over their treatment by the courts and court officers caused residents of the interior to rebel against the rule of appointed powers in Hillsborough and Alamance County. Dubbed Regulators by Royal Governor William Tryon, an expedition made up primarily of men from the coastal regions was mounted to put down the rebellion. Tryon appointed James Moore as colonel in charge of the army's artillery, and after a show of force the rebellion died without a clash of arms. That was not the case three years later. Troubles with the Regulators surfaced again in 1771, and this time Tryon was determined to crush the rebellion once and for all. Moore was again commissioned as colonel of the expedition's artillery, and performed well at the Battle of Alamance that saw Tryon's army of coastal North Carolinians defeat the insurrectionist Regulators of the interior. Moore would face some of these same men again in the campaign leading up to the Battle of Moores Creek five years later.

Despite defending the Crown in its attempts to squash the Regulator uprising, by 1770 James Moore had become convinced that the best hope for a bright future lay in the colony's break from English rule. At a June meeting of the Wilmington Sons of Liberty Moore lent his support to the formation of a committee to enforce a non-importation agreement along the Cape Fear. The colonies had decided that by refusing to import any manufactured goods from England they might force Parliament to realize how much of their economy depended on the American colonies. They hoped that realization might persuade the British to adopt more equitable policies regarding the government of its American possessions. That effort, along with many others, failed. The sentiment among many colonists in North Carolina and elsewhere was that only independence would remove the yoke of King George III from their collective necks.

In July of 1774, the decision was made to hold a Provincial Continental Congress, and Moore was elected a delegate to the body. It was the first predecessor to the Continental Congress, which would officially sever all ties of fealty to Great Britain two years later by publishing the Declaration of Independence. A year later, in 1775, James Moore and his brother-in-law, John Ashe, were both in the running to command North Carolina's new regiment of the Continental Army. Moore won the election by a single vote, then began assembling, provisioning, arming and training the regiment at Wilmington.

By January 1776, Royal Governor Josiah Martin had fled the Governor's Palace in New Bern to a confining yet safe berth aboard the *H.M.S. Cruizer* in the Cape Fear River. It was there he conceived the plan to raise a regiment of Highlanders from among loyalist Scots and former Regulators in the interior counties, march to Wilmington to link up with British regulars being sent from Ireland, and smash the American rebels' control of the South. Word of the plan caused James Moore to take command of patriot efforts to prevent the Highlanders from reaching the coast. Moore assumed overall command of the Continental Army and militia units mobilized to stop Brigadier General Donald MacDonald's Highlanders before they could reach Wilmington. In a chess match of a campaign that saw move and countermove all across southeastern North Carolina over almost a month, Moore's maneuvering put the Wilmington and New Bern militias under Alexander Lillington and Richard Caswell on the east side of Moore's Creek Bridge by February 27, 1776. In the brief but fierce fight that came shortly after sun-up, MacDonald's Highlanders were crushed and British plans for the domination of the Carolinas were destroyed for another five years until the occupation of Wilmington in 1781.

For two weeks James Moore and Donald MacDonald played a lethal game of chess that culminated with the defeat of the Highlanders at Moores Creek. For the Scots, the end of their two week march to the coast would be disasterous.

Recognizing the brilliant campaign waged by Moore, the Continental Congress promoted him to the rank of Brigadier General on March 1, 1776 and placed him in command of all Continental Army units in North Carolina. His first posting saw him consolidate his forces at Wilmington to keep a weather eye out for British sea borne incursions. Warships flying the Union Jack did not depart the North Carolina coast until October of that year. When General Charles Lee's regulars marched south to intercept Sir Henry Clinton's redcoats at Charleston, Moore's North

Carolina regiments were with him. Later Lee conceived a plan to attack British possessions in Florida and left Moore in command of the forces left at Charleston during his absence. When Lee was ordered back to the northern theater of operations, Moore assumed command of the war effort in the Southern Department.

Lee did not leave Moore with a sound command when he departed for points north. Shortages and no money to make them good plagued the Continentals. Moore found himself trying to fight a freezing winter and bottle up the British in Charleston at the same time. He spent the winter traveling between the South Carolina port city that had been his grandfather's seat of government two generations before, and the Carolina to the north that his own father had played such a big part in opening up for settlement. His goal was to drum up support in the form of food, blankets, medicines and the many other amenities needed to keep an army in the field over a harsh winter.

Those same supply problems would continue to haunt Moore into the new year. A year after Moores Creek, in February 1777, James Moore received orders to march his North Carolinians north to link up with General George Washington. Again shortfalls of clothes and equipment turned a routine movement into an ordeal. Moore took ill under the stress of shouldering the load of trying to keep his army in the field almost single-handedly. Having returned to the Cape Fear when his health began to fail in January of 1777, James Moore died in Wilmington of what was diagnosed as " a fit of Gout in his stomach." Moore left behind a widow, Ann Ivie Moore, sons Duncan and James Moore, and daughters Sarah and Mary.

Samuel A. Ashe, in his book of biographical sketches of notable North Carolinians, says that General James Moore died in the same house on the same day that his brother, Judge Maurice Moore did, and that they were buried together. Had he not died young, it is highly likely that James Moore would have been recorded as one of the new nation's best soldiers, and certainly one of the best military minds that North Carolina produced during the Revolutionary War.

Omar ibn Said, aka "Uncle Omar"

The Governor and the African Prince

By Jack E. Fryar, Jr.

My name is Omar ibn Said. My birthplace was Fut Tur (Futa Toro), between the two rivers...I reside in this country by reason of great necessity. Wicked men took me by violence and sold me to the Christians. We sailed a month and a half on the great sea to a place called Charleston in the Christian land. I fell into the hands of a small, weak and wicked man, who feared not God at all, nor did he read (the gospel) at all or pray. I was afraid to remain with a man so depraved and who committed so many crimes and I ran away. After a month our Lord god brought me forward to the hand of a good man, who fears God, and loves to do good, and whose name is Jim Owen and whose brother is called Col. John Owen. These are two excellent men. -I am residing in Bladen County."

In the beginning, home for Omar ibn Said was East Africa, in a Fula State of then-French Senegal. Of mixed African and Berber stock, the small-framed young man came from a family of minor aristocracy and was something of a prince among his people. Omar was born around 1770, to a father who was a man of influence and power among his tribe. He saw to it that his son had the benefit of all that power and wealth could provide. But Omar's life of privilege was cut short when his father was killed in one of the many battles that took place during the nonstop internecine tribal wars of the region. An uncle assumed responsibility for the young Omar, seeing to his education in Islam, reading, writing, and simple arithmetic.

Omar's studies continued for twenty-five years before the young man was of age to take his place as a man in the tribal hierarchy. Returning home to his village, Omar became a merchant, selling cotton cloth to customers throughout the region. It was during one such market gathering that Omar was captured in a surprise attack by raiders from a rival tribe and sold to slavers. Omar ibn Said took his last look at Africa as he was being loaded into the hold of a slave ship bound for America.

photo courtesy N.C. Dept. of Archives & History

The African prince's first glimpse of his new home came in 1807, as the hatches to the ships hold was thrown back and the captured slaves emerged into the bright sunlight of Charleston, South Carolina. The docks were a bustling place full of strange sights and smells that made the confused young man long for home. Rough sailors ushered the captive Africans down a gangplank to the wharf, where a factor took charge and led the slaves to a holding pen. Days later, Omar ibn Said, Prince of Arabia, was sold into slavery.

Omar's new master, by the name of Johnson, was an ill-tempered man given to strong drink and a sour disposition. The

Governor John Owen

work he assigned to the small-framed African would have been a chore for even a much bigger man, and was all but impossible for Omar to accomplish. When the work wasn't done with the speed or to the degree of competence his owner deemed appropriate, then Omar was punished with beatings and confinement. Complicating matters was the fact that Omar spoke no English. At night, Omar prayed fervently to his God for deliverance. He wondered what fate had caused him to be thrust into a living hell in a strange land where not even the other slaves could communicate with him. And day after day, the beatings got worse. Omar knew if he stayed, it was only a matter of time before he would die. The prince-turned-slave decided it was time to flee.

Stealing away in the dark, Omar didn't know what lay ahead of him. In a strange country, among a people he could not talk to, a runaway slave with no destination in mind, he only knew that continuing to live under Johnson's heavy hand was no life at all. He set out to get as far away from Charleston and his cruel master as he could. A month's wandering found the prince in Fayetteville, North Carolina. It was amazing that a black man who could speak no English was able to travel unchallenged from Charleston, South Carolina all the way to Fayetteville, in the North Carolina Piedmont; but through guile and good luck Omar had managed just that. But in Fayetteville his luck ran out.

Outside town, Omar ibn Said saw several of what he called "great houses". These were churches, and as Omar was a devout man, he went inside one to pray. A local boy was startled to see a black man enter into a white church, and rode off to alert his father about the runaway. The boy's father, a man named Handah (Hunter?) according to Omar, returned in the company of another man and a pack of dogs and took him into custody. The two whites led Omar twelve miles to Fayetteville and left him in the care of the county jail. It was a stay that would last just over two weeks, but it was a turning point in Omar's life.

Bob Mumford was not a cruel man, but the law was the law. As sheriff of Cumberland County, it was his job to hold on to runaway slaves until their masters came to claim them - even the ones who appeared to have been mistreated, as the whip marks on the back of the small man in his jail attested. There was something about the runaway, a quiet dignity at odds with the worn clothes and obvious desperation of the man that piqued Mumford's interest. The man had spoken in a strange language when taken into custody, but after it became apparent that none of the white men at the jail could understand him, he had become quiet. Not even other slaves seemed able to understand what the runaway said, and a close look at the man sitting erectly on floor of the cell made it obvious that the man did not share the same facial features of other Africans Mumford had seen. It was a puzzle that Mumford would find himself pondering at odd moments without coming up with any explanations. And the puzzle was about to get thicker.

Omar grew increasingly desperate to communicate with his captors - or anyone else, for that matter. In the fireplace grate he spotted a few odd pieces of charred wood and coal left over from past blazes and had an idea. Perhaps if these men could not speak his language, then maybe they could read it. Omar took up the charred fire remnants, and began to write on the walls of his cell. Using the Arabic alphabet, he wrote his name and his story. He wrote passages from the Koran that he knew from memory. He did ciphers to demonstrate his knowledge of mathematics. It got results.

Word spread of the strange little black man in the county jail who scribbled strange markings on the jail walls but spoke not a word of English. People began to drop by to see the oddity and speculate as to the meaning of the writings on the wall. Among those was Sheriff Mumford. One look at the wall of Omar's cell and Mumford knew he was dealing with no ordinary runaway. There was order to the markings, and intelligence in the eyes of the little man as he gestured to the writing that indicated education far beyond that which most slave owners would extend to their African chattels. It made Mumford even more determined to solve the man's mystery.

James Owen was a wealthy planter of Bladen County who had served in Congress from 1817-1819, later served as president of the Wilmington and Raleigh Railroad, and was a general of the state militia. His brother, John Owen, would later serve as governor of North Carolina from 1828 to 1830. They lived across the Cape Fear River from each other in northwest Bladen County. It was from a river man ferrying supplies from Fayetteville to Wilmington that the Owen brothers first heard of Omar ibn Said. The mystery of the runaway slave grabbed their imaginations, too, and in short order the two distinguished young men were bound for Sheriff Mumford's jail.

Mumford ushered the two men into the presence of Omar with eagerness, hoping that the two could shed some light on the subject. John Owen looked at the writing on the walls, and, while he could not read or speak Arabic, recognized the scribblings as being an organized alphabet. The man in the cell was obviously educated and no ordinary slave. A quick consultation with his brother and the two were decided. John Owen paid the $1000 bond for Omar, and took him back to Owen Hill, his estate in Bladen County.

Owen proved to be a kind master. Omar was immediately clothed and fed, provided a cabin of his own and generally made to feel at home in the Owen household. In Omar's words, "These are good men. What food they eat they give me to eat. As they clothe themselves they clothe me. They permit me to read the gospel of God, our Lord, and Savior, and King..." Through gestures, John Owen was able to finally determine that the new member of his household was named Omar, and the delight in the eyes of the little man was evident when the future governor first made the connection and said the name aloud. In the coming weeks, there would be a scare for the prince as a man named Mitchell came to Owen Hill and tried to buy Omar and return him to Charleston. Omar was vehement in refusing when Owen put the choice to him. "No,no,no,no,no,no,no, I am not willing to go to Charleston. I stay in the hand of Jim Owen."

Omar quickly grew to be an integral part of both Owen households. Between the two Owen brothers and the children's tutor, Omar began to learn English. Omar had found a home. He was given keys to all the doors in Owen Hill and began serving as major domo for the governor. The Owens provided Omar with a horse and buggy and the freedom to wander as he pleased within the confines of the plantation. The Owen children began to call him "Uncle Moro". As he learned, he was able to finally share his tale with his friends and - at least legally - masters. The children were treated to wonderful stories of the prince's boyhood and the land he had called home for so many years. And Omar was happy at Owen Hill. He would scribble notes on scraps of paper and tack them to the trees around the estate, telling neighbors they must not take him away from his "good master".

Omar was also able to begin learning about Christianity from the Owen family and local ministers. John Owen went to the trouble and expense of having a Bible made in Arabic for Omar, and soon the Mohammedan wanted to convert. He began attending Beth Car Presbyterian Church in Tar Heel, where he and another slave had special seats beneath the church's high pulpit. Omar became every bit as devout a Christian as he had been a devout Muslim. When Omar read from his new book of scripture, it was invariably the Twenty-Third Psalm. At the part where the verse speaks of going down into the Valley of Death, Omar, in his broken English, would recite, "Me no fear; Master, He is with me." Omar's Bible is now part of the collection of Davidson College.

After being baptized in Fayetteville Presbyterian Church, Omar was a member along with the Owen family there until Governor Owen moved to Wilmington and their church membership was transferred to the port city's First Presbyterian Church. On Sundays Omar would walk down the center isle, back straight and eyes looking only forward, to the front row of the church hall. Placing a chair in front of the minister in the pulpit, he would sit erect with his hands on his knees listening intently to the sermon until the final prayer. On the way out of the church, Omar would bow solemnly to the minister who greeted his congregation by the front door.

Governor Owen offered Omar his freedom on several occasions, but was always turned down by the prince. Omar feared that his wife and child in Africa had long ago moved on with their lives, and he adamantly refused to take a wife from among the other slave women of the Owen household, declaring that he could not in good conscience marry someone not of royal lineage. He contented himself with serving the Owen family for the rest of his life.

Omar ibn Said died in 1859 after a life of ninety years. He was laid to rest in the family graveyard at Owen Hill, and remembered as a cherished friend of the Owen family. Omar would have liked that remembrance. He thought himself fortunate to have ended up in the homes of John and James Owen, and was quick to declare it. "O ye people of North Carolina, O ye people of S. Carolina. O ye people of America, all of you; have you among you any two such men as Jim and John Owen? These men are good men."

Beaufort's Old Burial Ground is a treasure trove of coastal history, with graves dating back to the colonial period.

And They All Rest Together:
Beaufort's Old Burying Ground

By David A. Norris

photo & drawing by the author

T hey are quite a motley group of neighbors. A little girl buried in a keg of rum. A British naval officer buried standing up. Two star-crossed lovers separated for decades and reunited for a last few weeks of happiness. An American naval hero with a grave adorned with one of his own cannons. These people are only some of those whose final resting place is in the mossy, shaded grounds of the Old Burying Ground in Beaufort, perhaps North Carolina's most beautiful and interesting cemetery.

The Old Burying Ground has a long history. The oldest marked grave bears the simple inscription "A. P. 1756", but a 1731 deed records the addition of land to the cemetery. Some believe that the first people buried there were slain in the Tuscarora War of 1711. The burying ground takes up most of the block bounded by Ann, Craven, Broad, and Turner Streets, sharing space with three churches: Purvis Chapel A.M.E. Zion, Ann Street Methodist, and First Baptist. On sunny days, bright shafts of sunlight pierce the canopy of ancient live oaks and spotlight the old inscriptions on the gravestones.

The Old Burying Ground developed on the lots set aside for the new town's church and courthouse. The people of the small colonial village of Beaufort never got around to building an Anglican church. Laymen or occasionally visiting clergymen held services in the small wooden courthouse. In 1724, a hurricane tore off the roof of the first courthouse, and the rest of the building burned down the next year. A new courthouse was built in 1728, and Anglican services were held there throughout the colonial era.

The entrance to the cemetery, on a tree-shaded Beaufort street.

Eventually, three churches were built at three of the corners of the Old Burying Ground. Purvis Chapel, Beaufort's oldest church building, was built on the northeast corner of the cemetery as a Methodist church in 1820. In 1854, the congregation built a new church on the southeast corner, the Ann Street Methodist Church. The old chapel was given to a black congregation and became the Purvis Chapel A. M. E. Zion Church. The First Baptist Church was built at the southwest corner of the cemetery in 1854; its current building dates from 1953.

Stone grave markers were expensive and so fairly rare in colonial North Carolina. Many grave markers then and even later were made of wood, with carved or painted lettering. Cypress, which is strongly resistant to weather, was a common wood used in grave markers. Most wooden markers have long since disintegrated, taking with them the names and stories of those whose graves they noted. Several wooden markers, their writing obscured by the elements and dappled with moss, remain in the Old Burying Ground today. A few, such as one for a child named Luther Robinson who died in 1898, are still readable.

Early stone grave markers in Beaufort and elsewhere in North Carolina were imported from New England or elsewhere along the east coast. Gravestones became more elaborate during the 19th century, a feature of social history revealed by a stroll through the Old Burying Ground. Early headstones often have a distinctive and easily recognizable silhouette with a semicircular motif flanked by flat edges or smaller semicircles. Some graves are topped with ledger stones, which are large flat slabs measuring perhaps three by six feet and laid horizontally over the grave or vault. Ledger stones had more space for biographical information, Biblical verses, or poetry.

Brick vaults, based on British burial traditions, are a common feature in Beaufort and other coastal communities, where they prevented coffins from floating away in areas with a high water table. Some old brick vaults have rounded arch tops; others have gabled ends and the bricks are laid to resemble a peaked roof.

One of the most famous graves in the Burying Ground holds a man who was buried standing up. The original marker is long gone, but a replacement reads, "British Naval Officer buried standing in salute to His Majesty George II". The story goes that the man spent the last part of his life as an invalid. After years of confinement to a bed, he hated the thought of spending eternity lying down, and asked to be buried standing up. So, to honor his wishes, his coffin was tipped into his grave vertically. The man's name is long forgotten, and sources disagree on the date of his burial and even whether he was an officer in the British army or navy. Another legend of the Old Burying Ground is the "Little Girl in the Rum Keg." The daughter of a Beaufort merchant named Nathaniel Sloo, she died at sea while on a voyage with her father. Her father wanted to bury her in their hometown, so he placed her body in a keg of rum to preserve it. When his ship got to Beaufort, the barrel was taken straight to the Old Burying Ground and placed in her grave. Today, visitors decorate her grave with seashells, pretty trinkets, little toys, or coins as a remembrance. Coins from Canada and Europe, tokens of foreign tourists, are among the gifts *(the 18th-century Nathaniel Sloo House stands today on Front Street in Beaufort.)*.

The grave of a British soldier buried at attention in Beaufort Cemetery.

Beaufort's stained glass

Perhaps the most famous grave in the Old Burying Ground is that of Capt. Otway Burns. Burns was a successful privateer captain in the War of 1812. In 1818, he built the *Prometheus*, the first steamboat constructed in North Carolina. He served in the General Assembly, and was the keeper of the lighthouse at Portsmouth, across from Ocracoke. After his death in 1850, he was brought to Beaufort for burial. In 1902, Burns' descendants built a brick vault over his grave, which they topped with a cannon from his privateer ship, the *Snap Dragon*. Photographs of this unusual grave have appeared in many books and on countless postcards.

Veterans of many of America's wars rest in the Old Burying Ground. The cemetery has many headstones belonging to Civil War veterans. Visitors will notice graves with iron Maltese crosses, which designate graves of Confederate veterans. Among the Confederate dead is Sgt. Jechonias Willis, one of the two Beaufort Confederates killed in the bombardment of Fort Macon in 1862. Capt. Matthew R. Gooding, commander of the Confederate warship and blockade-runner *Nashville*, died in 1863 and is also buried in this cemetery.

Not every Civil War veteran in the cemetery fought for the South. Sgt. George Johnson, of the 35th United States Colored Troops, is buried there. His unit was one of several black Union regiments raised in North Carolina.

And not all burials during the Civil War years were directly related to the war. The grave of Ann Potter tells of a great tragedy that struck Beaufort during those years. She taught Sunday school at the Ann Street Methodist Church. In the yellow fever epidemic of 1864, she and her entire class of ten children died of the dread disease.

One gravestone in the cemetery came from Denmark. It is placed over the last resting place of Capt. Christian Wulff, a Danish naval officer who died of yellow fever in Beaufort in 1856 (Denmark owned the Virgin Islands until they were sold to the United States in 1917. A ship going from the Caribbean to Denmark would follow the Gulf Stream and therefore pass not too far from Beaufort.). Wulff's sister, Henrietta, had a tombstone carved in Denmark and sent to Beaufort for her brother. In 1858, Henrietta Wulff decided to come to Beaufort to see her brother's resting place. She never made it to Beaufort. Her ship, the *Austria*, caught fire during the voyage and was completely destroyed. She was one of the 300 passengers who perished.

The gravestone of Nancy Manney French (1820-1886) tells another sad story, one warmed by the glow of an undying love. Nancy Manney of Beaufort fell in love with Charles French, her tutor. Her family forbade her to marry French, and he left Beaufort to seek his fortune. French ended up in Arizona and was quite successful, rising to the post of associate justice of the territorial Supreme Court. He wrote faithfully to Nancy, but she never received the letters and thought he had forgotten her. Many years later, French wrote a query about Nancy to the town postmaster. The postmaster had a startling confession to make: as a favor to the family, he had intercepted and destroyed every letter French had sent her. French still loved Nancy, and upon learning what happened to his letters, he returned to Beaufort to see his old love. He found her dying of tuberculosis. They married and spent a short time together in the few weeks before she died in 1886.

Two different tales are told about the grave of Dr. Lafayette Leecraft, which is topped with a broken stone column. One says that Leecraft belonged to an odd fraternity of doctors, who forbade their members to have a grave marker over a certain height. His friends, so the story goes, broke the column to keep it within their regulations. It is more likely, though, that the broken column is simply a symbol of a life cut short.

As gravestones became more elaborate in the 19th century, more and more of them were adorned with relief sculptures or topped with statues. A tree trunk, broken off near its roots, symbolized an early death. Graves of children, tragically common in an era of short life expectancies, might have symbols such as lambs or a sleeping child. Ornate decoration also enhances many of the iron fences that surround some of the family plots in the cemetery.

One grave memorializes the victims of the wreck of the *Crissie Wright*, a schooner that was lost on January 11, 1886. The *Crissie Wright* ran aground off Shackleford Banks near Beaufort during a storm on a bitterly cold night. Ashore, people saw the wreck, but were unable to launch a boat in the heavy surf. Three crewmen were washed overboard, but four men managed to wrap up in a sail and lash themselves to a mast. By the time rescuers could get a boat to the wreck the next day, only one man was still clinging to life. The young sailor was taken ashore, wrapped in quilts, and warmed up enough to survive. The bodies of some of the crewmen were never claimed, and were laid to rest in a common grave near the Purvis Chapel side of the cemetery.

The Old Burying Ground is now on the National Register of Historic places. Located at Ann and Craven Streets in Beaufort, it is open to visitors from early morning to sunset.

Swiss Landgrave Baron Christopher Von Graffenreid

King Hancock and the Bloody Warpath

By Jack E. Fryar, Jr.

S wiss landgrave Baron Christopher Von Graffenreid could only listen in helpless horror to the whoops and cries of the Tuscarora braves as they executed his friend, John Lawson. The famed explorer of the Carolinas was condemned to die in a cruel twist of fate that saw the man who had been one of the colony's biggest advocates for the Indian tribes killed, while the man who was most responsible for bringing the offending settlers to the banks of the Neuse River was spared. It was one of the first clashes between two cultures seeking to claim the Carolina coast as their home. Before it was over, the colonization of North Carolina would nearly die in its infancy, and the waters of the Neuse River would take on an ocher tint from the blood of both white settlers and Indians alike.

Early in the life of the new colony political infighting between factions supporting Governor Edward Hyde and his predecessor, Thomas Cary, embroiled North Carolina in what amounted to civil war. By 1711 the southern Tuscarora tribe under the rule of King Hancock, as well as their allies among the smaller coastal tribes, recognized the weakness of the settlers and decided the time was ripe to rectify some of the indignities they had suffered at the hands of the encroaching whites. It was just bad luck that Lawson, Von Graffenreid, and two black slaves stumbled into the Indians as they were preparing for a dawn attack on September 22.

Trouble had been brewing between the settlers and the Indians for some time prior to the outbreak of hostilities in the fall of 1711. As early as 1703, the colonial government had declared the Coree and Nynee tribes living south of the Neuse River public enemies and waged a war that forced them to move inland, seeking refuge with the mighty Tuscarora. Both sides kept a wary eye on the other for a decade before things came to head and the blood began to flow in earnest. Neither

Von Graffenreid and John Lawson's capture by the Tuscarora.

side trusted the other, and that distrust manifested itself in irritating and inflammatory acts by both groups. The Machapunga tribe began threatening settlers, stealing livestock and accosting whites before retreating to the safety of their village, close by a wooded wilderness that afforded them a quickly reached sanctuary when settlers would mobilize to retaliate against them.

It's not like the Indians had no reason for suspicion. The site where Christopher Von Graffenreid settled his Swiss and Palatine German newcomers, at the junction of the Neuse and Trent rivers, was originally a Neusioc Indian town called Cartouca. When the whites came, the Indians were paid a paltry sum and quickly moved out of the area, an act that left many Indians disgruntled. According to Von Graffenreid, Surveyor General John Lawson found the site for the settlers, claiming it to be uninhabited. When the settlers arrived, Von Graffenreid said Lawson urged the landgrave to drive the tribe off without any sort of payment. If true, it was an attitude that would have been extremely out of character for Lawson, whose travels through the North Carolina backcountry had seen him in many encounters with Native Americans. Lawson, for the most part, was a sympathetic friend of the Indians.

Indian traders in many cases made it a practice to cheat the natives, often plying them with liquor before robbing them of their lands and goods. According to Lawson, many traders considered it a "Gift of Christianity" to not sell their wares to the

Indians as cheaply as they did to the whites. And of course, the settler's penchant for taking Indians and selling them into slavery was also a point of contention between the two cultures. It got so bad at one point that a year before the war broke out, the Tuscarora actually petitioned the government of Pennsylvania to let them move there to avoid the risk of slavery in North Carolina, especially in the area of Bath County. For whites, the trouble between Governor Hyde and Thomas Cary was a contributing factor in distrust of their Indian neighbors. In the summer of 1711 that distrust was intensified by rumors that Cary supporters were trying to incite the natives to attack Hyde's supporters.

So it was that by the autumn of 1711, the Indians of the central North Carolina coast had had enough. The Tuscarora weren't blind to the discord among the whites, and King Hancock began planning a surprise attack that he hoped would rid the Indians of the newcomers. Hancock sent emissaries out to enlist the smaller tribes and found willing allies in the Coree, Bay River, Machapunga, Neusioc, and Pamticough Indians. With the 250 warriors that they contributed, King Hancock was able to field a force of at least 500 braves. That was a lot of men, but the settlers actually caught a break that stopped it from being much worse. Hancock had sought an alliance with the northern band of the Tuscarora in the Albemarle region, but tribal leader Chief Tom Blunt chose to remain neutral. Had he allied himself with Hancock, the hammer that fell on the colonists in September 1711 would have been much larger.

John Lawson and his party were taken prisoner by a band of roughly sixty Indians and taken to King Hancock's village at Catechna, near modern Snow Hill. Hancock ordered the prisoners to be sequestered until he could bring them before a council of tribal leaders and question them about their presence in Tuscarora country. The next night, Lawson and Von Graffenreid were summoned before a war council made up of King Hancock and the chiefs of several nearby smaller tribes. After the white men answered questions from the chiefs, it was decided that they posed no immediate threat to the Indians' plans for a surprise attack on the settlements along the Neuse River and New Bern. Chief Hancock informed the relieved explorers that they could go free the next day.

As the captives prepared to leave the next morning, a few chiefs who had been unable to reach Catechna in time to participate in the war council the night before finally arrived at the village. Among them was the Coree chief, Cor Tom, whose people had been the previous owners of the land claimed by Von Graffenreid's settlers at New Bern. Ever since his tribesmen had been evicted from the site claimed by the whites, Cor Tom had harbored strong resentments towards the settlers and especially John Lawson, who he took to be a friend until the arrival of the Swiss and Palatines. When he saw the whites about to go free, a violent quarrel erupted between Cor Tom and John Lawson. Both Von Graffenreid and Lawson were seized again and returned to the lodge where the war council was reconvened. This time, with Cor Tom arguing for their deaths, Lawson and Von Graffenreid were not so lucky. King Hancock decided to assuage his ally and ordered the deaths of both men.

Von Graffenreid immediately protested that as landgrave his death would result in the wrath of the Queen of England falling down on Hancock and his tribe. King Hancock consulted with the neutral King Tom Blunt of the Northern Tuscarora, who advised him to avoid trouble with England by letting Von Graffenreid live. What Hancock did with Lawson, on the other hand, was up to him. King Hancock decided Von Graffenreid would be spared, but in a nod to his Coree counterpart, Lawson was denied a pardon. Indian braves locked Von Graffenreid away in a lodge as the execution of John Lawson took place. Hancock decided that while the

photo courtesy N.C. Dept. of Archives & History

John Lawson's death at the hands of King Hancock's men

landgrave would not lose his life, he would remain a captive until after the attack was under way, to prevent Von Graffenreid from raising the alarm. So it was that the Swiss nobleman listened to the war cries of the gathered tribes as one of North Carolina's best-known explorers went to his Maker. Accounts vary as to just how Lawson died. Von Graffenreid confessed he never heard Lawson utter a sound as he was killed, but was of the opinion that the Indians cut his throat with a razor. One of the two slaves who were also captured reported that the Tuscarora stuck his body full of lighterwood splinters and slowly burned him alive – a grisly demise Lawson had recorded in an earlier account of his encounters with Indians while exploring the Carolina backcountry.

On September 22, as settlers began their Saturday morning chores at farms along the Neuse and Pamlico rivers, five hundred Tuscarora warriors and their allies from the smaller eastern tribes launched the surprise attack that would tear through the white settlements with a fury unmatched by anything previously experienced in the history of the young colony. Terrified survivors wrote of seeing acts of savagery by the Indians without regard to age or sex. With one eye painted with a circle of black and the other with a circle of white, the war parties under King Hancock swept east. Houses were pillaged and set to the torch, while the owners were killed with a savagery unknown among European armies. Vital crops were destroyed under the feet of attacking bands of Indians, and livestock were killed or driven off to fend for themselves in the wilderness. The attacks seemed harshest along the Neuse and the south bank of the Pamlico, but all of Bath County felt the wrath of the Tuscarora.

Not all settlers were taken without a fight. The story goes that John Porter, Jr.'s Chocowinity Bay home was among the first attacked. Porter and his guest, Dr. Patrick Maule, fought off the attackers and escaped with Porter's family in a boat.

William Bartram

A Mr. Nevil, of Blounts Creek was not so fortunate. He and his family were not just killed by the warriors, but their bodies desecrated, as well. Christopher Gale, North Carolina's receiver-general, had barely missed being captured along with Lawson and Von Graffenreid. Gale had been invited along, but had to beg off when a relative fell victim to yellow fever. Gale wrote of women being "laid on house floors and great stakes driven up through their bodies. Pregnant women had their unborn children ripped out and hung up in trees."

Bath and New Bern became flooded with refugees seeking protection from the marauding Indians. William Brice's plantation on the Trent River was also a destination for the fleeing settlers. Brice was a blacksmith and one of the few settlers with the foresight to build a fort on his property. He had been at odds with Von Graffenreid earlier, and had drawn up a list of charges against the landgrave, going so far as to march against him at New Bern. Whatever disagreements the two may have had were put aside for later when the Tuscarora went on the warpath. Within a month of the first attacks, there were eleven such fortified redoubts along the rivers. But while the settlers may have found a temporary refuge from the Tuscarora, food and ammunition were in short supply. Much of the ordnance the settlers had on hand was used earlier during the Cary Rebellion. The same hands that wielded those muskets were also the hands that normally would have been put to bringing in the season's crops. While the fortified walls of places like New Bern kept the Indians at bay, the crops that rotted in the fields during the rebellion stood a good chance of accomplishing what native force of arms had not. Even if the white colonists did find a way of feeding the many hungry mouths gathered at their strong points, it was only a matter of time before they ran out of lead and powder to defend themselves. North Carolina needed help, and it needed it quick.

After the initial spate of attacks, the Indians took a break to return home with their plunder and the women and children of the colonists they had slain, captives who would become slaves to the tribes. Among those captives was the Bartram family of the Whiteoak River, whose descendents John and William Bartram became world famous naturalists. In their wake the Indians left roughly 140 dead settlers, almost half of who came from among Von Graffenreid's Swiss and Palatines. Only New Bern escaped the devastation of the Tuscarora warpath, as the landgrave managed to extract a pledge from King Hancock to leave it unharmed.

While the Indians took time to regroup, the settlers set about raising the alarm. Governor Hyde sent messengers to Virginia and South Carolina seeking men, munitions and provender for the beleaguered settlers huddled around their dwindling stockpiles at the Bath County garrisons. In the Albemarle, where Chief Tom Blunt's neutrality had spared the colonists the same horrors endured by their brethren to the south, Hyde called out the militia and prepared to march to Bath County's aid. Hyde's efforts to relieve the colonists in the Neuse region were hampered by lingering grudges from the Cary Rebellion. Quakers from the Albemarle also refused to bear arms in the fight, limiting the manpower pool available for the expedition. In the short term, the settlers of Bath County would have to fend for themselves.

Major General Thomas Pollock managed to raise 150 men from the Chowan Precinct to march to Bath's aid and join with the fifty or sixty men gathered by William Brice. In Bath, a fort of sorts had been built on a rise outside town that prevented the Indians from sacking the port settlement. Pollock ordered Brice's company to march out and link up with troops from Bath at an abandoned Indian village up the Neuse River. Brice did so, but the men from Bath never showed up. In lieu of orders to the contrary, Brice advanced deeper into the interior until he came up against a force of 300 Indians. Outnumbered and finding himself literally in Indian country, Brice was forced to withdraw to the relative safety of his plantation.

While Brice was beating a hasty retreat, North Carolina's neighbors were trying to come to their aid – at least to varying degrees. Virginia's Governor Alexander Spottswood immediately ordered a halt to all trade with North Carolina Indians in an attempt to cut off their supplies of arms and ammunition. Virginia militia were dispatched to the border to block warriors from traveling south to join the Tuscarora in their wars against the whites. The governor, while never going so far as to ask for troops to aid the North Carolinians, did persuade the legislature to appropriate money for material relief. Spottswood also tried to use the resumption of trade between Virginia and the tribes of the Northern Tuscarora as a carrot to persuade the warriors of Chief Tom Blunt's band to enter the fray on the side of the colonists. Chief Tom Blunt wisely chose to remain neutral despite the governor's overtures.

Christopher Gale, in his role as a major of the militia, had better luck in South Carolina. When word of the Tuscarora attack reached Charleston, the government almost immediately appropriated a healthy sum to help the North Carolinians. While the cash was appreciated and certainly needed, the most pressing shortage the besieged colonists had was for men to take the fight to the enemy. South Carolina answered the call by raising an expeditionary force of Indians from their own Yamassee, Catawba, Cheraw, Wateree, Wynyaw and Cape Fear tribes. Under the

Christopher Gale (right), attempted to bring men and supplies for Barnwell's expedition by sea, but was detained as a prisoner of war after his ship was captured by the French in the ongoing Queen Anne's War.

photo courtesy N.C. Dept. of Archives & History

command of Colonel John Barnwell, a young but veteran Indian fighter who had been the colony's comptroller, the force numbered over 500 Indian warriors led by 30 white men.

It was common practice among the European settlers to use Indians as their proxies when it came to fighting in America. Not only were white fighters unused to the guerrilla style of fighting employed by the Native Americans, but also the numbers of white colonists that could be mustered for a campaign were woefully small for the task. Using Indians to fight Indians also had the effect of deflecting lingering, post-war grudges away from the white paymasters and onto their Indian mercenaries. The colonists were well aware that after the fighting was over they would have to do business with the Indians again. One of the reasons the Indians were doomed to lose in their struggle against white encroachment was that they were never able to unite against the common enemy. Instead, traditional rivalries between the various tribes was used to good advantage by the whites, ultimately proving out the divide and conquer rule. White traders and governments encouraged Indian warriors by purchasing captured enemies as slaves and paying for scalps. The windfall a war with the Tuscarora represented made finding Indian allies willing to make the march north easy to find. A month after the Tuscarora lit the fuse that started the bloodshed, the Barnwell expedition was ready to go to the aid of the North Carolina colonists.

It took more than two months for Barnwell to make the trek to the banks of the Neuse, where Christopher Gale had promised to meet him with a force of North Carolina men to supplement the South Carolinians' numbers. Barnwell was eager to see the promised men, because many of his Indian braves had deserted on the way north. But when he arrived at the meeting place there was no sign of the promised North Carolina soldiers. Gale's force was supposed to have returned to North Carolina aboard a sloop carrying much needed provisions. Little did Barnwell know that European politics had interfered with the plan. Gale's ship had been captured by a French warship and made a prize in the still ongoing Queen Anne's War between England and France. It would be early November before Gale and his ship were allowed to resume their journey home.

Having come all that way for a fight, Barnwell swallowed his disappointment and, without any guides familiar with the local terrain, pushed on into the interior. At the Tuscarora town of Narhantes the South Carolina commander took the war to the Indians for the first time in any serious way since King Hancock's surprise attack twelve weeks earlier. Narhantes was an open town consisting of several farms that stretched over an area of several miles. Within the open fields and villages that constituted Narhantes, nine palisade forts made up an Indian defensive network that immediately became the object of Barnwell's attack plan. The South Carolinian sent his forces against the strongest of the nine redoubts and was surprised to find that much of the toughest opposition came from Tuscarora women, who displayed a handiness with a bow and arrow that would have done credit to King Hancock's ablest male warriors. The fight lasted for thirty minutes before Barnwell was able to enter the fort and survey its aftermath, including at least fifty-two Indians killed – including ten women – and another thirty taken captive. The South Carolina force suffered seven killed and thirty-two wounded. Many of Barnwell's Indian mercenaries loaded up with goods the Tuscarora had looted from North Carolina colonists and disappeared into the forest. When Barnwell left Narhantes a few days later he burned the town to deny it to the enemy.

Barnwell turned his force east, cutting a swath through the Indian towns and villages as he passed. By February 10, 1712, he was at Bath. As the month drew to a close, sixty-seven North Carolinians finally augmented Barnwell's force. What should have been a blessing for Barnwell's rapidly dwindling rolls was more like a fresh burden. With the North Carolinians, Barnwell's strength stood at 94 whites and 148 Indians. None of the new men had weapons or food, and Barnwell's stores were already dangerously low. The North Carolinians were something less than ideal recruits, too. Barnwell wrote of them that they were "the most impertinent, imperious, cowardly Blockheads that ever God created..." So much so that the colonel had to bind one of their officers and flog him every time one of the North Carolinians disobeyed an order. The South Carolinian commandeered what ammunition he could find among the garrisons dotting the Pamlico region to supply his haggard army. Leaving his baggage train behind, he left from Fort Reading on February 27 and set out for Hancock's Town, a short distance from Catechna on the west bank of Contentnea Creek.

At Hancock's Town, Barnwell found the village already deserted. The Tuscarora had withdrawn into Fort Hancock, a strong, palisade fort across the creek. Built with the help of a fugitive South Carolina slave named Harry, Barnwell described it as "strong as well by situation on the riverbank as by Workmanship, having a large Earthen Trench thrown up against the puncheons with two tiers of portholes." Four circular bastions anchored the corners, and all approaches to the fort were blocked with tree limbs and sharpened cane reeds to slow any attackers. Inside, 130 warriors waited for the army to attack, along with several of the captive women and children.

By March 5, 1712 Barnwell and his Indians were ready to attack. Wearing bundles of sticks called fascines for protection, Barnwell's men began to advance. As they did, the Tuscarora began torturing their prisoners. Terrible cries of anguish and pain echoed off the trees, and grown men among Barnwell's forces felt the cries stab at their hearts. Every time the white troops attacked, the punishment of the innocent captives checked their hand. Many of the North Carolinians in Barnwell's little army had kinfolk among those taken by the Indians, and each cry from inside the fort caused them to wonder if it were their wives and children suffering under King Hancock's knives.

Finally a woman emerged from the fort and stumbled to Barnwell's lines. Between sobs she related that she had five children still inside the fort, and that the Tuscarora demanded the attack end immediately, or they would kill their captives. In return, Barnwell would get the immediate release of a dozen hostages, and a promise to meet the colonial forces at Batchelours Creek, not far from New Bern, to discuss ending the war. Mindful of the fate of the hostages still inside the fort, Barnwell agreed to the terms and withdrew.

The March 19 deadline came and went, and the Tuscarora never showed up at Batchelours Creek to discuss peace. Barnwell took measures to strengthen the colonists' defenses by establishing a garrison across the river from Bath at Qurhous, and gathered his forces for a return to Hancock's Town. Staging out of Fort Barnwell, built on the remains of the Indian village known as Core Town thirty miles above New Bern, and only a few miles from the Indian fort, Colonel Barnwell surrounded Hancock's palisades. For ten days the soldiers lay siege to the fort, this time with the aid of a pair of three-pounder cannon provided by Von Graffenreid from Governor Hyde's residence. Inside, the Indians grew short of food and ammunition. It was just a matter of time before they would've been forced into unconditional surrender, but then something totally unexpected happened. Barnwell unaccountably accepted terms from the Indians that were much more generous than their military situation would've indicated. The Indians surrendered on April 17, after agreeing to a handful of terms that most white settlers found to be ultra generous. The agreement called for King Hancock and three other Indians to be delivered to Barnwell, plus an assortment of lesser demands.

The North Carolina legislature was less than pleased with the surrender. Instead of presenting Barnwell with the accolades and rewards of a conquering hero, the colonel found himself enduring the censure of the governing body. To be fair, the peace was made independent of any consultation with Governor Hyde. Even the centerpiece of Barnwell's surrender terms ultimately went unmet. King Hancock had already fled North Carolina for Virginia, so he couldn't be turned over. Barnwell's only excuse for ending the siege was "extreme famine" that he blamed on a parsimonious legislature. The South Carolinian said that had the legislature provided supplies for just four more days, he would have "made a glorious end of the war." Governor Hyde didn't buy Barnwell's reasoning, especially given that North Carolina reinforcements were on the way. Barnwell, exasperated at the failure of the North Carolinians to reward him for saving them, took some of the Indian prisoners as slaves and departed for South Carolina. Meanwhile, the Indians who had followed Barnwell to Bath County were unhappy, too. The lack of trophy scalps and captive Tuscarora to be kept as slaves prompted the warriors to kidnap some of their erstwhile enemies and return home along with the colonel.

The taking of now peaceful Indians by Barnwell's party left the Tuscarora and their allies that had opted for peace understandably distrustful of the whites, and suspicious of the treaty that had ended the fighting. In response, a fresh spate of fighting broke out in the Neuse and Pamlico regions. Governor Hyde, fed up with it all, determined to march at the head of a column of Albemarle militia and put an end to the uprising once and for all. Hyde intended to march to Bath Town and "end the war with honor or make such peace as shall not reflect upon the British Glory." It was a good plan, but Hyde wouldn't live to see it carried out. The governor died on September 9, 1712 after falling victim to the dreaded scourge of the coastal Carolinas, yellow fever. With his passing, command of the colonial militia and leadership of the government fell to Thomas Pollock.

While Pollock did his best to make sure the forces arrayed in Bath County had everything they needed to fend off the Indians, a second expedition was being pulled together in South Carolina. Governor James Moore dispatched a force commanded by his son, Colonel James Moore, to again travel north and help out their North Carolina brethren. Moore led a force of 33 whites and 900 Indians into Fort Barnwell early in December 1712. He immediately saw that Pollock and company were in pretty dire straits. Fort Barnwell's larder was empty, and munitions were few. Following the river down to New Bern, Moore discovered Von Graffenreid's colony wasn't in any better shape. Not even the supposedly fortified

Bath could support the needs of the relief force, so Moore headed into the Albemarle to try and find the food to feed 900 men.

By January 17, 1713 Moore was ready to commence offensive operations. He moved south out of Albemarle County, but was forced to call a halt when bad weather made going any further futile. Two weeks later the weather broke and Moore set out from Fort Reading to take the fight to the Tuscarora. The largest of the Tuscarora towns was Fort Neoheroka, a few miles up Contentnea Creek from Fort Hancock, the scene of Barnwell's showdown the previous spring. Moore made preparations for nearly a month before finally laying siege to the town. The preparations were necessary because Neoheroka wouldn't be a pushover. Constructed of thick logs and earthworks, the Tuscarora fort was a formidable target. Moore had his thousand-man force in place by the first of March. It took three weeks to do it, but by March 23 the last of the fighting was over. What was left of the Indians migrated to New York and joined kinsmen among the Iroquois. The Tuscarora were finished as a power in the south. Moore's force killed 392 Indians inside the fort and another 166 in fighting surrounding it. Another 392 prisoners made the total Tuscarora losses almost a thousand, or one casualty for every man in Moore's force.

While the Tuscarora had been vanquished, the other tribes of the region were not totally eradicated. The Machapunga and Coree continued to strike out at the white colonists around Mackays, near the Pungo River. Thomas Pollock asked Moore to turn his force against them as well, but by this time much of his force had begun the return journey to South Carolina. Gathering the hundred or so Indians still with him, he marched on the raiders in the Pamlico. Moore had less than complete success against the Machapungo and Coree as they retreated into the swampy wilderness between the Bath and Roanoke Island. Nevertheless, Moore managed to quell the attacks for a while, and by the fall he set out for home.

Periodic raiding occurred again beginning in the spring of 1714, and things in North Carolina remained unsettled until a peace treaty was signed in February 1715. The Indians agreed to move to a reservation near Lake Mattamuskeet, and life resumed its normal pace around New Bern and the rest of Bath County. In Bath especially things began to look up almost immediately. The colony's new governor, Charles Eden, chose to build his home in Bath Town and make it the seat of government. Christopher Gale also chose town living over the life of a country gentleman, selling his plantation and moving to Bath to become the colony's chief justice.

Even Colonel Moore succumbed to the charms of Bath, buying property there himself. Not long after, the Moore clan and others packed up bags and baggage and moved north to stake a claim along the Cape Fear, founding not just Brunswick but also many of the grand estates that would be part of the Cape Fear landscape until the end of the Civil War.

Wilmington's John A. Taylor house, formerly the W.L.I. Armory

When The Pot Boiled Over: 1898

By Jack E. Fryar, Jr.

Lieutenant Colonel Walker Taylor gazed out at the angry faces arrayed in front of the John A. Taylor house, the fortress-like building now finding new life in 1898 as the headquarters of the Wilmington Light Infantry. The chill running down his back had little to do with the cool November air. Taylor was looking into the face of the beast, and the North Carolina State Guard commander wanted nothing to do with it.

"Come on, colonel," shouted a voice from the crowd. Taylor couldn't tell whom it belonged to, as the faces of the five hundred armed whites milling about in adrenaline-fed anticipation seemed to somehow blur together. "It's time to make a stand. Lead us down to the Hall and we'll put things right once and for all."

Taylor slowly shook his head. Ugly things were about to happen in Wilmington, things that the soldier and civic leader wanted no part of.

"You all go down there in this kind of mood, you'll do it without me," he said. "I've been a soldier too long to be part of a mob."

A dark mutter went through the milling throng, and then the same voice addressed Thomas C. James. "How 'bout you, Tom? You're commander of the Light Infantry. You know how to lead!"

"What, me lead a mob? Never!" James declared.

At the end of the nineteenth century simmering racial resentments in the wake of the Civil War had made North Carolina's largest city a powder keg waiting to explode. Even as far back as the colonial period, Wilmington was something of a contradiction when it came to how blacks and whites interacted together. Though large numbers of slaves were employed to build and maintain the city and the many plantations that surrounded it, the bonds were relatively loose compared to the rest of the state and south. In fact, the state government enacted legislation as far back as the 1700's to reign in the freedoms allowed to Wilmington slaves – a freedom that other slave owners in North Carolina found entirely too discomforting. Many Wilmington slaves were allowed to have their own dwellings in town, and even take side jobs to earn their own money as long as they didn't neglect the chores set for them by their owners. Even fears of a slave revolt following the Nat Turner uprising in the 1830's didn't stop local slave owners from allowing their slaves to lease themselves out for a year at a time every January, at the Wilmington Market House at the foot of Market Street. This allowed slaves in the Wilmington area to achieve a level of independence not enjoyed by their brethren elsewhere.

Alex Manly, whose newspaper editorial provided the spark that set fire to the racial resentments of North Carolina's largest city at the end of the nineteenth century.

photo courtesy New Hanover County Library

Men like Elvin Artis, Jack Kellogg and Fredrick Cutlar Sadgwar used their skills in the construction trades to make better lives for themselves and their families, becoming artisans in high demand among white property owners building in the booming city.

After the fall of Fort Fisher sealed the death of the Confederacy and the institution of slavery, Wilmington blacks came into their own. Through a combination of shrewd voting and federal patronage following the war, Wilmington became something of a shining example of what reconstruction could do to further the lot of former slaves and bring about enforced equality between whites and blacks. By 1897 there were three black aldermen on a board that only seated ten, while blacks also served in leadership positions as justice of the peace, deputy clerk of superior court, and coroner. A black man sat on the Board of Audit and Finance, and as Superintendent of Streets. Black policemen patrolled Wilmington's raucous nighttime alleys, while two black fire companies helped to keep the city's imminently combustible homes and businesses safe from the flames that had been such a scourge throughout the town's history. There was an all-black health department, as well as federally appointed mail clerks and carriers. President William McKinley made twice as many black appointments to federal jobs as his predecessors, including John Campbell Dancy, who added to his sin of being a non-Wilmingtonian by replacing a white incumbent. Among the middle class, whites and blacks lived side by side in desegregated neighborhoods. Even in predominantly black Brooklyn, on the north side of town, whites shared space with black neighbors.

Resentment of the new status of blacks in the city was an undercurrent that simmered long and hard among much of the white community. There was a general feeling among lower class whites that Wilmington employers preferred hiring blacks for the menial jobs that both disadvantaged classes were competing for. In Dry Pond, on the city's south side, that resentment was especially high. With a high percentage of mostly unskilled and uneducated Irish immigrants living in what may have been Wilmington's meanest community, competition was keen for those service and manual labor jobs, which seemed to be the only kind they were suited for. The perception that white bosses preferred blacks fed racial resentment that swelled the ranks of organizations like the Ku Klux Klan and the Red Shirts. The Red Shirts were a group of men who actively opposed the rise of blacks in North Carolina, armed white horsemen who used intimidation to cow black voters and rally white support in communities across the state. They would play a central role in the destruction that descended on Wilmington on November 10, 1898.

Democrats saw their control of the government slipping away and into the hands of blacks and Republicans, and mobilized to halt the party's decline. In the months building up to the elections of 1898, white resentment over the gains made by North Carolina and Wilmington blacks had given rise to a series of legislative acts that would come to be known as Jim Crow laws, designed to disenfranchise black voters and create a defacto control of government by whites. The Democratic Party was the author of most of those provisions, which included a poll tax and a literacy test for voters. New Hanover County's representative to the state legislature, George Rountree, was a driving force behind the push for both measures, which would be voted on as amendments to the North Carolina constitution in a 1900 referendum. The Democratic status quo became even more tenuous when disgruntled agrarian voters who had been loyal to the party began to break away to form the new Populist Party and throw their support to Republican candidates, creating a blend of political factions that became known as Fusionist politics.

The racial violence that would erupt in Wilmington was not the first clash between blacks and whites in 1898. Raleigh, Lumberton, Ashpole, Fayetteville and Goldsboro all experienced racial discord that broke out in violent confrontations, though none would approach the levels of what would happen in the state's largest coastal city on the Cape Fear. Not even Governor Daniel Lindsey Russell, North Carolina's

Republican chief executive from Winnabow, elected with support from Fusionist voters, was exempt from the mob. On the way home from casting his vote in Wilmington on election day in 1898, his train was stormed at Maxton by a crowd of angry whites intent on lynching him. Only quick thinking by one of Lindsay's men saved the day when he hustled the portly governor into the mail car and hid him. Lindsay was a target for the crowd because it was Republicans who were responsible for the advances blacks were making in government, and it was the Republican Party that had won the allegiance of black voters.

In 1897 the mayoral election saw three separate men sworn in as Wilmington's chief executive, and the fight for the mayor's office went all the way to the North Carolina Supreme Court before Dr. Silas P. Wright was anointed the rightful winner

Alfred Moore Waddell (left) and Col. Walker Taylor (right) played pivotal roles in the events of November 1898.

photo courtesy New Hanover County Library

of the election by the justices. Wright, who had moved to Wilmington in the wake of the Civil War, was seen as a carpetbagger by local Democrats and judged unfit for the job. Dismayed that the argument went against them, Democratic leaders in Wilmington began to look to other means of regaining control of the local government. Beginning almost a year before the rioting of 1898, a secret group of nine influential Democrats began planning what amounted to an overthrow of the elected officials. Harry Hayden named the members of this clique as being J. Alan Taylor, Hardy I. Fennell, W.A. Johnson, L.B. Sasser, William Gilchrist, P.B. Manning, E.S. Lathrop, Walter L. Parsley, and Hugh McRae. Hayden named the group the "Secret Nine."

Members of the group, meeting in secret at the home of Walter Parsley, designed a plan that would utilize the burgeoning White Supremacy movement to provide the foot soldiers for the coming offensive. Block lieutenants were established in each of Wilmington's five wards to make sure that ballots were cast for the right candidates. Elsewhere, another similar group consisting of William L. Smith, John Berry, Henry G. Ferrell, Thomas D. Meares, and Walker Taylor were making plans of their own at Smith's Market Street home across from the Bellamy mansion.

Rioters and Redshirts outside the remains of Manly's newspaper.

Hayden's "Secret Nine" knew of the Smith group, and considered it something of an auxiliary to their own group.

The Secret Nine began orchestrating, with the help of sympathetic newspapers like Thomas Clawson's *Wilmington Messenger*, a campaign of innuendo and outright lies against blacks and the white politicians who supported them. Targets of the slurs included not just the mayor and Governor Russell, but also Police Chief John R. Melton, G.Z. French (who had been an orderly for Union General William T. Sherman), the New Hanover County Sheriff, and Judge David B. Sutton. Wilmington's four black attorneys – L.A. Henderson, William A. Moore, Armond W. Scott, and L.P. White – were particularly vulnerable. Blacks were depicted in the press as being the culprits in most crimes committed in the city, while editorials bemoaned the state of affairs under the Fusionist government that allowed blacks to become "insolent" and display "open malice" toward whites in public. The result was a feeling among many whites that a cancer was among them, threatening their entire way of life.

Those feelings fit well with the White Supremacy campaign of 1898, when relations between the races had a more immediate impact on North Carolina lives than did the war with Spain that was raging in Cuba and the Philippines. Championed by New Bern's Furnifold Simmons, white supremacy became the issue on which Democrats would stake their claim to office in the upcoming election. Newspapers like Josephus Daniels' *Raleigh News & Observer* became the mouthpieces of the Democrats, decrying government by blacks as a scourge voters had to defend against. The *Wilmington Messenger* again proved prophetic when it said, "the Democrats intend to overthrow the present political conditions – peacefully if possible, but by revolution if necessary." Among the rumors flying free and without substantiation was one that said there was a "colored conspiracy" to take over the reigns of each branch of the North Carolina government and make the state into a "commonwealth" for blacks from across the nation, where they could find refuge under a government run by their own race.

So it was that tensions between the races was running especially high as the autumn of 1898 came around. With things already at the boiling point, it wouldn't take much to cause an explosion. Alexander Manly, the black grandson of North Carolina's last Whig governor, Charles Manly, would provide the spark that launched the terror. In an editorial rebuttal to a speech given in Georgia by Rebecca Latimer Felton, *Wilmington Record* editor Manly provided the excuse the Secret Nine and the Red Shirts needed to take back their city.

Felton had given a speech at Tybee Island in 1898 that raised the terrifying specter of white women being raped by black men made bold by liquor and newly granted voting rights. Her speech declared that if to stop such desecrations drastic measures were needed, then "...if it takes lynching to protect woman's dearest possession from drunken, ravening human beasts, then I say lynch a thousand a week if it becomes necessary."

Alex Manly fired back in an August 18, 1898 editorial that derided the hypocrisy of Felton's speech, saying "We suggest that the whites guard their women more closely, as Mrs. Felton says, thus giving no opportunity for the human fiend, be he black or white...Our experience in the country suggests that women of that race are not any more particular in the matter of clandestine meetings with colored men than the white men with colored women...Every Negro lynched is called a Big Burly Black Brute, when, in fact, many of those who have thus been dealt with had white men for their fathers, and were not only not black and burly, but were sufficiently attractive for white girls of culture and refinement to fall in love with them, as is very well known to all." Manly's closing sounded particularly chilling to the ears of white Wilmington: "Don't think ever that your women will remain pure while you are debauching ours. You sow the seed – the harvest will come due in time."

It was all the ammunition the Democrats needed. Simmons gleefully declared it the key to a Democratic victory in the coming election, while publisher Josephus Daniels made sure the editorial was read in every corner of the state by printing 300,000 copies of it and distributing it across North Carolina. Despite the immediate repudiation of the editorial by the New Hanover County Executive Committee, the damage was done. Anger over what Manly had written was so high that Democrat George Rountree, who up until then had been among the leaders of those fanning the flames of white supremacy in an effort to regain political power, actually began backing away from incendiary rhetoric.

New peaceful attitude or not, Rountree helped Hugh McRae and the Secret Nine push through resolutions in the chamber of commerce that accused the "corrupt and incompetent" city administration of allowing Wilmington to descend into anarchy. Red Shirt activity began to spike, most notably with a march from Dry Pond to a rally at Thalian Hall in late October where Alfred Moore Waddell, a

Confederate veteran and former congressman, spoke for the crowd, declaring, "We will never surrender to a ragged raffle of Negroes, even if we have to choke the Cape Fear River with carcasses."

Many black Wilmington and North Carolina residents, politicians and businessmen distanced themselves from Manly. They disavowed the sentiments of the editorial, in many instances out of nervousness regarding the effect of the article in the racially charged state of North Carolina. Blacks in other parts of the country far removed from the brown waters of the Cape Fear River, however, often applauded Manly's words, serving to further convince North Carolina whites that they were the targets of a widespread black conspiracy. Meanwhile, Wilmington blacks reading the pulse of the town found keeping a low profile to be a good idea.

Manly quietly heeded the advice of friends, closing down the *Record* and slipping out of town with his brother in the dark of night. Thomas Clawson recalled going into Brooklyn shortly after the editorial was printed to warn Manly that his life was in danger and to reclaim the *Wilmington Record's* printing press, which he had sold to Manly when the black paper was started. Manly had only made one payment on the equipment, and Clawson was concerned about his investment. The white editor's warning went undelivered, however. Alex Manly had already slipped away.

In a letter written in 1954 by Carrie Sadgwar Manly, Alex's Wilmington-born wife, she told her children the story of Alex's escape from the city. In her letter, Carrie Manly said that a "prominent white" family friend sent for Alex and told him that "they were going to lynch him, and he must leave town that very night." The friend gave Manly a password that would hopefully get them through the patrols of whites spreading like ants all over Wilmington. The warning may have been right on the money. Hugh McRae, one of the Secret Nine, told after the riot of sitting on his porch when fifty Redshirts led by an unemployed Irish Dry Ponder named Mike Dowling came to his house, where Dowling dismounted and informed McRae that they were marching on the *Record*'s office to burn the building and lynch Manly. McRae realized such an action would upset the careful plans of the Secret Nine, and persuaded Dowling to turn around and save his zeal for later. Dowling, unconvinced, was finally swayed when St. Thomas Apostolic Catholic Church's Reverend Christopher Dennen made him promise to keep his men in check. Dowling agreed – for the time being.

Meanwhile Manly said a tearful goodbye to his family and, with just the clothes on his back, climbed into a horse and buggy along with his brother, Frank, and began his escape. Two friends, Jim Telfair and Owen Bailey, followed the Manly brothers in another carriage. All around, Manly saw armed white men milling about on horseback, patrolling the streets, riverbanks, railroads and steamboats. All wore the distinctive red shirts of Dowling's white supremacists and carried Winchester rifles. Manly and company didn't dally, and spurred their carriages along at a quick pace. Nearing a wooded area outside the city, Manly used the password to cross the Fulton Bridge, and immediately must have felt like he had jumped from the frying pan into the fire. According to the story told in his wife's letter years later, Redshirts were everywhere. Sentries came up to the carriages and, not recognizing the Manlys (who could pass for white, as could their friends Telfair and Bailey), told them they were "having a necktie party in Wilmington." The Redshirts then wanted to know where the strangers were going.

"We are going after that scoundrel Manly," a quick thinking Alex answered.

"What! With no guns?" challenged the white sentry. He ordered the carriage loaded with firearms and sent the Manlys on their way with the admonition, "If you see that smart nigger – shoot him!"

The election took place and saw a cowed black community casting far fewer ballots than they had in previous elections. November 8, 1898 saw Red Shirts, under the leadership of Mike Dowling, menacingly roaming Wilmington streets and polling places, an intimidation that gave the Democrats five thousand more black votes than they garnered in the 1896 election. The Democrats' scheming had

photo courtesy New Hanover County Library

Judge Armond W. Scott

succeeded, and they were on the brink of reclaiming the reigns of Wilmington government. But Republicans still held office until the election victors could be sworn in weeks later, and Democrats were unwilling to let Silas Wright and his Republican-backed administration hold the keys to City Hall for a minute longer. Alfred Moore Waddell chaired a mass meeting on November 9, the day after the election, and helped push through resolutions which put teeth in the white supremacy platform, among them a call for the banishment of Alex Manly (who had fled Wilmington days earlier), and another calling for the immediate resignation of the Wright administration. Dr. Wright complied almost immediately, resigning his office, which was immediately filled by Waddell. A deadline of 7:30am on November 10, 1898 was set for black leaders to comply.

In Brooklyn, black leaders saw no choice but to comply with the Democratic resolutions in order to avoid bloodshed. Ominously, on the eve of the election, trains leaving Wilmington were full with the wives and children of whites who knew of the reckoning that was coming. Black watchers could also read the signs. Armond W. Scott, one of the city's four black attorneys, was entrusted with their reply to the white ultimatums passed at the city's opera house the day before. But, afraid to enter Waddell's white neighborhood given the temperament in the city, Scott claimed to have mailed the reply instead. Whether he did or not, whether the post office failed to deliver it, or whether Waddell got it and ignored it, when 7:30am rolled around on the morning of November 10 there was no answer for Waddell.

By 8:00am five hundred armed men had gathered by the steps of the John A. Taylor house near the corner of Fourth and Market Streets. The white marble walls of the building, home to the Wilmington Light Infantry, lent a martial air to the proceedings. Walker Taylor, who had been a member of the second group of whites scheming to reclaim town government from the blacks and Republicans, didn't like the results of those efforts, standing before him now in the form of a gun-toting mob. Taylor refused to lead the men, whether out of fear for the consequences or because of the oath he had sworn as an officer of the state militia, and advised them against violence. Unheeding, the crowd looked elsewhere for leadership and found it in former Confederate officer Alfred Moore Waddell, who climbed the steps and assumed command of the milling throng. Forming up four abreast, the mob began marching towards the *Wilmington Record* office in Brooklyn's Free Love Hall. The city's new mayor was at the front of the column. By the time it reached its destination, witnesses say there were as many as two thousand armed white men and boys in the mob.

Free Love Hall was situated on Seventh Street, between Nun and Church, a scant twenty feet from Saint Luke's Baptist Church. The two-story frame structure was locked when Waddell knocked, and after a moment the door was broken and twenty men entered the first floor where the *Record*'s offices and press were located. Windows shattered as the Redshirts began destroying the office. The watching mob cheered as bits of furniture and other items were flung from the building into the street. Kerosene lamps were smashed on the floor and ignited by match, and

photo courtesy
New Hanover County
Library

During Reconstruction blacks filled many positions in Wilmington, including that of firefighter, of which they were some of the best.

soon flames licked the outside walls through busted window frames. Onlookers saw the fire inching closer to Saint Luke's Baptist Church and cast an uneasy eye towards the direction of the black fire brigade station at Sixth and Castle streets. When the firemen - some of the best in the city - failed to arrive, men from the mob began fighting the fire themselves to prevent it from consuming the religious property next door.

The fire brigade had been intentionally held up on the orders of Fire Chief Charles Schnibben, who had instructed white firemen to prevent the black fire brigade from leaving its station until word was sent that the fire was about to spread beyond its intended target. Once they were dispatched, armed whites lined the street on either side for two blocks. As the fire engine flew past, its horses at the gallop, the whites fired guns into the air. Upon arrival at Free Love Hall, the black firefighters sprang into action with a determination and focus that illustrated why they were among the best in the city. Having won medals and first prizes in fire brigade competitions across the state, the black firemen had the flames under control in short order, a feat that impressed even many of the whites that had caused the blaze in the first place. One witness attested that, "They were the best disciplined firemen I have ever seen." After the fire was out, the firemen pulled down the smoking remains of Free Love Hall's second floor. As the engine made its way back to its station, the white mob gathered by the blackened structure for a group picture. When the photographer was done, Waddell led his men back to the armory.

At the armory, the new mayor tried to restore order, telling the men of the mob to go home. But the men had their blood up and didn't want to lay down their arms just yet. Rumors swirled about, one of which claimed up to three hundred blacks had armed themselves and were gathered at the Sprunt cotton compress near the river, preparing to launch a counter-attack. Alexander Sprunt & Son's Champion Cotton Compress was not only the largest such enterprise in the nation, but it was also something of a progressive company when it came to its black employees. Sprunt expected his workers, both black and white, to behave themselves in a responsible way and to stand by their employer. In return, the company went to pains to stand by them. Sprunt often went so far as to post bail for his employees who ended up in jail after the occasional bender, and was always someone his employees could go to when they were in a jam. When flames darkened the horizon from the burning newspaper office, punctuated by occasional gunshots and screams, Sprunt's black employees became understandably nervous.

Jim Reeves, a cotton weigher who later became headwaiter at a Fayetteville hotel, remembered when the workers at Alexander Sprunt & Son realized trouble was headed their way. It had been a pretty fall day, with warm temperatures moderated by salty breezes from off the ocean. Men at the cotton compress were going about their jobs when ticket taker Henry Paschau came into the warehouse and whispered something into the ear of supervisor James D. Smith. Moments later the fire bell began ringing nonstop, and a black man ran into the building yelling that Redshirts

**The W.A. Walker grocery, where the first blacks were killed.
The "X" marks where they fell.**

had killed one black man and were on their way to kill the rest of them. Confusion reigned in the streets as armed whites rushed in the direction of the gunfire and black women, thinking their own homes had been set to the torch, implored their husbands working at the compress to come home.

Down the street came a crowd of armed whites, many of them soldiers recently returned from Cuban combat in the Spanish-American War. Among them was Donald McRae, an army officer who armed himself when the unrest began. At the cotton compress, black employees looked to their employer for help against the armed mob. James Sprunt, the son of company owner Alexander Sprunt, obliged by having himself hoisted atop a bale of cotton and placing himself between the mob's guns and his black workers. Sprunt had the doors barricaded, and the four guns of his yacht turned on the intimidating crowd of whites. Sprunt, who had faced the business end of guns before as a purser aboard Civil War blockade runners, then addressed the Democratic mob, telling them to "Shoot if you will, but make me the victim." Having a prominent man like James Sprunt stand up for his black employees gave the mob pause (and the four guns aboard his yacht didn't hurt his case, either). After a moment or two they moved on and left Sprunt's employees be.

Sprunt told his men to either go back to work or, if they feared for their families, to go home. Many chose to do just that, and Sprunt asked Don McRae to escort them through the lines of armed whites. Just as McRae was about to lead them off, it was a reported that fighting was going on between whites and blacks in Brooklyn. The remaining armed whites, including McRae, immediately set out to the sound of the guns. At what was then known as Dickinson Hill, McRae was asked to assume command of the whites trying to establish a line to repulse an expected attack from besieged blacks. The army officer did so, forming a line of battle that could sweep any attackers off the high ground and down towards the river, when

some thinking person among the Democrats in the group recognized the danger McRae's leadership posed. As an officer recently returned from the war, he was still a commissioned officer of the federal government. If he led any fighting, then he would be subject to federal charges should the Washington government investigate what happened in Wilmington at a later date. McRae relinquished command of the men and joined the ranks, but the expected mob of blacks never arrived.

With the press destroyed and Alex Manly nowhere to be found, the mass majority of Waddell's white mob returned to the W.L.I. armory and disbanded into the various neighborhoods where they lived, often next door

photo courtesy New Hanover County Library

Captain Donald McRae

or across the street from blacks. One of the ugliest incidents of the episode, and one that resulted in the single biggest loss of life, happened at the intersection of Fourth Street where John Brunjes' store was located in north Wilmington's Brooklyn neighborhood.

As a party of armed whites made their way up Fourth Street, a group of understandably angry black men had gathered on a corner across the street. Some in the party carried scrounged pistols or rifles, though most of them were unarmed. Packing a weapon or not, much of the talk centered on retaliation against the whites. When the homeward bound whites saw the gathering at Brunjes' store, they suspected an ambush and ordered the blacks to disperse. It was something the angry black men were unwilling to do, despite the pleading of people like Norman Lindsay, himself black, who begged them to leave if only out of regard for their families' well being. "I am as brave as any of you," Lindsay replied to the hissing from the crowd of dark faces, "but we are powerless."

Reluctantly, in the face of the white guns assembled on the opposite corner, the black crowd dispersed to the northeast corner of Fourth Street and a position near Saint Matthew's English Lutheran Church. The move wasn't a great one, and Aaron Lockamy, a white police officer on the scene, addressed the crowd, urging them to leave and avoid any trouble. While Lockamy was making his case, the first shot rang out.

"Hell broke loose," someone later said. In the group of whites, William Mayo spun to the sidewalk with a mortal gunshot wound that pierced both lungs before exiting his body. In the stunned silence immediately following the shot both sides tried to comprehend what had happened. Incomprehension only lasted a moment, though, and then the whites' returned fire at the blacks they assumed had fired the shot that killed Mayo. Rifles, revolvers and shotguns sent a curtain of lead across the street, and the gathering of black men scattered in the face of the onslaught. Two men died instantly, while another four managed to make it a few steps before bullets ended their flight. From there things degenerated into a running gunfight, with blacks fleeing and rifle-toting whites giving chase through the neighborhood. Some blacks that had managed to acquire guns returned the fire, but the overwhelming volume of shots came from white guns. Casualties were suffered all across town, the violence spilling out of Brooklyn and into other neighborhoods. At Third and Harnett, Swann, and the Carolina Central Railroad yard black men fell dead. The violence was the stuff of nightmares. Redshirt cavalry armed with Winchester rifles and plenty of ammo rode into Brooklyn with the force of a whirlwind, and chaos reigned once again.

In Raleigh Governor Russell was reading telegraphed reports and wondering what to do to restore order in his largest coastal city. His earlier brush with Redshirt violence gave him some first hand experience of what the mob was capable of. On the advice of Major Charles Davis, in command of the North Carolina State Guard, Russell ordered Walker Taylor to assume command of the local guard company and restore order in the port city. Similar instructions were approved for Wilmington's naval reserve, who Russell directed place themselves under Taylor's command. Elsewhere, guard units in Clinton and Maxton were ordered on the alert for possible deployment to Wilmington if needed.

While the state government under Russell was mobilizing troops to restore order, other towns across the state were offering to send men to reinforce Waddell and his white forces. Offers of men and guns from Oxford, Rockingham, Dunn, Lumberton, Monroe, Wilson, Mount Olive, Fayetteville, Macon, Winston-Salem, Clinton and Goldsboro all attested to a willingness among North Carolina whites and Democrats to come to the aid of Wilmington revolutionaries.

At the Wilmington Light Infantry armory, Captain William Rand Kenan supervised the mounting of a Gatling gun and two Hotchkiss cannons. With his heavy weapons ready, the W.L.I. moved out for Brooklyn. At the Fourth Street bridge, a crowd blocked the roadway, to the extent that the ambulance driven by the black Frank Shephard and carrying the wounded William Mayo was unable to cross on its way to the hospital. The local priest finally managed to get people to disperse enough for the ambulance to cross, which it did in a great hurry. Meanwhile the soldiers moved into Brooklyn. With military precision the infantry lined up in formation and began delivering well-placed volleys against targets that in virtually all instances were black. Cannon were trained on black churches while soldiers demanded that doors on the places of worship be opened to search. Homes were torched when fleeing blacks refused to come out and surrender. It was a long, bloody day, but by three o'clock in the afternoon the fury seemed to be spent. White sentries, some no older than twelve or fifteen, manned checkpoints on each corner and blacks returning home from work did so at their own peril unless accompanied by their white employers.

In the streets, dead and wounded blacks lay bleeding into the dust, while a lone Red Cross ambulance dashed frantically from body to body checking for those that might be saved. In days to come the official death toll would hover between twelve and fourteen blacks killed, while among the white Mayo had sustained the most grievous injury though several other white men suffered wounds. Doctors of both races busied themselves treating injured patients from both sides, while black coroner David Jacobs convened fourteen coroner's juries. In all fourteen cases, death was ruled to have been from "gunshot wounds inflicted by persons unknown."

Fear of retaliation prevented survivors from coming forward with an accurate counting of the fathers and sons who died during the rioting. To this day the numbers of those who are believed to have died stirs great debate. What can be said is that even among those who didn't die in the fighting, many chose to abandon their property and leave Wilmington forever. Alex Manly ended up in Washington, serving as an aid to a black congressman. Many had sheltered in the woods and swamps surrounding Wilmington, carrying with them only the belongings they could grab on the fly. In the wake of the riot Col. Taylor declared martial law. The city was thick with men carrying rifles, some in the uniform of the military, others sworn in as one of the 200 special policemen sworn in to keep order. No further trouble occurred. New mayor Alfred Moore Waddell oversaw the banishment of those he and the Secret Nine considered troublesome, mostly black but some whites, too. Men were escorted to trains and told not to ever return if they valued their lives. New Police Chief Edgar Parmele directed Police Captain John J. Furlong and Thomas Wright to round up the undesirables. Among them was deposed mayor Dr. Silas P. Wright and ousted Populist police chief John Melton. Thomas Miller, a black man to whom many whites owed money, was banished, as was federally appointed United States Commissioner Robert H. Bunting – principally because he was a white man married to a black woman. Armond W. Scott, the Wilmington lawyer sent to deliver the reply of the black community to white demands at the outset of the trouble, would leave and eventually become a respected judge in the nation's capitol.

A close call was avoided when respected men of the white community answered an urgent call to go to the jail and persuade drunken Redshirts gathered in a lynch mob to go home and leave the "prisoners" in the hands of the sheriff. Catholic priest Father Christopher C. Dennen literally stood in the doorway to the jail and told the mob, largely Irish from Dry Pond, that they would have to walk over his dead body to take the blacks being held in protective custody. Whether it was the rain that began to fall or the sixty armed soldiers detailed to protect the jail, the Redshirts soon turned for home. The next day the prisoners were escorted to the train station by soldiers carrying bayoneted rifles and put aboard cars, under guards with orders to take them out of North Carolina. These exiles often left without the rest of their families or any of the property and wealth they may have accumulated over years of hard work. Others were herded aboard steamers leaving Wilmington for someplace else.

photo courtesy New Hanover County Library

Police Chief E.G. Parmele

In the aftermath of the riots, white labor began filling the gaps in the workforce left by exiled or dead blacks. The new administration threw a few bones to the poor whites that had provided the muscle for their coup; but not long after the guns went back into the closets, class differences reasserted themselves. Whatever Mike Dowling and his followers from Dry Pond might have expected to gain from their aristocratic partners in revolution, what they got was much less than they were led to believe would be their due. A little over a year later, Dowling himself would be dismissed from his job as foreman of Fire Engine Company No. 2 for "incompetency, drunkenness, and continued insubordination."

The black exodus from Wilmington continued for a long time after the city had regained some semblance of normality. Despite the best efforts of Waddell's administration, local blacks could never again trust the white community or the Democratic government in City Hall. Those leaving sold their property at prices only a fraction of what they were worth. The city lost the services of the two crack fire companies, and had to make due with only three units instead of the pre-riot five.

In a city where more than four centuries of history has provided ample examples of the better nature of its residents, the riot of 1898 has gone down in history as one of our less than stellar moments. On a day less than two weeks from the day set aside as a national day of thanks, violence made blessings hard to come by for a great many of Wilmington's citizens. Men died, the rule of law was usurped, and the rights guaranteed all Americans by the Bill of Rights and the Constitution of the United States were flagrantly ignored, all in a bid by desperate men to maintain their grip on the offices of power in the city. The Wilmington riot, though the most glaring example of the burgeoning white supremacy movement in North Carolina, did not arise out of sentiments that were particular to the city. Similar movements were active all across the state and the south. Out of Wilmington came laws and legislation to limit the influence blacks could exert on the political processes of the state, the Jim Crow laws that would be the focus of the Civil Rights movement of the 1960's. The legacy of 1898 lives on even today, as Wilmingtonians of all colors try to come to terms with what happened in its most shameful episode.

Immigrant Louis Froelich contibuted to the Southern cause by manufacturing swords, lances and bayonets.

Swords For The South:
Louis Froelich's Confederate Arms Factory

By Robert L. Cooke

L
ouis Froelich had to be thoroughly dejected. A fire had swept through his
workshops and destroyed several buildings. Looking at the ruins located at
the southern end of the town of Wilmington, surely he must have thought
that all his work was for naught. Just who was this man who would become known
as the "Swordmaker for the Confederacy"? Even the pronunciation of his name is
something of a mystery. Correctly pronounced "Fray-lee," but more often
pronounced just as it reads (Fro-lick), he first immigrated to England from Bavaria
where, it was said, he worked on the steamship *Great Eastern* as a steamship
mechanic. After a stop in New York, by 1861 he was in Wilmington.

With the outbreak of war, Wilmington boomed as a center providing many of the
military goods required by the new southern enlistees. One of those companies
was Loeb and Swarzman's "N.C. Button Manufactory" which, "under the direction
of Mr. Louis Froelich, a thoroughly educated mechanic" turned out uniform buttons
and also brass patterns for cannon balls. Towards the end of the year, Froelich
began a partnership with yet another unknown: Bela Estvan (sometimes spelled
Eastvan). Estvan, a one-time Hungarian fencing master from Richmond, seems to
have been something of a boaster, but together, he and Froelich formed the "C.S.
Arms Factory." The site for the factory was located south of the modern Cape Fear
Memorial Bridge, "below the foundry" of the Clarendon Iron Works. In September,
an ad appeared in the *Wilmington Journal*, asking for thousands of pounds of copper,
brass, zinc, tin and "5,000 Hickory Lance Sticks, 8 feet long, 1 1/2 inches, to taper

to 1 inch," plus 5,000 leather straps for lances. The operation was to be a large one; the same advertisement offered jobs for 6 Brass Moulders, 30 Brass Finishers, 5 Machinists and 20 polishers. Shortly afterwards, the company's agent sought boarding for one hundred workers, "as near the sword factory as possible."

In the latter part of 1861, the factory was almost ready to start production. On November 2, 1861 they received the first boxcar-load of raw materials (and tools) that would be made into swords, bayonets, lances, pikes and Bowie knives. Later, ads advised the public that the factory was buying zinc, brass, copper and spring steel (sword blanks) 2 1/2 inches wide. On November 9, the Vice President of the Confederate States, A.H. Stephens, visited the factory. Stephens had been delayed in Wilmington and took the time to visit the budding industry.

"He was requested by the courteous agent, Mr. Newhoff, to lay the foundation for a new sword making machine, which he did, laying the brick and spreading on mortar in a most workman-like manner, taking the occasion to make a few...remarks respecting the welfare of the factory and its importance to the Confederacy," wrote the Wilmington *Daily Journal* of the visit. "[A] beautiful Sword and Lance were accepted by Mr. Stephens...Holding the Sword and Lance, Mr. Stephens made a spirited address...He complimented the firm on the patriotism and energy displayed in the undertaking."

It was something of an advertising coup! Stephens promised to bring the arms presented to him to other parts of the Confederacy so that they could "see what the Old North State was doing." In an attempt to foster more business from the State, the firm prevailed upon one of Wilmington's leading citizens, Dr. William George Thomas, who wrote a letter of introduction to his brother-in-law, North Carolina Governor Henry T. Clark.

One of the first orders, 128 lances and 220 "lance boots" were churned out by the factory and sent to Richmond. The total cost to the Confederate States was $1,054. By the end of that month, the factory was turning out 900 sabers every week; this was probably under optimum conditions, but was enough for an entire regiment. There were still some bugs to work out (there was a problem with the scabbards) but the operation was going smoothly, the blades were forged, ground and polished. After tempering and attaching handles, the swords were ready for the cavalry. The *Journal* commented "The factory has turned out...lances, saber bayonets, officer's swords, cavalry sabers, artillery swords and we suppose all other cutting, sticking and stabbing utensils." Pikes were not mentioned, but the Arms Factory also made them. Because of a scarcity of arms at the beginning of the war, pikes were produced and issued to some men, but never on a large scale. Regardless of what Vice President Stephens may have thought, the authorities were not pleased with the quality of weapons coming out of the factory. In a letter written by Governor Clark to Secretary of War Judah P. Benjamin on March 11, 1862, Clark railed against the lack of arms available to newly raised regiments.

"They are yet without sabers, though we spared neither effort nor money," Clark wrote. "We did engage from Estevan and Froelich sword factory at Wilmington, and paid high prices, but three-fourths of the swords proved worthless."

In February, Dr. Thomas was again prevailed upon to write the governor. "Mr. Froelich called on me this morning and requested a letter to you,' wrote the doctor. "He has not, some how been properly represented either in his partner Mon. Estevan, or perhaps the work which the State has rejected. He has difficulty in making himself understood...but...He wishes to satisfy you that he can & will do good work; and from what I have seen and know of him, I believe him to be not only a most competent and skillful workman, but an honest man also. He is, I suspect, unfortunate in the selection of a partner, who does not fairly represent Mr. Froelich in any respect."

At the same time, in Wilmington, Froelich was in the act of dissolving the partnership with Estvan. The man had been exposed as an imposter and had absconded with the company's funds. He made his way north, eventually going to London, where he wrote a book condemning the Confederacy and the "foul and treacherous conspiracy against an excellent, just and equitable government." He wound up at Franfurt-on-Main, Germany, probably very close to where he had started out. Froelich was forced to start over again. Being ever inventive, Froelich the mechanic devised a thirty-six-shot "repeating revolver." It was said to be "accurate and efficient" to 1,400 yards and was mounted in a one-horse wagon.

"The wagon is to have a bullet-proof shield of sheet iron in the form of a triangle, to defend the man and horse, when in action," related one contemporary description. "Loopholes in the screen will give room for the firing of the gun, which can be moved in any direction...It will be...well adapted to out-post or picket duty."

Although it was brought to Richmond for a demonstration, apparently nothing ever became of it. The men of the Eighteenth N.C., many of whom were Wilmington boys, could have used such a weapon on May 27, 1862 at Hanover Court House in Virginia. They were engaged in repulsing Union General Fitz-John Porter's troops and suffered nearly fifty percent casualties. Upon learning of the battle, the people in Wilmington donated foodstuffs and money to aid the stricken soldiers. Some seventy employees of the Sword Factory donated money ($328.25) and "a fine sword for the Colonel," Robert H. Cowan. Cowan wrote a letter of appreciation to Froelich and publicly thanked the workers at the "Confederate Arms Factory" for the money and the "very handsome sword and belt" given him. He vowed that it "shall never be sheathed...until the Confederate States of America are acknowledged among the nations of the earth [.]"

By 1862, the factory was in full operation, with about seventy employees. Among them was the company's bookkeeper, Heinrich Westerman, from Bremerhaven, who had come to Wilmington around 1856. Enlisting in the "German Volunteers" (a local militia unit which became Company A of the Eighteenth N.C.) he served for a year during the war but was released due to deafness. Another countryman,

George Grotjohan (also a bookkeeper) was from Hanover, Germany, but there were also Yankees and native southerners in the factory, both young and old. E.T. Lucas (age 43) was a tinner who hailed from Connecticut. W. Ulrich (age 18) was from Pennsylvania, while Allen B. Petterson (age 16) was from North Carolina. Brass finishers, blacksmiths and molders, carpenters, tinsmiths and common laborers were among the workers. By mid-1860, blacksmiths were making three dollars a day (later increased to 6-10 dollars per day). The big incentive for employment, however, was not the pay. More and more men were needed by the Army and employment in a "war related" industry allowed a worker to be exempt from active duty (although they were subject to militia duty, which as Froelich complained, "interrupts our work a great deal.").

Workers were not exempt, however, from yellow fever. That disease struck Wilmington in the late summer of 1862. Many businesses shut down, as did the Arms Factory. Wilmington became a deserted town, cut off from the surrounding towns by an embargo or "quarantine." On September 27, work ceased at the factory, the workers were "furloughed" and dispersed to safer areas. Froelich's agent, Mr. Newhoff, attempted to go to Fayetteville, but he was stopped at a quarantine station, where he soon fell ill and died. Notices in newspapers advised workers to report their whereabouts so that their furloughs could be extended. Towards the end of November, most businesses had started to reopen. The Arms Factory was scheduled to start production again on November 20, with the blacksmiths returning first, followed by the finishers. Not all smithies came back, so an ad was run for six blacksmiths and helpers (to be paid the "highest wages"). In an attempt to branch out, Froelich hired about twenty-five men to manufacture knapsacks and other leather goods. It has been written that the Confederate Sword Factory, from 1861 until March 1864, "furnished 18 sets of surgical instruments, 800 gross of military buttons, 3,700 lance spears, 6,500 saber bayonets, 11,700 cavalry sabers, 2,700 officer's sabers, 600 navy cutlasses, 800 artillery cutlasses, 1,700 sets of infantry accoutrements, 300 saber belts and 300 knapsacks." It was not all military work though, for in January 1863 the workers, who had organized themselves into a military company, paraded through the town with pennants attached to their lances and pikes.

The following month a fire struck the shops, putting Froelich and the men out of work. Perhaps looking for another location around the time of the yellow fever epidemic in October of 1862, Froelich had purchased property in Kenansville. The land, which would become the site of the Armory in Duplin County, contained two and a half acres situated just south of town. Located at the crossroads of the Warsaw and Wilmington roads and within a short wagon trip of the Wilmington and Weldon Railroad (or the Northeast Cape Fear River), Kenansville was chosen because it was thought to be far enough away from Wilmington to be safe. Major General W.H.C. Whiting had strongly urged people to leave the city because of a threatened

Union attack. By March 1863, Froelich moved to Kenansville where he thought the factory would be out of danger.

By the end of that month, he was back in operation, and in early May had an outlet in Wilmington. James McCormick, who operated a dry goods store on Market Street, would "take orders for Swords, Belts and Military Equipments...Mr. McCormick has now on hand...a fine assortment of the above articles manufactured at the Armory, which he will take pleasure in showing to all parties desirous of purchasing." Other arms manufacturers began to spring up in Wilmington, including one called Kidder's Mill on Front Street, run by a man named Steinmetz, who may have been a former Froelich employee fired for the poor quality of his swords. Another man named Douglas also began producing arms, and swords could be bought at Smaw's Bookstore in Wilmington by 1864.

It wasn't always military arms that Froelich produced. In April 1863, he sold two brass kettles to the Army quartermaster at Wilmington, for the use of the Medical Department. The foundry also turned out horseshoes and agricultural implements. Also that month, he contracted to provide 550 sets of infantry accoutrements, consisting of cartridge box, cap box and belt with bayonet scabbard. The sets were to be "equal in all respects to sample at Ordnance Depot, at the price of thirteen dollars per set."

The first installment of 150 sets were to be delivered on June 1, and "thereafter at the rate of 50 sets every two weeks," with payment made with one-third in Confederate Bonds, the rest in cash. Also included in the agreement was the buyer's option of canceling the order, "in the event of an armistice or public notice of peace."

It was not peace, however, that canceled the order. On July 4, Union cavalry from New Bern raided Kenansville and burned Froelich's factory. According to Union reports, "The Confederates had established an armory and a saddle manufactory at that place, both were destroyed, burning the former with a large number of sabers, saber bayonets, knives, and all kinds of arms of that description, a large and splendid engine and boiler...all the tools, saddles, and all the stock [.]"

Undaunted, Froelich rebuilt the factory and was again in business after the raid. An advertisement dated November 21, 1863 notified the public that the C.S. Armory was seeking to purchase metals to supply the factory. Also sought was 100,000 pounds of moss (probably to be used as a cushioning material for sword handles). Anyone who could supply the needed items was asked to contact Claus Tinkens at Wilmington. The raid certainly set back not only production, but profits as well. In early January 1864, strapped for cash, Froelich went into partnership with Jacob Henry Nicholas Cornhelson, of Wilmington. Cornehlson had been First Sergeant, Company A, of the Eighteenth North Carolina, know as the "German Volunteers." Jacob had gotten out of the army at the same time as his brother, Christian. Christian had been Captain of Company A, but had been defeated for reelection in April

1862. It is quite possible that Jacob obtained the money from Christian, who ran a "Billiard Parlor and Saloon" in Wilmington. Jacob paid almost $30,000, which gave him equal partnership in the firm. The last known correspondence between Froelich and Confederate authorities is dated June 7, 1864 and concerned a shipment of knapsacks to Richmond.

After the war, Froelich remained in Kenansville and involved himself in agriculture. In 1866 several prominent citizens of Kenansville met at Froelich's house to discuss the possibility of the large-scale production of wine. He proposed establishing a cooperative and hoped that several hundred acres could be brought under cultivation. It is doubtful that a consensus was reached, but Louis went into the wine business. In November 1869, he exhibited many of his farming products at the Cape Fear Agricultural Society Fair. Listed in the 1870 census as a "horticulturalist," he proudly displayed his scuppernong wine (and was especially proud of his " Sparkling Burgunda"). While at the fair he also showed off his shell and butterfly collection. Louis sold his wine commercially; in 1872 he brought a suit for $184 against the Southern Express Company for failing to deliver a barrel of wine to Hartford, Connecticut. He was awarded $187, but the company appealed the decision because Froelich had sued in the wrong court. Learning that the court he sued in only handled cases of losses over $200, he promptly increased the wine's value to $250! Upon appeal in the North Carolina Supreme Court, Froelich lost.

The house that Froelich lived in while in Duplin County still exists (although not in its original location across the street from the Armory). Leon H. Sikes, in his article *The Swords of Kenansville*, wrote, "Some citizens in Kenansville remember seeing an old photograph of the house that could have been made in the 1860s. They described seeing a fence along the front and sides of the house. This fence was different. It was made of dozens of sabers evenly spaced and partially thrust into the ground creating a fence made totally of Froelich's swords."

After the war, still in debt, Louis began to be hounded by creditors. Transferring ownership of his home to his wife Wilhemina only a few months before those to whom he owed money took his other properties, it may well be that he was trying to escape debt by moving out of Kenansville. Sometime after 1872, he moved to Enfield in Halifax County, and it was there, in 1873, at the age of 56, that he died of consumption. The Wilmington *Morning Star* wrote, "He was among the most useful men of his day and generation."

A highway historical marker denotes the site of the Kenansville factory at the junction of N.C. Hwy 11 and N.C. Hwy 24/50, on the south side of town. Part of the factory site is now occupied by a Dollar General store. Although crude even by 19th century standards, an authentic Froelich staff officer's sword with scabbard will fetch anywhere from $10,000 to $13,000 today, depending on condition. A Foot Officer's sword (with the lettering *CSA* on the guard) can bring from $15,000 to $20,000. The high prices are due to the rarity of the weapons and their Confederate origins. Several swords still exist today, most notably in the N.C. Museum of History in Raleigh, and one in Kenansville. The sword of Col. Thomas Kenan, on display at Liberty Hall in Duplin County, is a Froelich blade. Yet another may have achieved fame as the sword that was broken in two at Appomattox (it was *not* turned into a plowshare).

"49ers" flooded California when gold was found, and a fair number of Wilmingtonians were among them.

photo courtesy Library of Congress

Tar, Pitch and Gold: Wilmington's California Connection

By Robert J. Cooke

In 1846, conditions between Mexico and the United States rapidly deteriorated into war. U.S. troops moved into her southern neighbor and one of the first battles occurred in May, at a place called Palo Alto. Sterling Langdon, an eyewitness to the battle, described it in a letter home to his cousin in Wilmington, North Carolina.

"Such was the immense carnage on the side of the Mexicans that the prairie for nearly one quarter of a mile...was strewn with the mutilated bodies of the Mexicans, so dreadful was the fire from our lines that even in one small space around a piece of artillery 90 dead bodies were found, some with their heads entirely gone [,] others torn to atoms by grape and canister shot.

"Among our own lines, many a brave and gallant fellow 'bit the dust' [.] Lt. Chadbourne of the 8th Regt...fell while advancing in front of his company...Other officers were killed, among them Major Ringgold (of Fremont's Company) & Lt. Inge of the Dragoons...Capt. Page had his lower jaw and tongue shot entirely off...(by the by he was one of the greatest talkers in the Army)."

It would be later said that the "flying battery" of the Third U.S. Artillery was in large part responsible for the American victory. A Mexican cannonball mortally wounded Major Ringgold, who was in charge of the unit. As he fell from his horse, a young lieutenant named Sewall L. Fremont ran to catch him. Captain George Taylor was also at that battle. Both he and Fremont were West Point graduates who had become friendly while fighting Seminoles in Florida, and had been stationed together at Fort Johnston in Smithville, North Carolina (modern day Southport). Both had courted and would marry Cape Fear girls who were cousins. Fremont and Taylor took part in several more battles in Mexico, but soon after, Fremont was back at Fort Johnston preparing more recruits for service south of the border. His likely assistant in this duty was Paul Henry Langdon, a cousin of the woman Fremont was engaged to. Fremont was the Third's Quartermaster, and could hire a civilian clerk.

The war continued until February 1848, ending with the signing of the Treaty of Guadeloupe Hidalgo. With this, Mexico ceded its northern territories, which encompassed the states of California, Nevada, Arizona, Utah and parts of Colorado, New Mexico and Wyoming. Very shortly after the signing of the treaty, gold was discovered in California; this set off one of the greatest migrations of the 19th century. California at the time was sparsely settled by Indians, Californios and a few Anglos, but this would soon change. Those already in California found gold seemingly everywhere, with the simplest of tools – a shovel, or even "a butcher knife." Stories of fantastic gold finds made their way back east, with one miner relaying the good news of his strike to his brother in Wilmington in a letter.

"I have about $117,000 worth of gold," he wrote. "The first months of the excitement, myself and companion collected upwards of seventeen pounds, but as the sickly season had commenced, I have left the mines...I bought me a pair of boots yesterday and paid for them with two ounces of Gold...I could not get them for less."

Stories continued to stir the imagination of thousands back in "the States." There was the "runaway soldier" who discovered a "golden rock" which weighed 899 pounds! He didn't dare leave it, but began to get hungry and offered $27,000 for a plate of pork and beans; yet another man brought a pair of hogs with him to his fields, so they could root for the gold. It was said the hogs brought him from six to eight ounces every night "from their snouts." Such stories were dismissed by the folks back home until the Military Governor of California sent back a tea service full of gold (which was assayed as quite pure), then people began to get "gold fever." Even in North Carolina's biggest port city, the excitement was evident.

"Yesterday the California Cholera was raging in our midst with unprecedented violence," one Wilmington paper observed. "It was caused by two objects, the first was Col. Mason's report; the second, a placard affixed to a telegraph pole at the corner of Third and Market streets, written thus – WANTED: 150 young men to go to California to dig gold; 100 Dollars per month will be given."

The Great California Gold Rush began in 1849. It has been estimated that anywhere from 80,000 to 100,000 people migrated to California during the rush. All states, as well as all countries (except Russia and Japan – whose governments forbade emigration) were represented. The migrants were mainly young, overwhelmingly male and in their mid-twenties, men looking for adventure and a chance to strike it rich. They went by several routes, among them being overland. Jumping off from Independence, Missouri, they followed the "Oregon Route" or "California Trail," their wagons pulled by several teams of oxen. The trip could last from six to eight months, crossing both prairie and the towering Rocky Mountains. One story, verified by several diaries kept by the intrepid travelers, recorded a Scotsman who actually walked the entire route, toting his belongings in a wheelbarrow! This route subjected travelers to Indian attacks (quite rare) and disease (quite common). Cholera raged along the prairie for months, killing many of those who sought a new beginning.

Paul Langdon had gone west as an assistant quartermaster for an army expedition in the late 1840s. By 1850 he was in Wyoming, where he and several partners operated a ferry across the Laramie and Green Rivers. In a letter home he wrote of the immense numbers who had passed through Fort Laramie: up to July of that year there had been 37,280 men (but only 816 women). It would be some time before entire families migrated to find homes instead of gold. Paul was probably the only Wilmingtonian to go by way of the land route. In 1854, he brought a herd of cattle over the mountains from Fort Laramie into the Promised Land. Langdon and his partner would buy broken-down cattle from passing settlers then fatten them up again and resell them to needy emigrants.

Emigrants could also go by steamer from an east coast port to the Panamanian city of Chagres, cross the Isthmus, then reboard a vessel for the trip up the Pacific coast. This route was the quickest, taking from six to eight weeks, but was also the most expensive. The threat this way was malaria or "Panama fever." If one had more time (and a little less money) he could spend the entire journey aboard ship. For about $200 one could embark at an east coast port and sail around along South America, cross the Cape and travel up the Pacific coast to California. The trip was 17,000 miles and lasted from five to eight months. Once aboard, passengers were at the mercy of the ship's captain. There were many complaints about the poor food and unworthiness of the vessels pressed into service. After all, a ship needed to be seaworthy to pass Cape Horn. Many Atlantic coast residents chose this mode of travel.

Gold had been discovered in North Carolina as early as 1799, so it is little wonder that the Old North State had its share of those willing to take a risk to obtain their piece of the western wealth. Two of the first men from Wilmington to venture out (probably in early 1849) were John Dail and George Ferguson. They chose the Panama route and were still there in April, stuck because of the mass of gold seekers and the lack of ships at the Pacific port of Panama City. Not to be deterred, they obtained work on an English brig (aptly named the *Two Friends*) and in return for helping to convert the ship to accommodate more passengers, secured passage to San Francisco.

Stock companies were formed "...to be composed of sober, moral, and respectable citizens," varying in number from several to a hundred or more subscribers. The price of stock varied also, from two dollars a share to two hundred dollars. In Wilmington, Col. Gaston Meares, recently returned from Mexico, received a letter from a friend outlining a venture the Colonel had inquired about.

"I am the proprietor of 300 shares in the sea expedition and could sell any day at $5 per share," the friend wrote. "The vessel leaves in five days. It is the most complete and tangible scheme yet organized, and the most popular started in N.Y. I have no doubt but that yours and the Doct. venture will turn out profitable – take plenty of provisions."

Meares decided not to go, but the doctors did. Drs. Samuel Langdon, John Moore, William Cowan and a prominent planter, Thomas H. Ashe, left in May. They boarded the *Falcon* at Charleston for the voyage to Chagres. Once in Panama they hired "bungoes," a sort of dugout canoe, to take them forty miles upriver. Travelers might pay up to $40 for the trip and one could buy a chicken for as little as fifty cents, but a pot to cook it in cost two dollars! After crossing the mountains by mule or foot, they arrived (25 miles later) at Panama City. There were few buildings there, even fewer hotels; those few quickly filled up. Many travelers simply slept on the beach while awaiting transportation. Sickness (cholera, dysentery and malaria) was always near at hand. Once passage was obtained, it was on to California, 3,500 miles away.

Quite a few from the Cape Fear went by way of Cape Horn. George Walker, the new skipper of the schooner *John Story*, left in August 1849 with a cargo of lumber and several passengers. Irving Ballard, Eugene Drake and a Captain Scott were aboard for the lengthy trip and were safely in California by January 1850. Captain Walker didn't stay, but returned home. Yet another seafarer was Silas Martin, who rented his Wilmington home and packed his family aboard the brand-new bark *John A. Taylor*. Advertised as having room for 100 passengers, the vessel would be making its maiden voyage. Instead of people, she took lumber outbound (apparently there was more profit in the wood). After a bit of heavy weather, the bark put in at Rio de Janeiro and remained there for some time. It is doubtful Captain Martin ever reached San Francisco.

In December 1848, the *Wilmington Weekly Commercial* ran an ad for the schooner *Gen. Morgan*. From New York the vessel was to touch at Wilmington, but there was not enough passengers there, the city on the Cape Fear was bypassed, and the ship arrived in San Francisco carrying twenty-five passengers.

Lurid stories continued to stream back to the east coast, inciting even more risk takers. Early in 1849, a photographer named William J. Pickett moved into the same Front Street building occupied by dentist William Ware. The "California Cholera" quickly infected both men. A newspaper reported the symptoms as "...a nervous restlessness, a convulsive feeling of the inside of the breeches pocket made with the hands, a constant motion of the tongue, in which oro, dinero, San Francisco and a incoherent entanglement of curious words and ideas [are mentioned]." By November, both men were gone with the rush and headed for California.

When Samuel Langdon's younger brother Richard went west, it was by way of Panama. He traveled in the company of his friends, Guilford Dudley and Dr. John Walker (brother of George Walker). They left Wilmington in November 1849, taking "...with them what is better than the gold they seek – integrity of character and industrious habits" according to a local paper. They too remained in Panama for some time, leaving both the old year and Panama at the same time. Young Dick detailed the trip in a letter to his mother.

"We left Panama in a small canoe...to go to the steamer which layed [sic] out in the bay about a mile and a half and was about one hour getting out, and while on the way got wet through and through in the rain, when I got to the vessel (the steamer *Panama*) I got myself aboard, but there being so many canoes arriving with passengers that I did not get my trunk until dark, so I had to remain in them."

Dick also explained to his mother that he had been stricken with both "Panama Fever" and seasickness, but both maladies had passed. Langdon and his friends were in steerage aboard the *Panama*, one of the worst ways to travel, but these young Argonauts were facing trials they had not even thought of. Like many who made the trip, Langdon kept a journal and wrote home describing the sights they had seen in Panama and Mexico (including the eruption of a volcano on the Mexican coast).

Finally arriving in San Francisco, Dick wrote "San Francisco is entirely different from what I expected to find, it is built upon four high hills, running down to the bay...and it now being the rainy season (for there have been only two good days since I have been here) the streets are up to your knees in mud and you see persons with their pants stuck into their boots coming up to their waists [,] trudging along through as unconcerned as you please [,] women going along with men's large heavy boots on, and as many persons passing backwards and forwards as there are in the City of New York."

As Langdon noted, the streets were covered in mud. One anecdote repeated about this situation was "this street is impassable, not even jackassable!" San Francisco Bay was jammed with ships. At one point, there were over 500 ships in harbor, many of them long abandoned by their crews, who had run off to the mountains to try their hand at prospecting. Any supplies or provisions still on board simply rotted away. The U.S. Navy had its problems with runaways also; there were many stories of sailors deserting, including one party that stole a longboat and made their way to shore. The officer on deck quickly rounded up a few men to give chase in a second boat, but that crew deserted, too!

San Francisco was a tent city. Lumber was not readily available, so structures were erected and covered in canvas (from vessels no longer needing sails) One newcomer, standing on the dock with his luggage, noticed a miner, apparently down on his luck. He asked the miner to carry his bags to the hotel, and he would give him a quarter. The miner looked at him, reached in his pocket and threw down some change. "Here's fifty cents," he said, "take them yourself!"

The new arrivals surely noted that the town was "wide open." As Mexican law was no longer in effect and California was not yet a state (it joined the Union in September 1850) there was much lawlessness in the territory. Since the balance of free and slave states could be upset if California was admitted as a free state, Congress was hesitant to act. Many Southerners probably agreed with John Walker's sentiments when he wrote, "that if California cannot 'come to the South, keep her out'." However, one expatriate North Carolinian, Thomas Jefferson Green, who attempted to bring slaves to the gold fields, was told in no uncertain terms that miners would organize and drive him out.

The increase in crime gave rise to groups of citizens taking the law into their own hands. Justice was not always evenhanded; some thieves might be beaten and thrown out of camp, while others might be strung up to the nearest tree. Indeed, one mining town was known for many years as "Hangtown."

"You mentioned in one of your letters about Whitaker playing the rascal and what should be done with such rogues," Paul Henry wrote to his mother, expressing a California opinion. "Send them to Cal [,] a rope is cheap or at least you would have thought so could you have seen four men tucked up to one tree last week within five or six miles of my camp for stealing cattle [.] Last winter not too far from the same place three up to a limb for the same thing, and one or two since [.] Sheriffs, judges and juries are saved much trouble here...If a stock thief is caught some kind friends are always ready to save him the trouble of waiting for court time – he is hung up to dry pretty quick [.]"

There was a military presence in the form of 2,100 soldiers in Monterey, but the commanding officer, Lt. William T. Sherman, reported that about 700 of that number had deserted. Little wonder, when a private earned about six dollars a month and miners were averaging $16 a day! From time to time the War Department would send out companies of soldiers to fill the depleted ranks.

In 1849 there had not been much crime. There was still enough gold for everyone, but by 1850 things had begun to change. There were claim jumpers, robberies and murders. One who suffered a violent end was Dr. Charles Everitt. He was from Smithville (modern Southport, North Carolina) and had come to the fields to mine near the "Four Creeks" in Mariposa (near modern Yosemite National Park). In November 1852, he and his partner were playing cards when they began to argue. His partner pulled his pistol and shot Everitt in the head. Over a year later, Dick Langdon reached the spot and wrote home.

"We were eleven days reaching Four Creeks, I went to O.K. Smith's...and made inquiries wether [sic] I could find anything that had belonged to Chas. Everitt but could find nothing [,] he having nothing at his death but a bowie knife and a pistol which were sold to pay his funeral expenses. I saw the house in which he was killed...a little log house about sixteen by twenty."

Everitt is remembered in the Old Smithville Burial Ground with a memorial inscribed on the tombstone of Dr. Sterling Byrd Everitt, his father.

Such mayhem was widespread, so in 1853 Washington decided to send out more troops. Selected were several companies of the Third Artillery Regiment. Ordered from Fort Adams (Rhode Island) they would go by the cheapest route, by sea, around the Horn. Dutifully embarked in New York on the new steamer *San Francisco*, the soldiers and their families prepared for a six-month journey. The captain had brought aboard as much coal as he could, since it cost less in New York than elsewhere. In addition to the many provisions already stowed, horses, cattle, pigs and chickens rounded out the cargo list. The vessel left on December 21, intending to call at various South American ports along the way.

The first day out at sea was beautiful, but the next day turned ominous. They were headed directly into a violent storm, which was soon upon them. The steamer, overloaded as it was, soon broke down and was at the mercy of the waves. A huge wave crashed into the ship and carried away the uppermost cabins. Two of those washed overboard were Major Taylor and his wife, Emeline. They were seen in the frigid water, holding hands but soon disappeared beneath the waves. Also on board was Captain Fremont, his wife and three children. After several days of harrowing experiences, the Fremonts were rescued and brought back to New York. Of the 700 troops, some 200 were lost. New recruits enlisted later would go to California by the overland route.

Other Wilmingtonians continued to arrive in San Francisco. One who came was Navy Lieutenant Archibald MacRae. Having been ordered to California to survey the coastline, MacRae was in command of the revenue cutter *Ewing*. While on board, MacRae began to show "symptoms of partial derangement," which so terrified his clerk that he sent word to a nearby naval steamer. Two officers were sent over to talk to MacRae, who appeared to be recovered; however, "scarcely (had they) reached the deck when they heard the report of a pistol." The 35-year-old officer had committed suicide. Dick Langdon reported the news to the folks at home and was later told that Archy's brother was "still in possession of (his) letter giving the account of poor Archy's disease."

Such was life and death in San Francisco. Leaving that city, with its boardinghouses and brothels, saloons and gambling dens, many Wilmingtonians continued inland to Stockton. That port town was transformed into a supply center for the "Southern Diggings." These were the rivers and streams that fed into the San Joaquin River: the Calaveras, Stanislaus, Tuolumne and several others. The would-be miners had to take a steamer from San Francisco up the bay to reach Stockton (this trip could cost $200). In Stockton there were hotels, restaurants and of course, saloons and gambling halls. From Stockton, it was via horseback or by foot to where the gold was. Centuries of water washing down from the Sierras had uncovered the precious metal. In many places it was wedged in or under rocks in creeks, in old dried-up riverbeds or sometimes laying on top of the ground. It was very hard work digging or panning in the cold streams. Hours might be spent with a shovel, hoe or pickaxe, hauling dirt to a "rocker" or "long tom" where dirt could be washed away, leaving flakes of gold dust or nuggets where they could be gathered at the end of the work day. In some instances, amateur engineers diverted the stream itself from its natural course so the newly exposed riverbed could be mined.

"We reached the point on Tulare Lake where our work commenced on the 11th of May and I commenced my initiation into the mysteries of surveying," Dick Langdon wrote of the hard work in an 1854 letter. "On the following day [,] the 12th – spent my birthday, by acting as flagman. Monday...finished all the work on the east side of the lake...We have only finished about eighty-five miles.

"Tuesday 30th, we traveled up the slough to look for a crossing...Wednesday the same, on Thursday morning...came to a place...& found it practicable by cutting a road through the trees, thistle and nettles about one hundred yds...we packed the loads down to the edge on our backs...Mr. Gibbs being the only one...who could not swim [,] we had to fix a strap to a two gallon keg and haul him across on that.

"We were from ten o'clock Thursday until two o'clock Friday crossing the things and wagons over and...not stopping to cook dinner, eating cold meat and bread...The mosquitoes are very abundant and bite like the devil [.]"

Many of the other gold seekers toiled in the mountains. Gil Dudley was mining on the American River "turning a stream," while young Tom Laspeyre was at Scorpion Gulch, working the tunnel claim there. It would appear that the Langdons and Laspeyre were partners at that claim, and all of them had to do their share of the work. If a partner could not be there, he had to hire someone to do his work. Paul Henry Langdon, who arrived in California in August 1854, wrote about Tom, who was down on his luck.

"Tom took a splurge for some six weeks on his summer's earnings, and went back to work as soon as his cash gave out [.] He gets rather downhearted & sometimes thinks his (luck) will never take a turn."

Another townsman, Henry W. Bradley, had other things on his mind, according to Paul Langdon. "I do not think it is Henry's intention to go back to Wilmington to settle...He is established in a good and growing business, and will in time do very well [.] He still has a great mania for 'the dear girls'[.] Every one he passes, in the least bit pretty, he says 'ain't she sweet? Who is she? Let's follow her and see – by Jove, I'd give my right hand to kiss her – Well now, don't she take your eye? Now just look at her foot and ankle – ain't that nice? I swear I'll find out who she is'."

The "good and growing business" that Henry was in was photography. "Professor" Bradley started out in a "shanty" but was somewhat annoyed by the rats that climbed the tripod and gnawed up his camera's leather. Batavia rats, white and albino, Java bamboo rats, Shanghai rats, there were all kinds of rodents in San Francisco! Declaring war on the four-legged invaders, Bradley lined his room with flattened tobacco tins and kept them at bay. Despite the rats, Bradley was successful in his photography business, and in 1850 he had over 5,000 customers. As competition increased, he took it in stride. He had backdrops of the Sierras painted on the walls and always had miner's props (long toms, picks and shovels) available. It was said Bradley was the first to put the sign, "Don't Shoot the Pianist. He is Doing his Damndest [sic]!" into his photos.

Several other men tried other ventures when their luck ran out in the hills. Richard Savage had a job in the Customs House and by 1853 was appointed City Clerk in Stockton. He continued to work at a claim in which quartz was mined. That mineral was usually found to be streaked with gold, and when crushed it yielded more of the precious metal. Captain T.F. Peck, probably one of the oldest Wilmingtonians to reach California (he was born in 1760), left his wife and children at home and wound up in the sawmill business in Sausalito (and had been awarded $10,000 in a lawsuit against the U.S. government). Peck, who had been a steamboat captain back east, recognized a ship in San Francisco harbor and was "invited aboard and served with a glass of Cape Fear River water, then highly esteemed as pure and wholesome, which had been kept in one of the reserve tanks for more than twenty years." Peck pronounced the water the best he had tasted in a long time!

If Peck was the oldest, certainly one of the youngest was David Saul Levy. Born in New York City on the Fourth of July 1838, he left Wilmington (with his parents) at the age of eleven. In a biography written in 1901, he described coming via Panama, arriving in San Francisco in August 1849. After working at his father's store for a short while he, at the age of twelve, "joined a pack train at Marysville, bound to Trinity Mountain." Thus began Levy's mining career, one that wouldn't end until after the Civil War. David traveled all over the northern section of the state, to Horsetown, Jackass Flats and Hangtown. While at Oroville, he and others worked all summer to build a dam and "turn" a river. As luck would have it, they "were wiped out in a night" when the floods from an upriver storm destroyed their work. Moving to Portland, Oregon, David tried his luck as a bookseller. Portland, however, was "too slow for a Californian," so he sold out and drifted back to San Francisco. After a short trip east (where he attended school) he returned to San Francisco and became a proud member of the Vigilantes. Of all his jobs he said, "Mining is the only pursuit that ever keeps a man fully supplied with hope."

Of the doctors who went west (Cowan, Moore and Langdon) only Langdon appears to have done well (at least financially). Doctors in California worked both the mines and miners, charging as much as $100 per visit. However, California was reported as having the healthiest climate on earth. Paul Langdon wrote "this country is too healthy for doctors out of a large city...people (rarely) die up here unless they come with the seeds of disease in them from other places." Not all of the doctors did well. Dr. Moore, out hunting, was found dead in a snow bank shortly after getting to California. In June 1853, Dr. Cowan, who worked at the State Hospital in Stockton, took as his bride Miss Annie Biven. A few years later he was found, "bound [,] murdered and robbed near Mariposa." The following year his family was forced to depend on friends to secure passage home to North Carolina for them. But the profession prospered. Dr. John Walker had traveled around the country for several months trying to find gold, but eventually (in the fall of 1850) established a medical office in Sonora. Walker continued to dabble "in mines and mining (also) inventing machinery whereby gold may be better extracted from quartz."

In 1853 Doctors Langdon and Richard Porter Ashe (a brother of Thomas Henry) had an opportunity to practice their trade when the *American Eagle*, while laboring towards Stockton "when about twenty-five miles (out) her starboard boiler blew out...There were fifty-three passengers on board but only two of the passengers were scalded. Eight of the crew...were scalded and five of them died...There was on board a large quantity of exposed gunpowder and several large barrels of brandy."

Col. John "Jack" Hayes

The liquor had taken fire and the steamer was quickly engulfed. "Colonel 'Jack' Hayes, the famous Texas Ranger, was onboard and immediately rushed to extinguish the flames." As the alarm was raised in Stockton, a steamer was dispatched with several doctors aboard (including Ashe and Langdon) "...and passengers and wounded were brought to Stockton." It is likely there was a reunion of sorts between Hayes and former Texas Ranger Ashe!

In Stockton, in addition to seeing patients and working his claim, he was politically active, backing various Whig candidates (as well as securing a position at the State Asylum). He did gain employment there and in 1857 got into an argument with another doctor.

"It ended in a fistfight," one writer recorded,"...in the center of the city. From there it developed in a duel on Rough and Ready Island. The sheriff was tipped off and tried to get to the dueling place before it was too late. In the meantime the first shots were fired and both missed. On the second round of shots, Dr. Langdon was hit in the leg. It shattered his knee, which crippled him for the rest of his life. It appeared that neither intended to kill the other."

Dueling was a way of life in California. The decade following the discovery of gold was a bloody one, where "wounded honor knew no healing balm, save blood." If one was insulted or otherwise slighted, there was always a Colt's Navy revolver that could be appealed to. In 1855, Eugene Drake settled in the Sonora area and was mining at a place called Shaw's Flat. A dispute developed between mining companies, a conflict that soon brought the parties into court. Drake, a "well known and influential miner of the Shaw's Flat party," was called to testify. The opposition lawyer, a Mr. Hunter, badgered him. Hunter was "a well-known attorney...of the browbeating, swaggering stamp...He was a fussy little man...disagreeable in private life [.]"

"After the examination, which was so offensive to Drake, the parties met in the 'Palace' saloon," wrote another writer, "and came into personal collision, resulting in Hunter's being thrown by Drake, who was much the larger of the two. Following this, came another hostile meeting...when Drake seized Hunter, and pushed or threw him from the sidewalk." Another witness continued, "I was present at the difficulty between Drake and Hunter. [I] saw Drake in front of the Placer Hotel, talking with others. Hunter came up...(and) passed behind me...He was moving towards Drake. Drake shoved Hunter from the sidewalk. Hunter turned and said 'You have done what no man ever did, and what no man can do and live'."

The confrontation escalated with several people trying to keep the two apart. Shouting and struggling to get at his adversary, Hunter drew a pistol. He cocked it as he raised it, while Drake went for his gun. Drake's pistol snagged in his clothing, and as he tried desperately to free it, Hunter took aim and fired. Hit in the arm, Drake staggered backwards, doubled over and exclaimed, "Oh Lord". He tried to run for cover, but Hunter fired again and again. Running across the street, Drake knew he was seriously wounded. Hunter was surrounded by several onlookers while Drake screamed, "Get a doctor, I am bleeding to death!" Indeed he was. Hunter's first shot had severed an artery in Drake's left arm, while two other shots struck Drake in the leg. Doctors quickly attended to the wounded man, but it was necessary to amputate the limb. Amazingly, Drake recovered and went on to become a Justice of the Peace in Tuolumne County in 1857.

Yet another duel took place in Sonora, a few years later. Present to record the facts was Dr. Walker. A political quarrel broke apart a friendship and the challenge to a duel was issued. Dr. Walker and the "entire medical staff of Sonora was there to render aid." Unknown to one of the antagonists, the weapons had been loaded with "cork bullets covered with tinsel [.]" As prearranged, when the first shots were fired, one of the men fell to the ground, apparently wounded. As the sheriff approached, the other man quickly fled the scene, learning only later of the hoax. What added to the merriment in the eyes of many, was the concoction that had been mixed up by the doctors. Instead of gin, it was a noxious brew and many of those in attendance soon sought medical attention. So much for healthy climate!

Others, after finding little money in the hills, found work in town. Sam's brother Richard had, by 1855, found a position as a clerk at the Mare Island Navy Yard, eventually becoming the Commodore's private secretary. The work was easy and he was close enough to enjoy San Francisco's social life. He lived onboard the *U.S.S. Warren*, the Navy's Guard Ship, anchored at the yard. The vessel had been employed as a floating prison (until jails could be built in the city) and later as a storehouse. The Navy had selected Mare Island as a much needed navy yard early in 1853; work was begun on a dry-dock later that year. Completed in 1854, a ball

Admiral David G. Farragut

was "given here by the contractors for building the U.S. Dry Dock, through their agents here [.]" Dr. Ashe attended that ball in his roll as the U.S. Navy's agent for the project. He was responsible for seeing that the work was done, and also for paying the contractors. In this position he worked closely with the yard's first commander, David Glasgow Farragut. The two would become brothers-in-law when Ashe married the sister of Farragut's wife, Caroline Loyall. It is likely that Ashe helped Langdon get his job. John Dall probably owed him a debt of gratitude as well. Dall received the contract to supply bricks for the buildings on Mare Island, while Gil Dudley delivered them. All hailed from Wilmington.

One of those adventurers who find it hard to settle down, Ashe came to California by way of Texas. Born in Rocky Point, N.C., he attended schools in the northeast and in 1840 secured an appointment to the U.S. Military Academy at West Point. To honor a deathbed request of his father, he entered the Academy under the name of Richard Ashe Porter, but he did not graduate. Expelled for dueling with another cadet, he attended Jefferson Medical College in Philadelphia and after graduating moved to Texas. There when Texas rebelled and won its independence from Mexico, he enlisted as a private in the First Texas Rifles when war came again in 1846. He was shortly thereafter promoted to Assistant Surgeon and served until 1847. In June of that year he, in company of "twenty-seven Texans, mounted on horseback, crossed the plains and rode into California." Settling in Stockton, he was soon appointed Naval agent.

It is little wonder Ashe got the job. In addition to being suitable, he also had connections in Washington. His brother William was a congressman from the Cape Fear region, and in 1853 had prevailed upon the newly elected President Franklin Pierce to select North Carolinian James Dobbin as Secretary of the Navy. At times advising Dobbin on naval matters, William Ashe also served on the Naval Committee in Congress.

Those from the Cape Fear tended to stick together, but new friendships were also made. One of those befriended by the Langdons was David Farragut, the commander of the Navy yard. Commodore Farragut and his wife Virginia became lifelong friends of both Paul and Richard, who both served as Farragut's secretary. An evening supper at the Farragut's listed the three Langdon brothers, John Dall, Gil Dudley and Richard Ashe. Writing later of the affair, Paul Langdon reported Mrs. Farragut said of her guests, "Oh, you North Carolinians are the most clannish people I ever saw in my life." Paul later wrote, "We muster pretty strong in the neighborhood!"

There were, of course, other North Carolinians in the neighborhood. Colonel Daniel Turner, from Warrenton, had been selected to be the Civil Engineer for the construction work at Mare Island. Former Congressman Edward Stanly had relocated to California by 1853 and, in addition to looking for gold, dispensed legal advice to his fellow Carolinians. Another North Carolinian, William J. Jeffereys from Raleigh, reported "I am on the land where they get gold [,] as I am a cleark (sic) in a house here Which all the money passes through my hands...I have had at least two hundred thousand dollars pass through my hands for the last four weeks...if a man cant (sic) make his ounce a day...they are doing bad buzness (sic)."

In all how did the Argonauts do? Of many there is little known other than that they arrived safely in California. One who was doing well was Thomas H. Ashe, who returned to North Carolina sometime prior to 1855. It was said he "...was rapidly laying the foundations of an estate" when he died, due in part from the toll of the gold fields. He had been "Chastened by the trials and hardships of his early life" and thus had "much sympathy for the poor." Brothers Dan and Ezra Wood, grocers in Wilmington, were in the fields; Dan no sooner arrived than he learned that his wife, whom he left behind, had died. John Dall, after operating a brickyard that supplied the Navy Yard (usually delivered on Gil Dudley's back) did well in the real estate boom in San Francisco and very likely remained in Stockton until at least 1865.

Dr. Ashe was one of the first to help establish a public school in San Joaquin County. In 1850, when the Legislature enacted a revenue tax (in the form of license fees) to raise money for the building of a courthouse, mass meetings were held to protest the act. As he was active in politics, Ashe was elected to a committee that offered a resolution demanding the repeal of the tax. Yet another resolution declared, "if the above request (to repeal the tax) is not granted...we, the citizens of Stockton [will] resist the operation of the law even unto the shedding of blood." In 1850 Ashe began the first stage line to Mokelumne Hill (known as "Mok Hill") and in the first county election held that year, was elected sheriff of San Joaquin (probably serving from 1850 to 1853).

As sheriff Ashe was involved in a few "high-profile" cases. One of these was the hanging of a murderer named Mickey Lyons. Brought to the gallows and guarded by Sheriff Ashe, his was the first legal execution in Stockton. Ashe also chased the renowned outlaw Joaquin Murietta until that bandit left the county. He was quite active in the Law and Order party, in opposition to the Vigilance Committee, an organization Ashe believed was illegally taking over San Francisco. Together with his friend and fellow Southerner, State Supreme Court Justice David S. Terry, Ashe was involved in yet another case, this time as ex-Sheriff.

San Francisco was a veritable powder keg at the time. James King, a newspaper editor who railed against "vice, corruption, crooked politics and general skullduggery" had been shot and killed. His murderer had been tried, convicted and executed by the Vigilantes. Some 3,000 of them had marched on the jail and demanded that he be turned over to them. They had taken over the city (the Vigilantes had most of the men and all of the firearms) and the Governor viewed the city as in a state of insurrection. As one writer noted, "In support of the National Guard, the War Department made an annual distribution of weapons to every state...and on an unnoted June day [Ashe] went to Benecia to see General Wood about...the issue of guns." Ashe sent a party of men to secure the firearms and bring them to San Francisco. The Vigilance Committee found out and captured the vessel (and the guns); however now the Committee had stolen arms from the federal government! The Vigilantes sought a man named Maloney, one of Ashe's men, and it was learned that he was in Dr. Ashe's office.

"On the day following a meeting of the Committee was held...Mr. Hopkins of the Vigilance police, was detailed to [arrest Maloney]," one account related. "He, with two assistants, proceeded to the office of Dr.[R]P. Ashe...where they found Maloney in company with Ashe and...Terry. These two gentlemen informed Hopkins that no arrest could be made in their presence [they had drawn their guns]. Hopkins, therefore, returned to the Committee's rooms for reinforcements."

While he was gone, Ashe and Terry armed themselves with rifles and pistols and attempted to get Maloney to a nearby armory where Law and Order friends were located. But in the street Hopkins once again confronted them, this time with more Vigilantes.

"As they drew near to each other, Terry and Ashe handled their arms in a [threatening manner]...Hopkins sprang upon Terry, while another officer seized Ashe...Terry struggled...to free himself, and, before the struggle was ended, Hopkins received a severe cut in the neck from a knife in the hands of Terry."

Terry had stabbed the Vigilante with his bowie knife, and all three men escaped into the armory. The Vigilantes soon surrounded the place and demanded they come out. They did, were arrested and wound up in "Fort Gunnybags," the Vigilante prison. When Commodore Farragut received the news, realizing that with Ashe in jail, the Mare Island project would come to a halt, he moved to help his friend.

"Bright and early Monday morning, Farragut was on his way to San Francisco to see about getting Ashe out...but on his arrival learned that [another naval officer], Commander Boutwell, had moved first. That officer had demanded, and obtained, the release of Ashe [.]"

Hopkins eventually recovered and Terry was acquitted. Ashe and Terry were involved in several real estate transactions, as well. Ashe bought up a lot of land "...owning no less than ten ranches from the outskirts of Stockton down to large tracts of Fresno." The ranches were located along the route of what would become the Southern Pacific Railroad. One of those ranches became known as "Alabama Settlement," when after the war, Ashe colonized the area by providing land and money to poor Southerners trying to escape conditions in the South.

Young Tom Laspeyre's luck finally took a turn for the better when, in 1858 and 1860, he was elected to the State Assembly from Stockton. Most of the Legislature's work centered around land grants but in 1860, with Abraham Lincoln's election as President, there was talk of establishing a Pacific Republic, which would be sympathetic to the Southern cause. In 1861 the "Breckenridge Democrats" held their State convention in Sacramento and their delegate was Tom Laspeyre. He listened as a young Virginian named Edmund Randolph "made the speech of his life." Within two months Randolph (who was a friend to Ashe) was dead of consumption. Many resolutions were passed, including one that avowed, "we are opposed to the employment of force by the general government against the seceded states," and voted "in favor of recognition of the independence of the Confederate States, and treaty of amity and peace between them and the United States Government [.]" Returning to Stockton, the delegates selected Laspeyre the head of a committee to prepare for the upcoming campaign. One of its planks stated, "The Democratic Party has a mission to defeat...Republicanism under whatever name it rears its head."

Try as they may, these western democrats were unsuccessful. California would remain in the Union, but would never supply any great number of troops for the cause, and throughout the war "Greenbacks" were not accepted as legal currency anywhere in the state. As one writer said, "The young pioneers of Stockton were hot-headed and impetuous, even those who in later years became its best and most honored citizens."

When the war broke out, many emigrants returned to their native regions, leaving behind the new lives they had created. One who tried to get back east was Richard Ashe, who began organizing a band to return and take up arms for the South. Before he could complete his plans, he was arrested by federal authorities and imprisoned on Angel Island. Ashe was later released on the condition that he not try to leave California.

Gil Dudley, Dick Savage and the Langdons all returned to North Carolina shortly before the state joined the Confederacy. Both Paul and Richard worked as auditors for the Wilmington and Weldon Railroad before enlisting in the Confederate army (Samuel and his younger brother Walter enlisted as surgeons). Dudley and Dick Langdon enlisted in the First N.C. Regiment as quartermasters, while Dick Savage joined the 36th Artillery Regiment. Even Henry Bradley attempted to do his part for Southern independence. He was accused of trying to take pictures of Union forts in California. Although much greater events lay ahead, their experiences out west had prepared them somewhat. Indeed, whatever the future held, they had "seen the elephant!"

New Bern native Gabriel Rains, father of the modern land mine.

The Tar Heel and the Torpedoes

By Jack E. Fryar, Jr.

The blue-clad soldier peered into the morning fog at the deserted street that led into the rebel stronghold at Yorktown, Virginia. The bombed out windows of the dark buildings seemed to stare at him accusingly, daring the Yankee interlopers to come further into the city that had until so recently been in Confederate hands. His fellow soldiers, gray silhouettes drifting like ghosts around him, moved steadily forward. Step by step, his feet echoing loudly in his adrenaline-alert ears, the soldier advanced along with the other men of the Union Army of the Potomac. His breath came in ragged bursts, and his palms were sweaty on the stocks of his long rifle as he moved forward.

Across the way, a private from Pennsylvania used his bayonet to lift the edge of a basket holding sweet potatoes.

"Hey," the private exclaimed, "lookee here! Sweet 'taters. I expect they'll go purty good with our rations tonight. Mighty good of the rebs to leave us a treat!"

As the Pennsylvanian reached down to lift the basket, the soldier glimpsed a thin cord running from it that disappeared into the ground. His mind whirred and made the connection just as the rebs' real treat detonated with a roar that blew him off his feet. He was deaf when the smoke cleared and the dust settled, and a gaping hole in the ground marked the spot where the Pennsylvania private had stood moments before. The Union army had just been introduced to the genius of North Carolina's Gabriel Rains, father of the modern land mine.

Though mines had been used in America as far back as the Revolutionary War, the devices that Gabriel Rains built were something new. Constructed from common artillery shells filled with gunpowder, Rains' innovation came with the addition of a detonating primer that, combined with the creative uses of camouflage, made the

Rains' New Bern home, which still stands today.

Confederate land mine a weapon that had an impact far beyond the numbers of mines actually laid. Had the military leaders of the time embraced the new tool of war, the life of the Confederacy may have been considerably lengthened.

Gabriel Rains and his younger brother, George, were both born in New Bern, North Carolina, sons of Gabriel Manigault and Hester Ambrose Rains. Together with six other siblings, the boys were raised in a house on Middle Street before their father, who did upholstery and cabinet work, moved the family to Johnson Street in 1816. The new home was closer to New Bern Academy, where both boys would attend school before matriculating to the United States Military Academy at West Point.

The military life suited Gabriel Rains, who entered the famous service academy on New York's Hudson River in 1823. Starting out in a class of ninety-eight cadets, Gabriel finished thirteenth in a class reduced to a third that size by graduation. It was a class that saw the young man from the town at the confluence of the Trent and Neuse Rivers excel in drawing, chemistry and artillery, all in the company of fellow future Confederates Leonidas K. Polk and Albert Sidney Johnston. Rains drilled on West Point's parade grounds alongside future Confederate States President Jefferson Davis, Joseph E. Johnston and a young Robert E. Lee.

By 1827 Rains sported the new rank of second lieutenant and packed for duty on the frontier Indian Territory at Fort Gibson. His acquaintance with Jefferson Davis was renewed during the twelve years he spent there, and the friendship would bear fruit for him decades later when civil war twisted the nation apart. Rains took a bride while on the frontier, Mary Jane McClellan, the granddaughter of former North Carolina congressman John Sevier, who went on to become governor of Tennessee.

By 1839, Indians in northern Florida were causing problems for the government and white settlers, and Rains drew orders to assume command of Forts Micanopy and King. His mission was to suppress the warring Seminoles and provide protection for white settlers there. It was in combat against the Seminoles that Rains would first test his hypotheses about mines, then known as "torpedoes".

With thick woods, swamp and jungle making it easy for Indian war parties to sneak up on white garrisons, Rains outfitted a small torpedo with a sensitive fuse primer that would detonate the mine when something came in contact with it. Rains buried the mine a mile or so from Fort King, hoping that some hapless Seminole war party would trigger it and provide the early warning his soldiers would need to prepare for an attack. The experiment was cut short when Rains took a party out to investigate an explosion and was seriously wounded in a Seminole ambush. Rains suffered a lacerated lung that had doctors predicting his demise, but the tough officer fought through and recuperated. Though the experiment was a short one, it proved that torpedoes could serve a useful purpose in defensive roles.

Rains was promoted to brevet major for his "gallant and meritorious conduct under fire" during the ambush. When war loomed large on the southern horizon, Rains hitched up his pack and headed to Mexico, where he honed his soldier's trade in fighting at Palo Alto and Ressaca de la Palma. It was a place where many of the men who would assume command on both sides during the Civil War would perfect their knowledge of the soldier's craft. After the war, Rains returned to Florida for a brief stay and promotion to full major.

New York was the next assignment for Rains, where he headed recruiting efforts for the Fourth Infantry Division at Fort Columbus. By 1853 he was back in Indian Territory, fighting Yakima Indians in what would become Washington State. In

photo courtesy Brunswick Town/Ft. Anderson State Historic Site

A keg torpedo, one of Rains' havoc-causing explosive devices.

1856 he assumed command of Fort Humboldt on the California Bay with the new rank of lieutenant colonel. Four years later, on the eve of the Civil War, Rains was back on the eastern side of the Mississippi River, this time serving in Vermont. Rains was alarmed when he learned that North Carolina had joined its southern sisters in breaking away from the Union. He adopted a wait-and-see attitude until blood was spilled at the First Battle of Manassas in the summer of 1861. By the fall he had resigned his commission in the United States Army and was wearing the uniform of the Confederate States of America, with the rank of brigadier general thanks to a recommendation by former classmate-turned-president, Jefferson Davis.

Rains was given command of the rebel troops garrisoning Yorktown, Virginia, a city that was important because it guarded the road to the Confederate capitol in Richmond. George B. McClellan's Union forces landed on the peninsula by the spring of 1862 and promptly aimed their sights at Rains' position. April saw siege operations underway by Yankee troops seeking to reach the rebel seat of government by way of Yorktown. Gabriel Rains and his men stood in the way, enduring more than a month of bombardment from Union guns. Rains and his men fought with such skill and zeal that the troops and their commander were recognized for their gallantry in dispatches to General Robert E. Lee. Despite the strong showing of Rains and his men, army planners decided to consolidate the capitol's defenses in a perimeter closer to Richmond. On May 3, Rains began an orderly retreat from Yorktown, the general remaining to supervise the rearguard defense and the placement of several torpedoes.

For Rains, the torpedoes were a force multiplier, a devise that allows a commander with inferior numbers to counter the superior force arrayed against him. Rains assumed that a few well-placed torpedo detonations would bog down the pursuing Union soldiers, and he was right. When that first mine went off, the empty streets of Yorktown suddenly took on a much more sinister appearance. Yankee soldiers advanced much less quickly as they gingerly checked every pile of rubble and suspicious patch of dirt for more of Rains' devilish devices. The use of torpedoes infuriated Union Major General McClellan.

"The rebels have been guilty of the most murderous and barbarous conduct in placing torpedoes within the abandoned works near wells and springs, and near flag-staffs, magazines, and telegraph offices, in carpet-bags, barrels of flour, etc.," McClellan wrote in a statement carried by the *New York Herald* in May 1862. He went so far as to suggest using captured rebels to remove the mines "at their own peril."

McClellan wasn't the only officer who found Rains' devices distasteful. General James Longstreet, Rains' commanding officer, ordered the New Bern native to stop placing the torpedoes, which he regarded as neither "a proper or effective method of war." In Richmond the man charged with protecting the capitol, General Joseph E. Johnston, read McClellan's assertions in the *Herald* and was disturbed enough by the allegations to order an investigation into Rains' use of torpedoes against land forces. Rains readily admitted placing the devices in the path of the advancing Union forces, a move he justified by pointing out the much larger Yankee army he was charged with slowing down. Having far fewer men and resources to stop them with, Rains saw the torpedoes as means of carrying out his mission.

While he defended the use of the mines, he denied ordering them placed in places like barrels and wells. The denial didn't stem from any conviction that such placement was somehow unsporting, but rather because Rains considered hiding mines in such locations "incompatible with the invention." Nevertheless, Rains conceded that some of his men might have placed the mines in such places without his knowledge or consent. He justified placing four shells along the Richmond road to allow his hungry, weakened and outnumbered men to withdraw to new lines nearer the capitol while carrying out their sick and wounded. Rains also pointed out that using the mines was, to his mind, no more shameful than the Union navy's bombardment of innocent civilians at Yorktown.

"Without a word of warning to innocent women and children as at New Bern, N.C., my native place, they (Union naval forces) commenced to pitch into town...beams of iron 18 inches long and enormous shells (which they continued for a month)..." wrote Rains to D.H. Hill in May 1862, "...scattering their death-dealing fragments among the innocent and unoffending...reversing the scriptural text that it is better for ninety-nine guilty persons to escape than for one innocent to suffer."

General James Longstreet

Johnston was not swayed. Rains was ordered to stop placing the mines, but the resourceful officer continued lobbying for the weapons. He urged his superiors to plead his case to officials in the Confederate War Department. "Subterra shells," Rains argued, bought time for rebel troops too often outnumbered and outgunned by the Union forces they faced. Torpedoes were useful in defending against night attacks, demoralized the enemy, and were certainly at least as legitimate as ambuscades and masked batteries. "Believing as I do the vast advantages to our country to be gained from this invention," Rains asserted, "I am unwilling to forego it."

The Confederate secretary of war was a man who understood the power of judiciously applied high explosives, having been chief of artillery in southeast Virginia prior to assuming his cabinet post. George Randolph recognized in Rains' invention a tool the South needed badly in the face of a superior enemy with virtually unlimited industrial capacity. Taking into consideration D.H. Hill's recommendation supporting Rains, he ruled that while using subterra shells just for the sake of killing was not proper, their use in defensive rolls was acceptable. Nevertheless, he decided that Rains should bow to the wishes of his superior officer, General Longstreet, and stop deploying the torpedoes against land targets. Randolph offered to let Rains transfer to the river defenses, a post that he considered eminently suitable for Rains' explosive devices. Rains refused the transfer, preferring to stay with his command, defending Richmond and taking part in the Battle of Seven Pines on the last day of May.

Joseph Johnston, commanding the Army of Northern Virginia, was badly wounded at Seven Pines, and command of the southern army fell to fifty-five-year-old General Robert E. Lee. The native Virginian made a careful survey of the assets he had and the enemy he faced, and decided one of the most imminent threats was that the Union navy, with more than one hundred warships gathering there, might seize the James River. Such a move would leave Richmond open to attack from the water, something that would be disastrous to the Southern cause.

"We think they are about to make an advance that way upon Richmond," Lee told Rains when he summoned him to his office, "and if there is a man in the whole Southern Confederacy that can stop them, you are the man."

Rains accepted the challenge, and assumed command of the "submarine defenses of the James and Appomattox Rivers" by June 1862. Rains found that Commander Matthew Maury of the Confederate States Navy had already begun a modest program to mine the James a year before. After Maury was reassigned, Lieutenant Hunter Davidson, CSN, filled the billet. When Rains was given the task of mining the James River, he began building on the navy's earlier efforts. Rains' devices were easier to build and deploy than those built by Commander Maury. His submarine mortar batteries did not require the electrical charge that Maury's weapons did. Rains built his devices from ordinary artillery shells affixed with primers and mounted on wooden frames that kept them anchored just below the surface of the water. The shells exploded when the hull of a ship ran over them and made contact with the primer. Rains also sealed common beer kegs and added primers to turn the wooden casks into barrel torpedoes filled with sixty pounds of powder with two metal conical heads. These were also deployed in the rivers.

By late summer 1862, McClellan's peninsula campaign ended, and Gabriel Rains found himself with new orders that sent him back to his home state. The general assumed command of the District of the Cape Fear, including the series of fortifications from Brunswick County to New Hanover County designed to protect the vital shipping port at Wilmington. His orders to build new shore batteries near Fort Caswell and strengthen the river defenses helped make the Cape Fear a place Yankee warships feared for more than just its shoals.

By now the Confederacy had to face some hard facts. It was becoming more and more apparent that as the war stretched on, the shortages endured by the South would only increase. More and more, commanders had to face bigger, better-equipped enemies with fewer and fewer fresh men and supplies of their own. In the face of the ongoing degradation of Confederate forces, Rains' torpedoes began to look a whole lot more palatable to rebel war planners. The Confederacy even went so far as to give torpedoes and submarine batteries official sanction by creating departments to manage their use. Still, the distaste of using the weapons must have remained strong among commanders, because when Rains assumed command of the army's Torpedo Bureau in December, his official post was as superintendent of the Bureau of Conscription. Men assigned to the Torpedo Bureau had to take an oath not to reveal information about Confederate torpedoes, even though they were civilians.

A sample of Rains' spar torpedo, used against enemy shipping.

Rains kept experimenting with fuses, injuring himself in one accident that left one of his hands damaged, but coming up with a device that would set off a mine at the slightest pressure. He quickly put the new fuses into action on torpedoes deployed in the waters of Charleston, Wilmington, and Savannah, Georgia. The floating mines did the trick, as Union naval commanders declared Charleston to be impregnable.

"Here...the ghosts of rebel torpedoes have for two months past paralyzed the efficiency of the fleet authorities,' wrote the rear admiral commanding the U.S. Navy's South Atlantic Blockading Squadron, "and the sight of large beer barrels floating in the harbor of Charleston added terror to the overwhelming fear." General P.G.T. Beauregard credited Rains with a large part of his successful defense of the South Carolina city where the war had started. "I place great reliance...on three things: heavy guns, Rains torpedoes, and in deep water rope obstructions."

Rains' work with torpedoes and explosives led him to prepare a book detailing his success for Jefferson Davis, the Confederate president. Davis was impressed, and the rebel chief executive made it known he wanted Rains to work on torpedoes full-time. By late spring 1863 he was officially relieved of his duties with the Bureau of Conscription and reassigned to Vicksburg, where Ulysses S. Grant's Union forces were trying hard to take the river port and secure control of the Mississippi River in the process. Rains didn't want the job, as he would fall under the command of General Joseph E. Johnston again, the same man who had initiated the earlier investigation into Rains' use of torpedoes in Yorktown and on the road to Richmond. Jefferson Davis insisted that Rains go to Vicksburg, however, and in the end Rains did what soldiers do – he shut up and packed his bags.

Rains arrived in Mississippi and set up shop in Jackson, but before he could do any good Vicksburg fell. Johnston, who had been admonished by the Confederate secretary of war that Rains' devices should be considered legitimate weapons of war, nevertheless showed a reluctance to utilize the great tool the president had placed at his disposal until five days after the town had fallen into Union hands. Finally Johnston ordered Rains to mine a riverbank to cover the retreat of the Confederate army fleeing Vicksburg. The results were impressive even to Johnston, who wrote that Rains' mines "stopped and stampeded Grant's army," and resulted in high enemy casualties.

Sometime after August 1863 Rains was summoned to Charleston, S.C. by Jefferson Davis, where Union gunners were making life hell with a near constant bombardment of the city. Rains deployed subterra shells in the waters of Charleston harbor to keep Union guns at a distance, and planted the devices on the approaches to Fort Wagner battery on Morris Island. The success of the mines drew notice of Alexander Boteler of the Committee on Ordnance and Ordnance Stores, who suggested to cavalry Colonel John S. Mosby that they might be useful against railroads ferrying supplies to Union troops in Virginia. Mosby and General J.E.B. Stuart both thought the mines a good idea. The two commanders asked for some shells and a man to show them how to deploy them.

Meanwhile Rains was envisioning a new use for his weapons. He thought it possible to discourage Union raids against southern cities by mining the approaches to the towns with his subterra shells. The large-scale deployment of the explosives could be accomplished with a minimum of manpower, and would make the task of capturing a protected city a nightmare for Union troops. He contacted southern governors directly with his idea, as he realized the official Confederate government was still skittish about the use of mines to a large degree. President Davis backed the plan, and Rains was assigned a small cadre of men to implement the defensive mine scheme.

By 1864 desperation made the use of torpedoes much more attractive to Southern generals trying to fight a war with ever shrinking resources. Rains, from his post in Charleston, continued to mine the waters between the city and the Yankee fleet offshore. One Union general described the proliferation of mines deployed at Rains' command: "Torpedoes were as abundant as blueberries," he said, "they floated ashore from the ocean, were discharged in the currents of the river and inlets, dug up in the sand or found...in the parapets of Wagner and Gregg." Rains had stymied the Union efforts at Charleston, and now he was called to do the same at Mobile, Alabama.

In February he reported for duty under Lieutenant General Leonidas Polk, who asked Rains to do what he could to keep the Union navy out of Mobile Bay. Rains immediately began submerging his torpedoes. In August 1864 his devices would score a kill when the *U.S.S. Tecumseh* struck one and sank while supporting Admiral David Farragut's capture of the port. The sinking would have delighted Rains, but he wasn't there to see it. By May he had been summoned back to Richmond to supervise all the Confederacy's torpedo programs. The writing was on the wall and southern commanders were grasping at any straws that might stave off the northern victory that was becoming more evident each day.

Rains' first step was to mine the James River again. A young naval lieutenant named J. Pembroke Jones, who would become one of the wealthiest men in the world after the war, helped him. Jones would build a great estate off Bradley Creek in Wilmington, N.C. that would evolve into modern Airlie Gardens. The mission was vital because Richmond had become a city under siege. Its continued survival depended on somehow slowing down the men and supplies that Ulysses S. Grant was steadily pouring into the area through the City Point supply depot.

Rains not only sowed his canisters of death in the waters around City Point, but he managed to beard the Union lion in his own den. In August 1864, torpedo operators John Maxwell and R.K. Dillard managed to pass a smallish box to a worker assigned to load a federal ammunition barge. The box contained a twelve-pound torpedo set to detonate an hour after placement. It performed as advertised, and 25,000 rounds of artillery ammunition ignited, along with 100,000 rounds of small arms ammo. The barge was destroyed, roughly fifty men were killed, and another 130 were wounded. The blast almost scored a lucky hit on General Ulysses S. Grant, who was nearby meeting with staff officers.

By October Rains was able to tell his superiors that 660 shells had been deployed around Richmond. A month later the number had grown to more than 1,000. Before he was finished, that number would grow to more than 2,300. But while Rains' inventions could slow the coming onslaught, they couldn't stop the blue tide pressing down on the Confederate capitol and the rest of the South. First Savannah, then Charleston, and Wilmington fell. General Robert E. Lee was forced to evacuate his lines at Petersburg, and advised Jefferson Davis and the rest of the government to flee. Jefferson Davis and his cabinet boarded a train for Danville on April 2, and on April 3 the Union flag flew over the rebel capitol. Gabriel Rains caught the train in Danville and managed to hitch a ride to Greensboro, N.C. for himself and his family. A week later Lee surrendered at Appomattox, and two weeks after that

Joseph Johnston surrendered the last southern army to Sherman at Durham, N.C. The war was over.

Rains became a chemist for a Georgia fertilizer company after hanging up his sword, a job he held until becoming a clerk with the U.S. Army's Quartermaster Corp in Charleston in 1877. He continued to tinker with torpedoes, and was awarded at least one patent for his innovations. In an article on torpedoes published in the Southern Historical Society Papers, he showed pride in his accomplishments. "Ironclads are said to master the world," he wrote, "but torpedoes master the ironclad."

As to whether or not the weapons were legitimate in warfare, Rains took the long view. "There is no fixed rule to determine the ethics of war," he observed. "Each new weapon in its turn, when first introduced, was denounced as illegal and barbarous, yet each took its place according to its efficacy in human slaughter by the unanimous consent of nations."

Three years later Rains moved to Aiken, S.C. hoping a drier climate might improve his deteriorating health. He died there on August 6, 1881, and was buried in the cemetery of St. Thaddeus Episcopal Church. Jefferson Davis lauded Rains in his history of the Confederacy, and journalist Thomas Cooper DeLeon wrote of Rains' military career and explosives genius that, "It was a service of science and perseverance; frequently of exposure to every peril. It required culture, nerve, and administrative ability; and it was managed in the main with success."

Today mines are, for good or bad, an accepted and integral part of warfare worldwide. Whether considered conscienceless devices of death and disfigurement, or defensive weapons that save soldier's lives, New Bern's Gabriel Rains changed the face of war forever.

Brigadier General Ambrose Burnside

Burnside's Military Trains of the Albemarle

By David A. Norris

Many years ago, on a miserable rainy day, a young Bostonian named James Gardner was on his first trip to North Carolina. The rain had started when Gardner left his steamship in Morehead City and boarded a train for New Bern. The train slowly chugged through a quiet landscape of forests, interrupted only with occasional camps of soldiers and lonely charred chimneys that marked the sites of what had once been homes. Cold and wet, Gardner and hundreds of other Union soldiers from Massachusetts were riding open flat cars along what had once been the Atlantic and North Carolina Railroad. Now, this captured line was part of the U.S. Military Railroad system.

Gardner was cheered by the thought of his canteen, filled with whiskey. It was a new model, suspended by a shoulder sling that contained a rubber tube. Gardner could drink his whiskey from the tube without opening his canteen. Unfortunately, he naively mentioned his secret stock to one of his buddies. Thereafter, he was pleasantly surprised by his friends' concern for his welfare. "The boys huddled together to keep warm," he wrote, and "nearly all of the boys in Company D seemed to have a particular desire to keep me warm." By the time Gardner decided to take a sip of his whiskey, the canteen was empty, drained by his "concerned" friends.

During the Civil War years, most Union soldiers stationed in eastern North Carolina took the same trip as Gardner. When Union Brigadier General Ambrose Burnside and his forces captured New Bern and Morehead City in March 1862, they found themselves in possession of half of the newly built Atlantic and North Carolina Railroad. Built between 1855 and 1858, the line was constructed to link the coast with the older North Carolina Railroad, which ended in Goldsboro. The Union flag waved over the tracks from Morehead City to Batchelder's Creek, the limit of Union control about eight miles west of New Bern. This portion was officially known as the Morehead City and Goldsboro Line of the U.S. Military Railroad. The Confederates controlled the rest of the line, running to Kinston and Goldsboro. Confederate troops pulled up several miles of rails west of Batchelder's Creek to cut the line and to furnish badly needed rails to repair other Southern railroads.

So, Ambrose Burnside had a railroad. The problem was, he had almost nothing to run on it. Before the fall of New Bern, the Confederates managed to get away with every engine and nearly all of the rolling stock of the Atlantic & North Carolina Railroad. Burnside had the foresight to bring some handcars along with his expedition; he used one to travel between New Bern and Morehead City until new engines and cars could be sent down by sea from the North.

photo courtesy Library of Congress

Burnside took advantage of the miles of southern railway in the central and Albemarle regions to create a military rail system.

After taking New Bern, Burnside's next objective was the capture of Fort Macon. His siege guns, three 30-pounder Parrott Rifles and four 10-inch siege mortars, had to be taken from New Bern to Morehead City. Because the retreating Confederates burned the railroad bridge across the Trent after the Battle of New Bern, the guns were carried by water to Slocum's Creek, where they were brought to the railroad. Once the line was repaired, the siege guns were loaded on cars and pulled by horses down the railroad to Morehead City. Four more 8-inch mortars were likewise brought a few days later to strengthen the force investing Fort Macon.

Even getting new engines to North Carolina was an ordeal. To start up Burnside's railroad, fifteen schooners sailed from Baltimore carrying four locomotives and an assortment of fifty cars. One schooner, carrying two engines, was lost in a gale off Cape Hatteras. Two more engines arrived in another schooner, but one of these promptly broke down and had to be sent back for repairs.

Repairs to the Trent River bridge took some time. The woodwork of the bridge was much damaged, but the brick piers were not. The log bridge carried not only railroad tracks, but a parallel wagon road as well. It was June 12 before the first U.S. military trains chugged into New Bern. The *Newbern Weekly Progress* reported, "all the town rushed to the wharves, and there was a veritable locomotive with cars, kicking and shrieking like mad, through from Beaufort. This gave pleasure to the citizens, for we could see it depicted in their countenances...Puffing along our streets, away she sped up in the pine woods toward Batchelder's Creek."

Locomotives in those days were given names, just like ships. Some of the engines that ran on the U.S. Military Railroad in North Carolina for the Union Army were the *Chief*, the *Vulcan*, the *Grape Shot*, the *Commodore*, and the *Ancient*, along with the *Blue Bird* and the *Reindeer*. Appropriately enough, the *Ancient* was too worn out for use on the road and was limited to use as a switch engine at Morehead City.

In the flat coastal plain, a locomotive could pull up to 25 or 30 cars, as opposed to perhaps 10 in piedmont or mountain country. In December 1862, a train of 31 cars carrying 2,000 soldiers ran from Morehead City to New Bern in one hour and forty-five minutes. Usually, one train a day made the New Bern - Morehead City run, which was scheduled to take two hours. Two trains a day ran from New Bern to the large outpost at Batchelder's Creek.

For protection, a number of strong log blockhouses were built near bridges and other vital points. By an important bridge over the Newport River, the Union established a fortified outpost called Newport Barracks. Cavalry and infantry units were stationed there, with artillery pieces inside earth and log fortifications.

Besides their stationary strong points, the railroad had mobile protection from the "Monitor Car", an iron-plated boxcar with two swivel guns and loopholes for small arms. This car was named after the famous ironclad Union gunboat. The Monitor Car's cannon were a pair of 2.6" Wiard rifled guns. The car was built by mid-July, and was used with every train running between New Bern and the coast.

A telegraph line was set up along the line of the railroad in June 1863. A Captain Shelton and a crew of six men had the 42 miles of telegraph wire up and working in one week. Seven operators, three of whom were killed by yellow fever in the epidemic of fall, 1864, staffed the telegraph line.

The railroad was plagued with attacks and sabotage attempts. In one case, a train running from Morehead City was derailed in August, 1864, when some men of the 67th North Carolina pulled off a couple of rails. Two Union soldiers were injured, one of whom was run over by the cars. The train pulled into New Bern at midnight, eight hours late. Another time, what was described as a "torpedo" (land mine) exploded just too late to damage a passing train.

Even without "help" from the Confederates, railroad accidents were common. For example, on June 30, 1864, the train from Morehead City wrecked six miles from New Bern when an axle broke. A Yankee reporter wrote for the *North Carolina Times* that when he "visited the scene of the disaster", he "found the cars piled on top of each other like miniature Alps. Flour, butter, molasses, lemons, oranges, filberts, peanuts, marble dust, and everything...was stirred up in one delectable mess. Two or three cars were completely stove to pieces." Two men were injured; one of the poor fellows was on his way out of North Carolina for a furlough.

A much more catastrophic accident happened at the Batchelder's Creek outpost on May 26, 1864. Soldiers crowded around the newly arrived train from New Bern, looking for letters from home. Meantime, what looked like three large wooden pork barrels were being unloaded from a freight car. They were each crammed with two hundred pounds of gunpowder, and were intended to be set as mines in the nearby Neuse River to guard against the Confederate ironclad *CSS Neuse*, under construction upriver above Kinston. The engineer officer in charge of the mines left the train, and a quartermaster sergeant, thinking they were simply two more supply barrels, had them unloaded. First one barrel, then the second, rolled down a gangplank from the car. The third barrel thumped into the others, setting off a detonator. All three exploded with a mighty roar heard in Kinston, twenty miles away. The log depot, the station platform, and a 90-foot high signal tower were "shivered to splinters". Thirty soldiers and ten civilians died, and forty wounded men were loaded onto a flat car covered with straw and taken to hospitals in New

Burnside traveling by hand cart.

photo courtesy Library of Congress

Bern. Nothing recognizable was left of the unfortunate quartermaster sergeant except his little finger, which was identified by his ring. The news was reported in newspapers as far away as New York.

A few days later, a fireman was injured when a locomotive crashed into a "platform car" (what we would call a flatcar) in Morehead City.

Early in 1865, General Sherman's army was preparing to enter North Carolina. The invading army was to be supplied by the Cape Fear River (now that Fort Fisher no longer guarded the mouth of the river), and North Carolina's railroads. Sherman sent Colonel W.W. Wright to get the military railroad ready to handle the greatly increased traffic that would flow when his army arrived.

Wright found quite a mess at New Bern. The railroad had only five locomotives, and two were broken down. The tracks were in bad condition, and traffic was badly impaired by the lack of sidings along the single line of track. The wharf at

photo courtesy Library of Congress

The Union trains were a frequent target of sabotage.

Morehead City was far too small to handle the cargo that would soon be brought in for the army. Rails, spikes, and even firewood were in short supply.

The colonel quickly put men to work repairing the tracks and building new sidings, as well as starting a massive new wharf at Morehead City. Ships brought more engines and cars, bringing Wright's total to thirteen locomotives and over 150 cars. For the rest of the war, the railroad was used to supply Sherman's troops. Union control of the line was extended westward as more territory was captured, and Wright's crews followed, repairing tracks and rebuilding burned bridges.

It would seem to be about this time that an inspection train bearing a photographer set out along the line. The U.S. government sometimes used photographs as proof that contractors did indeed complete the buildings or bridges they were hired to do, and that they were of the size that was being paid for. Without a photo, an unscrupulous contractor (and there were plenty of them) might build a 50-foot bridge and bill the army for a 500-foot one. Two photos of the military railroad line in North Carolina that survive today (shown with this article), depict what appears to be the same train halted on bridges across the Little River and probably the Neuse. A "conductor's car," an adaptation of a wooden boxcar, is shown on each picture of the train. This car, which housed the conductor and crew, was the ancestor of the caboose.

The U.S. Military Railroad system eventually absorbed several other stretches of railroad in North Carolina, all of which required extensive repairs after four years of war. The Atlantic & North Carolina Railroad remained in federal hands until it was handed back over to the company on October 25, 1865. From aiding the Union war effort, the 85 miles of track from the coast to Goldsboro went back to helping the future growth and prosperity of a new North Carolina.

The massive brick piers of the Trent River railroad bridge at New Bern survived until they were demolished just a few years ago in order to build a new bridge.

Dr. Jean Prosper Formy-Duval

The Strange Legend of King Louis' Doctor

By Jack E. Fryar, Jr.

Plese help them." Dr. Jean Gerome Formy-Duval still heard the woman's plea in his ears, even though the words had been uttered days before. Morning sunlight lit the cobble streets on the outskirts of Paris, and the scarlet tendrils announcing the new day washed the scene from his window in blood hues. Fitting, given the times.

Paris was a city gripped in revolutionary fever. The excesses of the French court of Louis XVI and his wife, Marie Antoinette, had tweaked the noses of the great-unwashed French masses until violent change had become inevitable. Revolutionaries, encouraged by the fledgling United States' success at throwing off the yoke of royal oppression, fanned the fires of independence in the streets and inns of the French capitol. Citizens Committees, ostensibly dedicated to liberty and equality, pledged to root out those loyal to the monarchy and redistribute the wealth from the haves to the have-nots. If in the process a few lingering grudges were settled, well, what goes around certainly comes around.

Dr. Formy-Duval was not a revolutionary, just a physician assigned to the royal court from his native region near Rouen, in the north. The fact that he was a healer made him useful to both sides of the growing argument, but didn't raise him totally above the suspicions of the committees. His assignment to the royal court assured that. No one tainted by royal contact or favor could escape the ever-emboldened proletariat seizing control of the country. Nevertheless, Dr. Formy-Duval was a healer, a man pledged to save lives. It was his reputation as such which caused his immediate discomfort.

As unrest began to turn into open defiance and revolution in 1789, those with royalist sentiment were being targeted for execution, sometimes for real offenses

The execution of King Louis XVI

against the people. In other instances people were targeted to settle old scores or to clear the way for new, more republican-thinking owners to claim the property of those executed for their purported ties to royalty. One such group accused and found guilty of loyalty to King Louis was scheduled to be executed for their real or imagined sins. The doctor knew the people to be shot, and knew that whatever their crimes, they did not rise to a level that called for their deaths. Dr. Formy-Duval came to a risky conclusion that was the only one his sense of honor would let him make.

For all their zeal, few among the revolutionary rank and file knew anything about law or the protocols of government. When the educated and distinguished Dr. Formy-Duval offered his services as examining doctor for the executions, the Citizens Committee accepted, thinking his participation would lend an air of legitimacy to their proceedings. Having a physician of the royal court volunteering in the service of the revolution would also be a coup that they could point to as an example of the broad range of people backing their efforts for change. Dr. Formy-Duval was accepted gladly.

Now the sun had risen high enough that the doctor could make out the pockmarked wall that had served as backdrop for other killings in the name of liberty. Each gouge in its brick face represented a blow struck on behalf of the masses, and each dark stain underneath marked where another life had been lost to the revolutionary tide sweeping the country. Dr. Formy-Duval could not in good conscience let his friends become another notch in that wall, or see their blood soak into those rust-colored cobblestones. Making his way downstairs, he approached the corporal of the guard in charge of the execution detail. He was a young man, with the cockade of the revolutionaries his only insignia of rank. Though he had a grave responsibility, Dr. Formy-Duval detected no malice in the boy. He was simply a soldier doing a job, the right or wrong of which was a debate for those ranked above him. It was a simple matter to convince the novice executioner that as examining doctor, Formy-Duval was responsible for inspecting and loading the weapons to be used by the firing squad.

A short while later the condemned were led from a nearby building and arranged against the wall. Tearful family members sobbed off to one side. Dr. Formy-Duval forced himself not to look them in the eye, afraid it might give him away. The air seemed to stand still, and around them the sounds of a city waking up for a new day seemed to stop as the corporal's first command to the firing squad rang out in the morning air. The file of soldiers clumsily raised their muskets and took aim at the men standing blindfolded thirty feet away. When the command to fire came, a volley of flame leapt from the gun muzzles, and black-gray smoke obscured the wall. When it cleared the condemned were all laying on the ground, arms and legs akimbo, some staring sightlessly into space. Dr. Formy-Duval knelt beside each body, using a stethoscope and mirror to be certain each was dead. Satisfied, he looked to the corporal and nodded, then motioned for the waiting family members to come and claim their fathers and sons for burial. The corporal of the guard gathered the death certificates signed by Dr. Formy-Duval and marched his citizen soldiers away.

At their homes, grieving families carried their burdens inside to prepare the bodies for burial. At the gravesides, weeping children lamented the loss of their dearly departed. At the citizen's court, satisfaction was taken that enemies of the people had finally gotten their comeuppance. And in secret rooms and barns, the men who were supposed to be filling those graves gathered their belongings and escaped into the countryside, away from Paris and its prying eyes, to rendezvous with their families after things had died down. Each and every one of them said a silent prayer of thanks for their friend, Dr. Jean Gerome Formy-Duval, a man who had put his own life at risk to save theirs.

The subterfuge would have worked perfectly, and the Citizens Committees would never have learned the truth – that Dr. Formy-Duval had loaded the muskets of the firing squad with blanks, then pretended the executions were successful – had one of the supposed dead men not been captured later on. Curious as to how a man who had been shot weeks before had managed to be caught walking around in good health, the committees began investigating. The corporal of the guard recalled that Dr. Formy-Duval had inspected the muskets prior to the executions, and sheepishly admitted he hadn't actually check the bodies himself after the firing squad did their job. The investigators put two and two together, and suddenly Dr. Formy-Duval was a wanted man.

Word reached the doctor that there was an arrest warrant with his name on it being issued by the Citizens Committee, and he wasted no time fleeing the city. Paris was no longer a safe place for him. He headed north, hiding by day and traveling at night until he came to the lands near LeHavre, a short distance from where his friends and family lived in Rouen. Some family members say the doctor hid in the swamps, using a bullwhip to hunt birds for his dinner. However he sustained himself, his main goal now was finding a way out of France for himself and his kin. Sitting in the green darkness of his swampy shelter, he thought of his wife, known to descendants only as "The Princess," possibly because of some kinship to the king and queen. One good thing in the doctor's favor was that he and his wife were childless. Spiriting just the two of them out of the country would be a much simpler task than if they had to figure children into the equation, too. King Louis XVI had granted Formy-Duval lands in Haiti, half a world away. If he could secure passage there, it might just be far enough out of reach of the Citizens Committees that he could live life as something other than a marked man.

LeHavre is a coastal city long noted as a major port, with merchantmen calling there to drop off and pick up cargo from all over the globe. It was the perfect place for Formy-Duval to find a fast ship away from his troubles. Always careful to remain at arms length, aware that the committees had eyes even among the wharves and docks of the coastal city, the doctor sought a captain who could provide him and his wife a berth. He eventually found such a man and ship, sailing for Haiti on the next tide. Dr. Formy-Duval and his wife gathered together only their most precious possessions and made their way to the ship under the cover of night. The captain whispered orders, and the two fugitives were brought aboard and hidden in a dark corner of the cargo-laden hold. The Princess paid for their passage with gold pieces from a sock of coins she kept on a leather thong that dipped between her breasts. The couple held their breath as they waited for the ship to get under way, worried that someone may have seen them climbing aboard the ship in the dead of the night, or that someone in the ships company might betray them. The Formy-Duvals gave a sigh of relief when they felt the deck cant over as wind filled the sails and the ship began making for open water. They didn't dare venture out onto the deck for a last look at their homeland. Whatever memories of France they carried in their minds would have to suffice. Home was now some unseen land beyond the horizon.

For weeks the fugitive couple had time to consider the future, the days taken up by speculation as to what lay ahead and daydreaming while the ship skipped over the ocean swells. Finally a low green smudge on the horizon brought a cry of recognition from the lookout atop the ship's main mast. The Formy-Duvals had made it safely to their new home. Once ashore the doctor and his wife set out for St. Domingue, where King Louis had granted him lands in the 1780's. Some say he owned a sugar or coffee plantation there, though little is known about the time the Formy-Duvals spent in Haiti. The couple settled into a life as country planters, and not long afterwards the family grew with the birth of John Gerome Prospier Formy-Duval around 1789, and again around 1790 when Henrietta Formy-Duval was born. Alexander, the last of the children born to Dr. Formy-Duval and The Princess, was born in 1792.

For a blissful while it seemed the young family would finally be able to live a free and prosperous life, unencumbered by the lurking threat of the executioner, but the happiness was short-lived. Trouble seemed to follow Dr. Formy-Duval, and in Haiti he once again found himself surrounded by discontent and danger. Haiti in 1791 was an island with 30,000 whites ruling over more than a half million blacks whose simmering anger would erupt into violence in what became known as the Haitian Revolution. For fifteen years the violence raged, ultimately killing half the black and mulatto population. The white population became almost nonexistent, with half killed in the fighting and the other half fleeing the island violence for new homes in America, many of them settling in South Carolina.

The white population of Haiti was decimated during the Haitian Rebellion, providing a big incentive for the Formy-Duvals to find a new home.

Dr. Formy-Duval tried to make a go of things in Haiti despite the violence. When Great Britain saw an opportunity to seize new territory in the confusion and disarray caused by the Haiti Revolution, the doctor may have seen a chance to rid himself of the death warrant hanging over his head once and for all. When British troops mustered near France's colony of Jamaica with an eye towards seizing key real estate in southern Haiti, Jean Gerome Formy-Duval may have offered his services in the English cause. The memoirs of a British officer involved in the Haiti action mentions a "Monsieur Duval" who came to the redcoats in 1793 and offered to raise a body of men to help them take the southern seaports of Jeremie and Tiberon. The British accepted the offer, and then marched on the two towns. Monsieur Duval's promised men never materialized, and the redcoats found themselves in a nasty fight, which they lost along with many men. The British were understandably displeased, and the officer's papers say that the Duval in question later left the island for America.

Exactly how the Formy-Duvals came to America is something open to debate, with differing versions of the story depending on who is doing the telling. Family legend claims the doctor was warned that slaves on a rampage during the rebellion had targeted the French plantation owner, and that he and his family fled with a few trunks of belongings, including the doctor's medical equipment, to a ship that took them to America. Another version points out that if the family had escaped just ahead of a lynch mob, they would hardly have had time to pack and transport several large trunks with family valuables. In this second version it's claimed that Dr. Formy-Duval made arrangements with an American sea captain to transport his and a few other French families to America and away from the bloodshed in Haiti. Fearing reprisals from revolutionary French officials, the captain made the Formy-Duvals and the others meet him in a dory at sea, where he took them aboard two days later and transported them to the fledgling United States.

The ship finally dropped anchor at Georgetown, S.C., but the rice plantations and large numbers of black slaves were a discomforting reminder of the bad times in Haiti. Dr. Formy-Duval and his family reboarded the ship and took their search for a new home north. The ship made its way up to the Cape Fear, where the captain was scheduled to call on the port at Wilmington, N.C. Afraid to discharge his passengers at the town for fear they might be arrested and sent back to France, the captain put the fugitive Formy-Duvals ashore at the sleepy little village of Southport.

Once on dry land, Dr. Formy-Duval moved his brood up the river and settled for a while in Wilmington. Coming to the town by land avoided the awkward questions that an arrival by ship might have raised, and the family was able to settle in for a time and catch their breath. Still, Dr. Formy-Duval was uncomfortable in the port town, exposed to the prying eyes of curious neighbors. Every time a new ship dropped anchor along the bustling waterfront, Formy-Duval wondered if a passenger or crewmember might be someone who recognized him from France or Haiti. In 1798 the United States government passed the Alien and Sedition Act, aimed specifically at keeping French immigrants out of the country. It felt to the doctor as if his family's newfound safety might be snatched away at any moment. Wilmington was just too crowded. Dr. Formy-Duval began looking for a more discreet place to set down his new roots.

South of Wilmington in what is modern Columbus County is Lake Waccamaw. Virginia patriot Patrick Henry owned land there once. After the war, the property was seized when its owner went into arrears for back taxes. Dr. Formy-Duval saw in the land a place where his family might finally settle down for good. He bought the 8,000 acres of property, much of it in the Green Swamp, and near Dupree Landing built a home. The Formy-Duvals had finally quit running.

Many residents of Crusoe Island in Columbus County claim to trace their lineage back to Dr. Formy-Duval, although he and the Princess never lived there themselves. By 1800 she had apparently died, and the doctor was remarried to Penelope Baldwin by 1802. Still a young teen when she became a bride, Penelope and the doctor had six more children. Dr. Jean Gerome Formy-Duval's children would play prominent roles in the history of southeastern North Carolina and Florida, where two of his sons moved. One became a politician there, and another started growing orange groves. It may be that Duval County in Florida is named after one of them. Back in

North Carolina, the doctor added another first to his name by becoming the first person to grow cotton in Columbus County, using Jonothan Price's cider press to produce a bale in 1815.

Jean Gerome Formy-Duval died while attending a sick patient in Fair Bluff in 1821. Coming down with the plague on the way home, one story says he was buried where he fell beside the road, while another account has him being interred at Porter's Swamp Baptist Church. The story goes on to say that whatever inheritance the doctor's children had coming was lost to crooked lawyers, leaving the once wealthy family penniless save for what they owned in southeastern North Carolina.

How much of the story about the immigration of Dr. Jean Gerome Formy-Duval is true and how much has grown out of embellishment over the years is a matter of some debate. Descendents like Mike Formy-Duval have devoted a great deal of time and money over the years to uncovering the tantalizing details of how their ancestors first came to call North Carolina home. Regardless of how many of the details are true, at its heart is a fascinating story of how one courageous family braved uncertainty and possible death to reach a place where they could have a better life, here along the North Carolina coast.

Blackbeard fell in bitter fighting with Lt. Robet Maynard and his men off Ocracoke Island.

King of the Pirate Scourges:
Blackbeard and the Carolina Coast

By Jack E. Fryar, Jr.

Have a seat, mate. Share a mug wi' yer captain." The man's sun darkened skin was framed in a wild mane of greasy black hair, his teeth a dull yellow in a face exuding innocence through a brotherly smile. The table in the captain's cabin was piled with roast pig and a pitcher of ale from the ship's galley. Israel Hands' belly rumbled at the sight in spite of himself. Tongue sliding across wind-chapped lips, he slid onto the seat across from his captain, Edward Teach, more widely known as the pirate Blackbeard.

"That's a lad," Teach said, pouring a mug of the cool liquid for the man sitting across from him. "How long have we been sailing together?" he asked.

Hands took a long pull at the mug and wiped his dirty sleeve across his mouth before replying. "Must be nigh on two years now, cap'n." He ventured a cautious smile. When Blackbeard was in a generous mood he could be quite expansive in his generosity. When he wasn't his smile could cover a mean streak as deep as the ocean itself.

"Two years," Blackbeard mused. "That's a long time for two blokes to share a deck."

"Aye, sir," Hands, the master of Teach's ship *Queen Anne's Revenge*, agreed.

"Long enough for there to be a certain amount of trust between two shipmates, eh?" Teach suggested.

The sailor swallowed hard, then allowed as to how it might be so.

"Good!" exclaimed Blackbeard. He leaned over and slapped the sailor on the back, then slid one hand under the table. Teach quickly blew out the lantern sitting on the table, dropping the cabin into blackness. A second later a pistol shot rang out, and Hands fell backwards out of his chair, screaming as he clutched his crippled knee while the cabin filled with the pungent smell of gun smoke.

"Come get this scum out of here," Blackbeard called to another lieutenant waiting outside the cabin door.

The pirate officer quickly came into the captain's cabin and spied the injured Hands lying in a pool of his own blood. "Lord, Cap'n! Why'd ye go and shoot him for?"

The black mane of hair turned so that two coal-dark eyes peered at him from blood red rims. The man trembled a bit at the scrutiny.

"You have to shoot one or two of your crew every now and then," Blackbeard explained. "It keeps 'em honest and reminds 'em who's in charge!"

Born in Bristol, England, Edward Teach (or Thatch, among several other last names and aliases said to have been used by Blackbeard) started his life on the high seas sailing under a letter of marquee issued by England during Queen Anne's War. Serving aboard a privateer against French shipping during the conflict, Teach was disinclined to resume more sedate activities once the war ended. Captain Benjamin Hornigold saved him from the dull life of a peacetime sailor when Teach signed on with the famous pirate about 1716. In 1717 the two made their way across the Atlantic to Providence, in the Bahamas, and from there began to prey off the coast of America and the Caribbean. Teach so impressed Hornigold that the captain put him in command of a prize sloop they had taken. The hunting was good, with Teach and his mentor Hornigold taking a shallop from Cuba carrying 120 barrels of flour, and a Bermuda sloop carrying wine. They hit the jackpot when they captured a Spanish ship bound for South Carolina carrying a sundry cargo of valuable items. On the way back to the West Indies, the pirates captured a French ship bound for Martinique. Hornigold put Teach in command of the prize, and there the two parted ways, with Teach taking the large Dutch-built ship off on a solo cruise, while Hornigold returned to Providence and took the king's pardon.

On his own with an independent command, Teach set out with a vengeance to make his mark in the pirate trade. Mounting 40 guns, his *Queen Anne's Revenge* was a match for just about any merchantman sailing the Atlantic, and was a formidable challenge even for warships of the Royal Navy. Blackbeard took his first prize off St. Vincent, plundering the cargo and setting the crew ashore before burning the ship to its waterline. The attack didn't go unnoticed, and days later the British warship *H.M.S. Scarborough* engaged the pirates in a fight that lasted for hours. To the consternation of the British, Blackbeard's ship gave as well as it got and forced the *Scarborough* to withdraw.

While enroute to what pirate chronicler Daniel Defoe called "Spanish America" Teach came across another pirate whose name would become well recognized along the North Carolina coast, Stede Bonnet. Bonnet, a former British army major who had resigned his commission to manage a sugar plantation in Barbados, took up the pirate trade to get away from a nagging wife. He bought a sloop, armed and manned it (something unheard of in the world of pirates), and went to sea. Bonnet preferred risking a hangman's noose than living with his spouse a day longer. The trouble with his plan lay in his inexperience. Bonnet had been a soldier, not a sailor, and knew virtually nothing about commanding a ship at sea or governing a crew – especially a crew of pirates.

Blackbeard saw an opportunity in Bonnets inexperience and immediately took steps to install his own man, a Lieutenant Richards, as master of the henpecked Bonnet's ten-gun sloop, the *Revenge*. Teach convinced Bonnet that having an experienced sailing master aboard to handle the mundane chores of running the *Revenge* would free Bonnet up to learn the sailing craft at his leisure. In effect though, Bonnet ended up being a hostage aboard his own ship. Blackbeard, through Richards, was calling the shots now. With his small two-ship flotilla, Teach set out for Honduras. Richards and the *Revenge* captured the Jamaican sloop *Adventure* while Teach and company had stopped to fill their water casks, expanding Teach's fleet to three ships.

Blackbeard was a man who enjoyed contests where the stakes were high. In the pirate world the toughest and cruelest man was often the top dog, and Teach was always holding contests and exhibitions to make sure his crew knew who was boss. Defoe recounts a tale of one such contest in which Blackbeard and several of his crew were locked in the ships hold with burning sulfur pots closed in with them. "Come, let's make a Hell of our own!" he said. The hold quickly filled with the suffocating smell of brimstone, and soon everyone had bolted for the fresh air of the main deck. Everyone, that is, except Blackbeard. He emerged last, laughing at the weakness of his men and further cementing his reputation as the Devil incarnate in their minds.

Over the next weeks, Teach and company took another dozen or so ships of varying sizes and with a wide range of cargoes. Teach was very successful in a short period of time, much of it due to his fierce appearance. He was a big man, barrel-chested and tall, with long hair the color of a raven's wing and a beard that began just below his maniacal eyes and extended down to his chest. When in combat he plaited the beard and tied the ends off with red ribbon, then stuck burning quick matches out from under the band of his hat. The smoking, hairy apparition he presented when he boarded a merchantman, a bandolier stuffed with three pairs of pistols across his chest, was sufficiently terrifying that many crews surrendered rather than find out if Teach was as wicked as his look suggested. The result was that despite his reputation, Blackbeard actually had to resort to murder relatively rarely.

By the time Blackbeard sailed away from Cuba, his men were beginning to show the effects of their efforts in the form of sickness and injury. Teach turned his flotilla north, towards the Carolinas. Lying off the bar at Charleston, Blackbeard played the part of shark to the South Carolina merchant fleet's prey for a week that had the residents of the colony's capitol keeping a fearful eye on the harbor. The first victim was a London-bound merchantman commanded by a Robert Clark. Several other vessels trying to leave Charleston fell to the pirates in short order. Blackbeard and his men had successfully bottled up the largest city in the Carolinas.

The response of the government and citizens of Charleston might seem unreasoned, given that it was the largest city in either Carolina and had at least some military strength by virtue of being the Crown's seat of government. But the appearance of Blackbeard off the bar came at a time when the resources of the colony had been strained almost to the point of depletion. Not long before Teach's *Queen Anne's Revenge* began taking ships off Charleston, another pirate named Vane had made life risky for ships coming and going from the South Carolina port. Too, the colony had appropriated men, money and materials to go to the aid of their North Carolina brethren around New Bern, who were being massacred by local Indians in the Tuscarora Wars. Charlestonians were stretched thin on all counts by the time Blackbeard appeared to hold the town hostage.

The London-bound ship the pirates initially seized contained a number of prominent Charleston citizens, including Samuel Wragg, a member of the ruling council. Once Teach had inventoried his prisoners and the ship's cargoes, he ordered them unceremoniously dumped back aboard the eight ships they came from and locked in the dark holds for safekeeping. Hours later the hostages were brought back aboard the *Queen Anne's Revenge*.

"My apologies for the unseemly delay," Teach said mockingly to the fine ladies and gentlemen, whose shine had become somewhat tarnished by their rough treatment. "I had t'consult with me colleagues in private. See, my shipmates have become a bit peeked of late, and unfortunately my surgeon tells me our supply of herbs and potions is somewhat lackin'. So it is my intention to send a list of medicines ashore with two of my officers. We'll be holdin' on to you fine folks to make sure they get the audience at Government House that they ought to. If'n we get the medicines, all's well. If'n we don't, well, then I reckon the good people of Charleston will be spending a great deal of time in the cemeteries."

A gasp went up from the terrified hostages. "But what if the medicines you seek can't be found in town?" a woman wailed.

"What if the governor refuses to treat with your men?" a man demanded from beneath an askew whig. "What of us then?"

Edward Teach surveyed the hostages coldly, a wicked gleam in his eye. "Let's just hope that doesn't happen – for all your sakes."

Samuel Wragg stepped forward and made a proposition. "Let me go ashore with your men. That way I can attest to the good condition of the rest of your hostages, and insure the safety of your officers. The council and governor would not dare jail them with me to speak for them and the rest of us here aboard your ship. You may even keep my son aboard to guarantee my return."

"Oh, may I, really?" Blackbeard asked. "Would yer lordship grant me that favor?" he turned and spit over the railing. "Tell ye what, Mr. Wragg. I'll give yer idea a try, but it won't be you going ashore. Yer just a bit too slick a sea snake fer my tastes. Besides, I know just how big a catch you are, Mr. Wragg. So you'll be stayin' aboard. Never let it be said Edward Teach separated a boy from his dear ol' dad. No, I'll be pickin' someone else to go ashore with our demands."

Teach cast his gaze over the group of prisoners before resting them on one man in the middle of the pack. "You. You'll do. Come up here and tell me your name."

The man reluctantly made his way forward until he stood in front of the pirate captain. "My name is Marks," he said.

"Very good, Mr. Marks. You be on your best behavior, now, when you and my boys get into Charleston." Blackbeard stepped forward until he was looming over the smaller man. "We don't want any unfortunate accidents or misunderstandings to cause any untimely incarcerations or anything. I realize that some of the good people ashore might be a bit high strung over our little visit. It'll be your job to remind them of their kinfolk stayin' aboard as my guests. Remind them that any inhospitality on their part might force me to stop bein' such a genial host. You've got two days to be back with the medicine."

The delegation from the pirate ship climbed down into a small boat and began pulling for Charleston harbor. Blackbeard and his hostages stood on deck watching until they disappeared in the hazy sunshine to the west. Then the hostages were herded back into the ship's holds to await their fate.

When the sun slipped low on the horizon on the second day, Teach stormed out on deck in an ill humor that had his crew scurrying to get out of his way. "Bring me Wragg!" he shouted. Moments later the Charleston council member stood before the pirate, flushed from the speed at which he'd been hustled up from the hold.

"So ye think I'm a man to be trifled with, is that it?" Blackbeard's question was even more sinister for the soft voice he used to ask it. His face was close to that of Samuel Wragg, and it was all the prisoner could do to contain himself under the assault of the pirate's fetid breath. "It's been two days, matey. Still no sign of my shipmates and the medicines. I'm afraid things are about to go badly for you!"

Wragg forced himself to speak up in spite of the fear for his son that suddenly gripped his heart. "Please, captain, let's not be hasty! The time limit has yet to expire, close though it may be. And any number of things could account for the delay. There could have been a mishap with the boat either going or coming. Or perhaps your men decided to linger a bit for their own amusement. Charleston is, after all, a city with a wealth of pleasures for men who've been long at sea."

"Maybe. Just maybe. It wouldn't be the first time those scurvy dogs were waylaid by grog and a shapely ankle," Teach mused, one calloused hand absently stroking his beard. "Alright Mr. Wragg. You've bought yerself another sunrise. But mark me, mate. If the boat hasn't returned by this time tomorrow, ye'll not see another."

Twenty-four hours later, many of the hostages were beginning to make peace with their Makers. On the quarterdeck Blackbeard alternated dark mutterings with loud outbursts of profanity. Still the boat did not come.

"You'd better pray that boat shows," Teach declared to the hostages gathered on the main deck. "If it doesn't, you'll not live two hours more."

"Deck there!" came a sudden cry from the *Queen Anne's Revenge* forecastle. All heads swiveled to see the lookout pointing towards Charleston harbor. "A boat coming fine off the starboard bow!"

Teach ran to the taffrail and snapped open his glass. The long missing boat was coming, for sure, but the men pulling at the oars were not familiar to the pirate.

Edward Teach was a fearsome sight for those who felt his wrath off the Carolina coasts.

Teach immediately suspected a trick by the people of Charleston. Yet one man in the bow was waving a red cloak Blackbeard had given to one of his men as a signal that all was well. He checked his temper and allowed the boat alongside. His rage began to grow afresh when he saw none of the men in the boat were his, and that the medicines he'd demanded were missing, too.

"Please, sir," stammered the envoy from town who had been waving the red cloak, "grant me leave to explain. Your men suffered a mishap on the way to town. They said a rogue wave capsized their boat, and it was all they could do to make it to a close by island. After no one had found them for a day or so, they finally had to lash together some flotsam and try swimming in to Charleston. They didn't make it that far, but they did manage to beach themselves at a village not far away.

From there they made their way into town with your demands. Knowing that the deadline would soon pass, they sent us to explain their tardiness."

Blackbeard nodded for the man to continue.

"If it please you sir, we are at this very moment trying to assemble the medicines you seek. However not all of the potions are readily available. It is taking time to find suitable substitutes. The friends, relatives and neighbors of the good people you hold ask that you forgo harming any of them until such time as the ransom can be paid."

Teach considered, and then came to a decision. The hostages would live two days longer. But at the end of that time, the boat still had not returned. Blackbeard fell into a wicked rage.

"Damn all fine lords and ladies for the blackguards they are!" he stormed. "Three times I've extended their deadline, and three times they've abused my generosity. Well, I'll not do it again. If I have to I'll sail into Charleston harbor and use broadsides to bring all their fine houses down around their ears!" He whipped around to point an accusing finger at Samuel Wragg. "And if it comes to that, fine sir, you'll all be swinging from the yardarms when I do."

Wragg stepped forward with his palms in front of him in a placating manner. "Captain Teach, I beseech you. Let us weigh anchor and stand in towards the bar. That way we'll be in a position to see the boat at the first opportunity. I trust fully in the good will of our friends ashore, but if there *is* perfidy, then we'll stand with you and cheer as you reduce them to rubble!" Around him fearful heads nodded in agreement. As annoying as the delays were for the pirates, for the hostages they were sheer agony.

So it came to pass that the good citizens of Charleston came to share in some portion of the terror the shipboard hostages suffered under as eight sets of pirate sails were spotted ranging in close to the harbor. The dark holes of gun ports gapped like dead eyes holding only the promise of death, pain and misery. On the waterfront startled onlookers raised a hue and cry, and men scrambled to grab guns and powder horns and report to militia rally points. Women and children ran helter skelter through the streets, terrified that pirate cannon would begin barking their deadly challenge at any moment. It was with a collective sigh of relief that the boat was seen pulling towards Blackbeard's flotilla with the medicine chest aboard.

Once back aboard the *Queen Anne's Revenge*, the truth of the numerous delays became known, when it was revealed that while the hostage, Mr. Marks, was trying to get the medicines demanded by Teach as ransom, the pirates who had been sent along made their way to the nearest taverns. When Marks went looking for them, they had wandered off and couldn't be found. Once the medicines arrived, Blackbeard released his prisoners and made his way back to sea, sailing for North Carolina.

North Carolina in the early eighteenth century was a poor cousin to its southern neighbor. Lack of settlement, a devastating war with the Tuscarora, apathy on the part of the Lords Proprietors, and a tricky coastline that made marine commerce difficult left North Carolinians with a much reduced standard of living compared to people who lived in Charleston. Governor Charles Eden presided over the colony at the town of Bath, in the Albemarle region. While he had the authority of the King, he did not have the crown's resources, and England was a long way away. As a result, North Carolina, especially at Bath, was pretty much at the mercy of Teach and his crews, who used the town as a base of operations. It was to Bath that Teach was destined, but first he decided to thin out the number of hands looking for a share of the plunder.

Blackbeard sailed his ships to Topsail Inlet, off modern Beaufort, North Carolina, on the pretense of cleaning his hull and making repairs. As he entered the inlet, Teach intentionally ran his ship aground and signaled for the larger of the two sloops in his small flotilla to come and help get him off. Israel Hands, commanding the sloop, ran the ship hard aground and so both ships were lost. Blackbeard and his handpicked crew boarded the smaller of the sloops and sailed for Bath, leaving seventeen other pirate sailors to die on a deserted island. Days later, pirate captain Stede Bonnet rescued the stranded men. Bonnet had since regained control of his ship and was in search of Blackbeard in an attempt to exact a little revenge, but he was always a day late in the chase.

Teach and his cohorts sailed into Bath and immediately went ashore to take advantage of a pardon offered by the king for any pirates who would come ashore and renounce the pirate life. Blackbeard recognized a get out of jail free offer when he saw it, and contented himself with life ashore for a time after swearing to Governor Eden that his pirating days were over.

It was a vacation the people of Bath were anxious to see end. At Bath, Teach was a force unchecked, doing pretty much as he pleased. He made it clear to Eden and the townspeople that any attempt to capture him would result in his crews pummeling the town with cannon fire from the pirate ship moored in the harbor. Blackbeard went from plantation to plantation, helping himself to not just material goods like food and spirits, but according to some accounts, to the women of the houses, too. He even took a wife, one of as many as fourteen he had all at the same time in different places. The girl was a young teen from one of the better Bath families. One story says that after Teach enjoyed their honeymoon bed, he turned the girl over to his crewmen for a turn.

Teach was a canny rogue, buying the reluctant cooperation of some Bath town officials with bribes taken from the loot captured in his pirate raids. One such recipient was Tobias Knight, Governor Eden's secretary. By June of 1718 Teach was once again plying the seas in search of booty, and came upon two French ships off Bermuda. One was empty, but the second ship carried a rich cargo of sugar and cocoa. Blackbeard herded the crew of the second ship aboard the empty ship, then placed a prize crew aboard the laden vessel and made for Bath. Once ashore Teach demanded that Governor Eden convene a prize court. In testimony before the court the pirate claimed to have found the ship adrift with not a soul aboard her. With no evidence to the contrary, Eden was forced to declare the ship a derelict and award Teach ownership. Knight stored his and the governor's share of the plunder from the French ship, amounting to roughly sixty hogsheads of sugar, in a warehouse on the waterfront. Soon after, Teach sailed the ship upriver and burned her to the waterline to prevent anyone from coming into the harbor and recognizing her. For months the people of Bath, including the colony's governor, suffered the abuses of Teach and his men. Sooner or later it had to come home to roost.

Elsewhere in the colonies, North Carolina's neighbors to the north and south were outraged at the shelter afforded the pirate. Merchants were losing money from the cargoes Teach was taking, and Governor Charles Eden's inability or unwillingness to bring him to heel was unbearable. It was a sentiment that was echoed by planters and merchants in Bath, too. Representatives of the merchants and planters in the Albemarle who suffered most directly from Blackbeard's presence sent a delegation to see Virginia Governor Alexander Spotswood via an overland route to seek help. If North Carolina was not able or willing to protect their interests, then maybe Virginia, who also suffered loses to the pirates, would.

Spotswood heard the petition and readily agreed that something had to be done. In the James River, two British warships lay at anchor, and the governor summoned their captains for a consultation. The captains of the *HMS Pearl* and *HMS Lime* devised a plan in which Governor Spotswood would hire two shallow draft sloops that would be crewed by seamen from the heavier navy ships. Renting smaller ships was necessary because the shallow inlets around Ocracoke, where Teach was reported to be, would not allow the *Pearl* and *Lime* to undergo the chase themselves. Lieutenant Robert Maynard, of the *HMS Pearl*, would assume overall command of the expedition to finally bring the notorious Blackbeard to heel. To provide legal grounds for what amounted to a raid on the territory of a sister colony, Governor Spotswood issued a proclamation offering a bounty for the capture or killing of Edward Teach, a.k.a. Blackbeard, and his crew. On the morning of November 17, 1718, Maynard and his small command hoisted anchor and sailed from Hampton on the tide.

By November 20, Maynard's sloops had arrived off Ocracoke. Above the low dunes, lookouts could spy the topmasts of Teach's ship. In the inlet, safe for the moment with the dangerous Ocracoke shoals between himself and the newcomers, Blackbeard made his preparations. Spotswood's bounty and the departure of Maynard's two ships for Carolina waters was not news to the pirate. Fishermen of the Albemarle saw Maynard's expedition pass, and some say the secretary to North Carolina's Governor Eden, Tobias Knight, sent a message to Teach warning him to be on his guard. Whether out of arrogance or disbelief, Teach did little to safeguard himself and his ship. Claiming to have forty men aboard, in reality there was only twenty-five on Teach's ship. Despite being woefully undermanned, Blackbeard chose to spend the night before facing the British ships drinking with the master of a local sloop.

Sunrise saw the three ships separated by a spit of land and shallow waters that no captain would take his ship into haphazardly for fear of shoals. Lt. Maynard ordered the ship's boat lowered and sent ahead of the sloops to sound out the channel. Barely making way, the sloops followed under just enough canvas to make steerage. In time, the unarmed British ships came within range of Blackbeard's long guns. Though Teach only had twenty-five men, the deficit didn't seem like much of an advantage to Maynard and his crew as they ducked the grape shot and canister being sent their way by the pirates. Sailors scampered up the rigging to return fire with muskets and pistols. From the stern the crimson flag with the blue and white Cross of St. George unfurled in the quickening morning breeze, and any subterfuge was gone. Blackbeard now knew without doubt he faced King's ships.

Blackbeard knew he stood a better chance if he was under way. With maneuvering room, his cannon could chop the British sloops to pieces while staying out of range of the small arms wielded by Maynard's crews. Grabbing an axe, he split the anchor cable with one mighty blow. Blackbeard's sloop began making way under a small spread of canvas. Light-handed as he was, there was barely enough men to work the guns and the ship at the same time. Each time the pirates peered over the taffrail Maynard was still there, inching ever closer as his men added oars to supplement sail power in the chase. Trying to sail and fight with an undermanned company, the pirates did neither well. It wasn't long before the sloop lurched to a halt as she ran aground. A stalemate ensued as the British sloops, drawing more water than Teach's ship, prowled menacingly in deeper water.

"All hands lighten ship!" Maynard shouted. Officers began directing ordinary seamen to toss overboard any and everything that added an extra ounce to the ship's weight. Ballast stones, anchors, water barrels – everything went in an effort to buy the precious inches at the waterline that would allow the British to close with their prey. After what seemed an eternity, Maynard stood in for the pirate ship.

"Damn ye for villains! Who are you?" Blackbeard demanded as the ships drew near. "Who sent ye?"

"You may see by our colors we are no pirates," Maynard replied, his saber pointing to the flag at the stern.

"Well come over with yer boat and let's parley," Blackbeard urged.

"I cannot spare my boat at the moment," Maynard shouted back over the din of small arms fire, "but I shall come aboard you as soon as I can with my sloop."

Blackbeard took a long pull from a jug on the quarterdeck, then spit overboard in the direction of the British. "Damnation seize my soul if I give you quarter, or take any from you!"

"And damn my soul if I ask it," Maynard answered. "Nor shall I grant it. Your day of reckoning is at hand, Teach. I shall be with you directly."

Meanwhile, the rising tide finally put water under the pirate ship's keel and Blackbeard floated free of the shoal just as Maynard's sloops came along side. Teach saw the low waist of Maynard's ship and gleefully ordered his starboard batteries loaded with a deadly mix of shot, broken glass and nails. When the guns fired, the devastation aboard the British sloops was horrific. Maynard's ship suffered twenty killed or wounded in the broadside, while the second British sloop added another nine victims to the butcher's bill. But still the British Tars kept to their oars, their officers urging them on in the face of the pirate cannon fire. If they quit, it was a certainty that Blackbeard would escape once again.

To fire the broadside the pirates had to move men from working the ship to manning the guns, so after the cannons went off, the recoil and lack of steady hands on the rudder caused Blackbeard's sloop to fall off a couple of points until the starboard guns were facing the beach. This took them out of action and allowed the British to close the gap. But only one of them was able to take advantage of the situation, as the sloop *Ranger* was badly damaged in the broadside and forced to fall astern of the pirates to make repairs before rejoining the fight. Maynard, however, was willing and able to close with Teach.

"All hands get down below the waist!" Maynard ordered as they closed the distance to Blackbeard, fearing the toll another pirate broadside would exact on his already depleted crew. "Helmsman, you stay on the quarterdeck with me to man the wheel - but make yourself a small target. There's hot work still ahead, and I'll be needing a steady man to guide us to the job!"

In the hold, Maynard's men readied pikes and sabers, pistols and belaying pins, knotting together at rally points and waiting for the crunch that would tell them the two ships had come together and they could finally go toe to toe with their pirate foe. From below deck level, men could hear the shriek of grape shot and muskets tearing the air, and they cast worried looks at their brave lieutenant on the quarterdeck. Despite the hailstorm of death crackling all around him, Maynard coolly stayed at his post beside the helm, determined to bring his sloop alongside the pirate vessel even as grenades sailed onto his deck from pirates in the rigging of the enemy ship. Finally the British sloop drew abreast of the pirates. Grappling hooks sailed out and the two ships were made fast.

As the British came alongside, Blackbeard saw only Maynard and the helmsman standing upright. The decks were strewn with the dead and wounded from the earlier broadside, and Teach took it to mean that the British were fatally undermanned. Never one to let opportunity pass him by, Blackbeard ordered his men to board the British sloop.

"At 'em boys!" he yelled. "Let's jump on board and cut them to pieces!"

Fourteen men followed the pirate captain across to Maynard's ship, its decks covered in smoke from the exploded grenades. Maynard heard a great yell, and through the haze saw the dark forms coming aboard his bloodied command from the bow. In the lead, a great hulking brute lurched forward with bandoliers crossing his chest and pistols in each hand, the shaggy mane of his beard and hair alight with quick matches tied into his locks. The lieutenant gave the order for his own concealed men to charge the deck.

Pistols rang out from both Blackbeard and Maynard as the two traded the first shots. Blackbeard's went wide of the mark, but Maynard's struck home. Nevertheless, Edward Teach barely flinched as his great torso absorbed the missile. Tossing the spent firearms aside, the two commanders drew their swords and came together with a bone-jarring clash of steel. Maynard struggled to parry the pirate's

Maynard sailed back to Virginia with Blackbeard's head on his bowsprit as proof of the pirate's demise.

thrust at close quarters, his nostrils filling with the sulfur stench of the burning punks in Blackbeard's hair. With a great push the lieutenant managed to deflect the blow and immediately raised his arm to ward off the follow up. Blackbeard's sword came down with a mighty crash that cleaved Maynard's blade just above the hilt. The pirate captain cast a cruel sneer at the weaponless officer and stepped forward to deliver the kill stroke.

Maynard's mind was paralyzed in that instant, a moment that seemed to stretch into days. There was Blackbeard looming over him. And now there he was bringing his right arm across his body, preparing to deliver a backhanded stroke that would surely chop Maynard's head from his neck. Maynard scrambled to cock a pistol, but his fingers felt thick as sausages. In slow motion Maynard finally managed to cock the pistol and pull the trigger, sending another half-inch ball into Blackbeard's chest. Still he came on. In the pirate's eyes Maynard saw a glee and emptiness that told the true nature of the evil in the man. Then the arm holding the sword began to swing forward – and suddenly stopped.

The lieutenant and Blackbeard both had become so caught up in their own fight that they forgot about the larger action going on around them. Fortunately for Maynard, one of his men had kept a weather eye on his commanding officer. As Teach began to deliver the deathblow to Maynard, the British sailor had lunged forward with his own sword, striking the pirate in the side of the neck. Blackbeard gave a grunt and checked his swing. Maynard seized the moment to regain his balance.

Fourteen pirates grappled with thirteen British seamen on decks awash in blood and gore. Blackbeard raged and bellowed each time he took a wound that would have been the end of a lesser man, but still he fought. Blades slashed the air to slice soft flesh and lead shot erupted from pistol muzzles to be buried deep in enemy bodies. Maynard was in the thick of it all, and time after time he saw the pirate captain take another wound. The British officer wondered if Blackbeard would ever die or if he was the devil incarnate people

Some Members of Blackbeard's Crew and their Fates:

John Rose Archer – served aboard *Queen Anne's Revenge* and later tried making an honest living as a fisherman. It didn't take, and Archer returned to piracy.

James Blake – Hanged in Williamsburg, Virginia in 1718 after Maynard defeated Blackbeard at Ocracoke.

Joseph Brooks, Sr. – Killed on November 22, 1718, in battle with Lt. Maynard's crew.

Joseph Brooks, Jr. – Taken to Williamsburg by Lt. Maynard and hanged in 1718.

Caesar – A black pirate who Blackbeard trusted as much or more than anyone else he knew. It was Caesar's job to blow up the ship if Maynard's crew got the upper hand. Two other pirates stopped him, and he was taken to Williamsburg and hanged.

John Carnes – Hanged at Williamsburg.

Joseph Curtice – Killed in the Ocracoke fight with Maynard.

Stephen Daniel – Hanged at Williamsburg in 1718.

Thomas Gates – Hanged at Williamsburg in 1718.

Garrat Gibbens – Was bosun aboard Teach's sloop, the *Adventure*. Died fighting Lt. Maynard at Ocracoke Inlet.

John Gills – Hanged at Williamsburg in 1718.

Richard Greensail – Hanged at Williamsburg in 1718.

John Husk – Killed at Ocracoke in 1718 during the Maynard fight.

Nathaniel Jackson – Killed at Ocracoke in the November 22, 1718 fight with Maynard's crew.

John Martin – Hanged at Williamsburg in 1718.

Thomas Miller – Blackbeard's quartermaster. Killed in action against Maynard's crew at Ocracoke.

Philip Morton – A gunner killed at Ocracoke in action against Maynard.

Joseph Phillips – Hanged at Williamsburg in 1718.

James Robbins – Hanged at Williamsburg in 1718.

Owen Roberts – Blackbeard's ship's carpenter. He was killed in the Maynard fight.

claimed him to be. At last, as he grabbed for another pistol from the last brace in his bandolier, Teach's eyes seemed to lose focus. He fell to his knees and looked up at Maynard one last time, and then fell face-first to the deck. The pirate Blackbeard was dead.

Before the battle ended, eight more pirates would give up the ghost, preferring to go down fighting rather than endure the slow death of prison and the hangman's noose. It was a fate that would be suffered by their fellows who jumped overboard and begged for quarter. Maynard ordered Blackbeard's head severed from his body and hung from the British sloop's bowsprit, a trophy to attest to the pirate's demise. The rest of Teach's body was thrown overboard, and legend has it that it swam around the ship three times before sinking into the murky depths of Ocracoke Inlet.

Back in Virginia, thirteen of the fifteen prisoners Maynard returned to face trial were hanged. Israel Hands survived the fight and its aftermath by having the good fortune to be ashore when Maynard's ships came for the pirates. Captured after the battle, Hands was condemned to die as well, but before the sentence could be carried out, a ship arrived bearing news of another amnesty for pirates. Hands took advantage of it and escaped the fate he deserved. He ended his life begging for his supper on the streets of London.

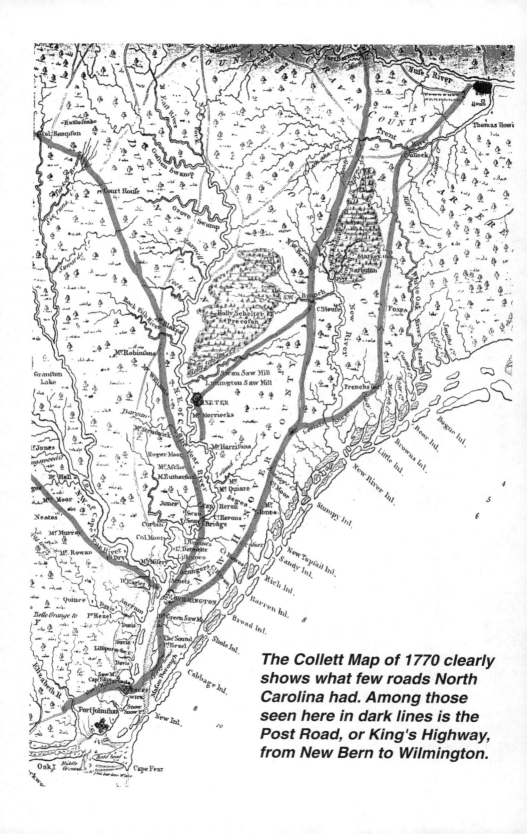

The Collett Map of 1770 clearly shows what few roads North Carolina had. Among those seen here in dark lines is the Post Road, or King's Highway, from New Bern to Wilmington.

You Can't Get There From Here: Travel In Colonial North Carolina

By Jack E. Fryar, Jr.

Interstate highways. High-span bridges. Commuter airplanes. The Intracoastal Waterway. If you were trying to get from one place to another in the American colonies in the eighteenth century, none of these things existed to make the journey easier. Getting around in coastal North Carolina was often a major undertaking, made more difficult by a combination of geography, poverty, and lack of industry.

Coastal North Carolina in the 1700's was a place of thick forests and swamps intersected by streams, creeks and rivers that made moving around tough for most people. There were just a few roads, and most of those were a far cry from the smooth, asphalt ribbons the state has today. North Carolina has been known as "The Good Roads State" for the miles of roads reaching into its every corner, from the coast to the mountains. In the grand scheme of the state's history, that is still a fairly recent moniker. When the first Europeans set foot on the white sands of the Outer Banks, there was nothing that passed for a roadway except the occasional animal path or Indian trail.

The first explorations followed those trails and waterways, with whites venturing into the bays and sounds along the coast, and taking first looks at the Carolina interior via Indian trading paths and game trails. John Lawson was among the first explorers to make an extensive survey of Carolina country, when he embarked on a more than five hundred mile walking expedition that he eventually chronicled in a book that spurred on further settlement by Europeans. Still, due to the fact that North Carolina's coastal geography has a dearth of good ports, newcomers tended to gravitate to either the Cape Fear or Albemarle regions. Settlers putting down roots along the central coast at places like New Bern and Beaufort were especially isolated, as the only practical way of reaching their northern and southern neighbors was by sea.

The lack of roads was a handicap that would play a big part in the development of the   colony. That was especially true of Baron Christopher Von Graffenreid's settlement at New Bern on the Trent and Neuse Rivers during the Tuscarora War in the early 1700's. When the violent uprising by King Hancock's tribe fell on unsuspecting settlers in 1711, calls for help immediately went out from the besieged Swiss colonists. While South Carolina answered the call readily enough, the task of getting the relief columns to New Bern was complicated immensely by the fact that there were no roads they could use to get there. Roadways in the colonies as a whole would develop slowly and be mostly local in nature, connecting plantations and inland settlements with major cities like Charleston, S.C., and seldom ranging more than thirty miles into the interior. Through the mid-1700's it was the ocean that would carry people and cargoes to and from North Carolina ports.

The one road network that did exist in most communities along the coast was the Post Road. Getting mail in the colonial era was not a regular affair. In most places, riders would wait until enough mail had accumulated before either placing it aboard a ship headed in the direction of the intended receiver, or saddling up a horse to follow what were essentially barely marked game trails running north or south along the Carolina coast between Norfolk and Charleston. To facilitate communication between his English possessions in America, King Charles II had instructed his governors in the New World to create the New England trail that would become known as the Boston Post Road as early as 1664. That road would be linked to other such postal roads along the coast and become the King's Highway by 1750. When the weather was good, it could accommodate wagon and stage traffic moving between Charleston and New England, but it was still an arduous journey and required as many as thirteen weeks to travel from one end to the other. Despite being something far less than a modern interstate, the King's Highway was indispensable to American patriots when war broke out with Great Britain during the American Revolution. Without it, the colonies would have found it difficult, if not impossible, to communicate with each other and coordinate troop movements. It was the only option open to patriots, as the British navy controlled the sea lanes. During the war many Americans began referring to it as the Boston Post Road once again, after the Declaration of Independence severed our ties with kings.

The King's Highway followed much the same course as Highway 17 does today, between New Bern and Wilmington and then south into Brunswick County and South Carolina. Travelers using it did so in anything but comfort. Stagecoaches of the day had no springs in their suspensions, and seats seldom had backs, much less cushions. The horses and oxen pulling these uncomfortable stages and wagons

Ferries have played necessary roles in coastal North Carolina transportation since the colonial days.

photo courtesy New Hanover County Library

were tired and often past their prime, and the roads themselves were rutted, bolder-strewn, and dotted with tree stumps. The paving surface in North Carolina, where it existed, consisted of rough-sawn pine planks. Most times it was just a sandy path, the air around it infested with sand gnats, mosquitoes and flies during the warm months. It's no wonder most people who could afford it opted for sea travel instead. But the great majority of people didn't have pockets deep enough to pay for much travel, and most of them lived their whole lives within thirty miles of the place they were born.

Branching off from the King's Highway were other routes that led into the interior. The King's Highway itself ran from north to south, passing through and below Wilmington, to William Dry's ferry at The Haulover (modern Sugar Loaf, in Carolina Beach State Park), to Brunswick Town and then south to Georgetown, S.C. But along the way other thoroughfares led into the interior and other destinations. One such road followed closer to the coast, paralleling King's Highway through Snead's Ferry and north to New Bern. Another road began at Exeter, the failed township on the Northeast Cape Fear River just below Holly Shelter, and ran northeast before joining up with the King's Highway near the Onslow County Courthouse, then on into New Bern.

One exception to the rule that roads of the colonial period were slipshod affairs bearing little resemblance to even the worst modern roadway was the Great Duplin Road. It ran from Wilmington across Heron's Bridge and into Duplin County at the place where Interstate 40 crosses from New Hanover to modern Pender County today. Janet Schaw, the young tourist from Scotland who visited North Carolina just prior to the outbreak of the Revolutionary War, recalled in her journal that the road compared favorably with the Perth of Tay in Scotland, one of the great roads of Europe. According to her, the road was wide enough to "march fifty men abreast," and ran all the way to Duplin Courthouse, near modern Warsaw.

A significant feature of the Great Duplin Road, which was also called simply "the Big Road," was Heron's Bridge. In a time where private individuals obtained concessions from the government to construct bridges, most spans were hardly worthy of the name. A concession holder would build the bridge, then charge a toll to cross it based on the number of people and type of conveyance making the crossing. Benjamin Heron received such a concession from the legislature in the mid-1700's. He built his bridge near where modern Interstate 40 crosses into Pender County across the Northeast Cape Fear River. Heron's Bridge was unique in the colonies because it was one of only two drawbridges in America at the time of the American Revolution. Spanning the river for a distance of more than four hundred feet, it was the scene of several clashes between Lillington's militia and the British redcoats of Major James Craig, who occupied Wilmington for most of 1781. Craig's mission was to ferry supplies up the river to Cross Creek, where they would be picked up by General Cornwallis, who was campaigning up through the Carolina interior. Craig tried several times to reduce the choke point on his resupply route created by Lillington's men at Heron's Bridge, but was never successful. The British managed to burn part of the bridge, but local patriots still held their ground on the Pender County side of the river. Craig was never able to get around that choke point, and after the battle of Guilford Courthouse, Cornwallis was dismayed to find no supplies at Cross Creek. That forced him to march to the coast. He stayed in Wilmington for two weeks before marching north to Virginia, hoping to link up with other British forces in the Chesapeake area. When he did, Washington's Continentals and the French fleet bottled the British up at Yorktown and forced their surrender. That might never have happened had Craig been successful in getting Cornwallis' much needed supplies past Heron's Bridge and on to Cross Creek.

At the place where the Cape Fear River splits off to become the Northeast and Northwest branches, another road terminated at what some call Point Peter, but which most people of the colonial period called Negro Head Point Road. Meandering southeast from Cross Creek (modern Fayetteville) to Wilmington, the road ran roughly parallel to the Northwest Cape Fear. It was the route used by Donald MacDonald's loyalist Highlander army in their march to the coast to fulfill their part of Royal Governor Josiah Martin's scheme to retake North Carolina for the British crown. It passed through swampy lowland near modern Currie, N.C. and across Moores Creek. It was there that the first patriot victory of the Revolutionary War was won in 1776, when militia under Alexander Lillington and Richard Caswell routed the Scots. The battle lasted all of fifteen minutes, but it kept the British out of the south for another four years. The road takes its name from the holding pens at its Wilmington terminus, where slaves being bought and sold at the markets there were kept segregated from the free blacks and slaves of the coastal port town. One story says that a slave revolt in the 1700's resulted in the heads of the instigators being lopped off and displayed there on spikes to discourage similar ideas in the slaves confined there.

Not even the rudimentary road system of the colonial period could have existed without the numerous ferries that provided a means of fording the many streams, creeks and rivers of coastal North Carolina. In the Wilmington area, William Dry obtained a permit to operate one of the first ferries on the Cape Fear at the Haulover, from Sugar Loaf to Brunswick. He also was granted a concession to operate a ferry at the foot of Market Street in Wilmington, which carried people and cargo from the town on the east bank of the Cape Fear to the causeway he and Benjamin Smith built on Eagles Island, connecting New Hanover with Brunswick County. Ferries played a part in the cat and mouse game between MacDonald's Highlanders and Whig militia during the Moores Creek Campaign, when the Scots were able to steal a march on the patriots by refloating a ferry sunken by the militia and use it to cross a creek that brought them that much closer to reaching Wilmington. Still, the slow growth of ferries in the colony inhibited travel for decades. By 1700, only one documented ferry was operating in the Albemarle, despite North Carolina's having more miles of inland waterways than any other colony.

Farther south, along the central coast, ferries had become fairly numerous by the 1720's, with one established at Bath's Core Creek and at New Bern. Dry's ferry at the Haulover forded the Cape Fear and completed the King's Highway through the colony. Nevertheless, service was hit or miss, with operators often absent or boats too few or in bad repair. The government tried to force ferry owners to be more diligent, but with only varying degrees of success. Often the vessels used as ferries were inadequate to the task, unable to operate in anything except the best weather and water conditions. One traveler wrote of the ferry at Snead's Ferry as being "the most ordinary Bawble of a Boat (which) did not float above two or three inches above the surface of the Water." Colonial Postal Inspector Hugh Finlay confirmed the poor quality of the north coast ferries, describing adverse winds that made passage across the Albemarle Sound "impassable for days," in boats that "are not very good." By the 1760's ferry service along the coast was readily available, even though the service still tended to be somewhat spotty. Their importance grew as settlers sought less difficult ways to reach the distant courts and militia musters.

With water the preferred means of travel during the colonial period, every town, plantation and home along the rivers and creeks had a dock or wharf of some sort. Planters in the southeastern interior would harvest and bundle their crops of rice and naval stores, load them aboard great rafts, and float them downriver to the markets at Wilmington. These cargoes were often left in the charge of slaves, who became masters of the Carolina waterways. This knowledge of the water would come in handy a century later, when enslaved watermen traveling to and from coastal markets smuggled escaped slaves out to waiting Union warships.

The range of vessels plying North Carolina's waters was great. In the Cape Fear, ships, boats, canoes and perriaguers were the craft seen most frequently. The ships ranged from two-masted schooners to single-mast sloops, both weighing less than fifty tons and crewed by four or so men. To transship naval stores, bigger vessels were required. Brigantines filled this role, weighing in at 100 tons and manned by a crew of seven. Snows were next up the pecking order, weighing in at around 150 tons, with two large masts and a smaller third mast at deck level flying a tri-sail. At the other end of the spectrum, cypress canoes – sometimes capable of carrying from 30 to 100 barrels of goods - were regular sights on the rivers and creeks. These large canoes were known as perriaguers, and were made by hollowing out a cypress log, splitting it down the middle, inserting planking for a wider deck, and then sealing the whole thing up again to make it water tight. Timber rafts and scows were also plentiful.

It took many years for North Carolina to earn its nickname as The Good Roads State, with countless miles of asphalt crisscrossing the landscape and reaching into every nook and cranny of its one hundred counties. But the waters that now are primarily sources of recreation for today's Tar Heels were once the ribbons that connected us to each other and the rest of the world, at a time when an animal path was considered a road for colonial settlers.

*If you had the courage, blockade running could make you rich
- or kill you.*

Threading The Needle:
Running the Union Blockade

By Jack E. Fryar, Jr.

The sleek steamer split the water like a knife as it sped on towards the gauntlet set to catch it off the coast of southeastern North Carolina. Federal warships lay like the jaws of a bear trap in three ranks that cordoned off the two entrances to the most important port left to the South. Wilmington, guarded by the hulking Fort Fisher and its sister installations on the river at Smith Island (Bald Head), Smithville (Southport), Fort Caswell (Oak Island) and Fort Anderson (Brunswick), had quickly become the lifeline of the Confederacy, without which Robert E. Lee readily admitted he could not keep his army in the field.

The night was moonless and the sea rolling with slight swells. There is no light to be seen aboard the blockade runner. Even the hatches providing precious ventilation for the Black Gang in the engine room were shuttered by thick canvas covers, making the Stygian darkness below decks a smoldering hell for the firemen and engineers. Lookouts on the bow gazed through salt spray to spot the silhouettes of Yankee blockaders, looming just a shade darker than the surrounding night's blackness. At the ship's wheel stood three men: the helmsman, Captain Reed, the ship's master, and James William "Jim Billy" Craig, the pilot who would lead the *Lynx* through the treacherous shoals off New Inlet at the aptly-named Cape Fear. Their feet were spread shoulder width apart, anchoring each of them to the deck as the ship rose and fell in the gentle Atlantic rollers.

"Soon there is added to the incessant noise of wind and waves the ominous roar of the breakers as the surf complains to the shore, and the deep-sea lead gives warning of shoaling water," fellow blockade runner James Sprunt later described, from Craig's recalling of the *Lynx's* run. "'Half speed,' is muttered through the

The Florida, *a former blockade runner captured and converted to a Union warship, was typical of the vessels that took on the Yankee cordon.*

speaking tube; a hurried parley; a recognized landfall – for Reed is a fine navigator – and 'Are you ready to take her, Pilot?' 'Ready, sir,' comes from Jim Billy in the darkness. Then he whispers orders through the tube: 'Slow down'; as there looms ahead the first of the dread monsters of destruction. 'Starboard,' 'Steady,' and the little ship glides past like a phantom, unseen as yet. Then 'Port,' 'Port,' 'Hard a-port' in quick succession, as she almost touches the second cruiser. She is now in the thick of the blockading squadron; and suddenly, out of the darkness and close aboard, comes the hoarse hail, 'Heave to, or I'll sink you,' followed by a blinding glare of rockets and the roar of heavy guns. The devoted little Confederate is now naked to her enemies, as the glare of rockets and Drummond lights from many men-of-war illuminate the chase. Under a pitiless hail of shot and shell from every quarter, she bounds full speed ahead, every joint and rivet straining, while Jim Billy dodges her in and out through a maze of smoke and flame and bursting shells. The range of Fort Fisher's guns is yet a mile away. Will she make it? Onward speeds the little ship, for neither Reed nor Jim Billy has a thought of surrender. A shell explodes above them, smashing the wheelhouse; another shell tears away the starboard paddle-box; and as she flies like lightning past the nearest cruiser, a sudden roar from Colonel Lamb's artillery warns her pursuers that they have reached their limitations; and in a few minutes the gallant little ship crosses the bar and anchors under the Confederate guns. The Captain and his trusty pilot shake hands and go below, 'to take the oath,' as Reed described it – for the strain must be relaxed by sleep or stimulation. 'A close shave, Jim,' was all the Captain said. 'It was, sir, for a fact,' was the equally laconic answer."

Surprising as it may seem, there probably were a lot of southerners and British speculators who could have kissed Abraham Lincoln when he ordered a blockade of southern ports at the beginning of the Civil War. With the stroke of a pen on the order, he created a new industry that would make many men rich, produce dashing heroes, and make sleepy coastal hamlets into boomtowns from Hampton Roads to the Gulf Coast. Wilmington was one such town, and because of its unique geography it would become the pre-eminent port of the Confederacy, and the last and toughest nut for Union forces to crack in their struggle to isolate the South from the rest of the world.

The agrarian South went into the war with its Northern neighbors knowing that the fight had to be a short one, because they simply did not have the industrial base to go toe to toe with the Yankees in a drawn out conflict. When it became obvious that the contest would be measured in years rather than weeks or months, Jefferson Davis' government had to look outside the North American continent for the things they would need not just to fight the war, but also for the things needed to simply survive from day to day. Davis' government found the answer they needed in Europe, where merchants and speculators saw a chance to rake in serious profits by supplying the Confederacy. It was definitely a seller's market. Everyone knew the South was fighting for its very survival and could get the things they needed nowhere else.

James Sprunt

Union war planners knew the South would have to buy what they needed to fight, too. As a result, closing Southern ports became a priority, though at first its implementation was poor and haphazard. That was because when the war started, the United States Navy was still relatively small, old and slow. Many of its best ships were on station overseas, far away from where they were needed along the South's Atlantic and Gulf Coasts. The territory encompassed by the eleven Confederate states had a combined coastline of over three thousand miles, in North Carolina's case much of it consisting of shallow coves and bays that would be beyond the reach of most Union warships and their heavy drafts. The coast at Wilmington was especially hard to bottle up, having many inlets leading to the mainland and two huge access points to the Cape Fear River. Once a blockade runner made it into the river they were safe, as not even the best Union gun could hurl a shell far enough to cross the Federal Point peninsula and hit targets steaming leisurely towards Wilmington. Still, President Lincoln's order meant they had to try.

The sun rose blazing and hot on the July morning in 1861 when the *U.S.S. Daylight* took up a lonely single-ship patrol off the Cape Fear, in a blatantly futile attempt to stop contraband from reaching Southern armies through the port at Wilmington. Part of the reason for the single ship patrol was that Yankee strategists knew just by looking at a map that Wilmington's port would be extremely difficult to close. That being the case, they decided to direct their still meager resources at ports that could be reduced with a lot less effort.

Three things made Wilmington such a formidable target for the Union. One, there were two entrances to the river for blockade runners to choose from. The oldest was at Old Inlet, between Smithville and Smith Island (modern Southport and Bald Head Island). It was guarded by auxiliary batteries at Fort Holmes on Bald Head and Forts Caswell and Campbell on Oak Island. The other inlet was just south of Federal Point, under the guns of the rapidly growing Fort Fisher, whose great sea coast guns could range out as much as five miles against any Union blockaders. New Inlet had been created by a hurricane in the 1760's. It was fairly narrow and shallow, with enough water to float the sleek little blockade runners, but not the heavier U.S. Navy ships pursuing them. The second thing was Frying Pan Shoals, a ship-killing obstacle that ran from off the southern tip of Bald Head Island southeast for more than forty miles into the Atlantic, right between the two inlets. A blockading ship on one side of the shoals could never make it to the other side in time to assist in stopping a fast blockade runner making for New or Old Inlets. That meant that though the straight-line distance between the Cape Fear's two entrances was a matter of only a few miles on a map, the actual distance a ship would have to travel to go from one side of the shoals to the other was much greater. That, in turn, meant that to effectively close off both entrances, double the number of ships would have to be used. In 1861 the U.S. Navy simply didn't have enough keels in the water to do that. The third element in the Confederacy's favor was Wilmington itself. Situated more than twenty miles upriver, it was well out of reach of even the biggest Union naval guns. The city could not be reduced by naval bombardment like Charleston, S.C., to the south. To take Wilmington meant putting troops on the ground, and that meant taking Fort Fisher and control of the Cape Fear River. It was something that the Yankees could not do at that early stage of the war.

So Wilmington became a favorite port for blockade runners willing to risk death or imprisonment for the handsome profits to be earned by bringing illicit supplies of arms, food, medicines and mercantile goods to the South. It turned North Carolina's largest city into an even bigger boomtown, with a mixture of locals, speculators, soldiers, railroad men, slaves and sailors crowding the streets. Sometimes those streets ran red when lawlessness and alcohol combined in rough men who settled disagreements with guns and knives. Soldiers and dock workers, sailors and dandies all often resorted to violence to make their point, and the loser was left lying in the street, his hands clutching at a mortal wound. Wilmington husbands and fathers kept their women folk inside and away from the dangerous gazes and hands of the newcomers to their city, and more than one household kept loaded shotguns and pistols close at hand – just in case.

For Robert E. Lee, the city was his main source of food and supplies. As such, railroads ran directly from Wilmington to Petersburg and Richmond. Once a cargo was off loaded from a blockade runner, it was quickly put aboard rail cars and shipped to Virginia, where it was so desperately needed. The empty blockade runners would then fill their holds with bales of cotton that would be carried back to Nassau or Bermuda, and then transshipped to Europe for resale. From January 1, 1863 to October 31, 1864, Wilmington's export trade earned investors over sixty-five million dollars. Imports, those finished products so desperately sought by the South, amounted to a bit less due to the difficulty of breaching the blockade by the later stages of the war.

photo courtesy N.C. Maritime Museum at Southport

Sometimes blockade runners like the **Modern Greece** *(above) would beach themselves in an attempt to salvage their cargo for the South.*

It was a profitable business that made men rich. A pound of cotton shipped from Charleston sold for five cents, but sold in England for fifty-five cents. Ten dollars worth of quinine purchased in Nassau sold in Charleston for between four hundred and six hundred dollars. The incredible sums of money to be made, plus the adventure of the enterprise, brought many Englishmen into the blockade running business. The U.S. Consul at Liverpool, England wrote to his superiors in Washington that, "Nine tenths of all vessels now engaged in the business (blockade running) were fitted out in England by Englishmen and with English capital, and are now owned by Englishmen." In fact, many of the ships that ran the blockade were known as Clyde steamers, after the river in Scotland where so many of them were built.

By 1864 the blockade was tightening. In North Carolina, Union forces under Ambrose Burnside had successfully occupied the northern portion of the coast from New Bern to the Virginia border. That meant that the U.S. Navy could concentrate its forces around the half of the coast near the Cape Fear. Admiral

David Porter constructed a blockade plan that relied on three concentric rings off the Cape Fear coast. The innermost ring was made up of shallow draft lighters and gunboats capable of pursuing blockade runners into the very mouth of the river and over the shoals that kept out bigger ships (but even these small craft were wary of the big guns of Fort Fisher). The middle ring was made up of warships that could lend fire support to the small, fast ships of the inner ring and interdict incoming and outgoing blockade runners on their own. The outer ring, called the Cruiser Line because it was made up of the navy's biggest deep water ships, patrolled the Gulf Stream some twelve miles out, acting as a safety net for blockade runners that slipped past the first two lines on the way out of Wilmington, and looking for inbound runners coming from the West Indies.

Still, the blockade was never sewn up tight, not while Fort Fisher and its sister installations hovered like guardian angels at the entrances to the Cape Fear. Enough of the little blockade runners managed to thread the needle of Porter's blockade to make it worth a daring captain's while to run the risk. Approximately 130 runners were lost to the blockade due to wreck, capture or destruction by U.S. Navy guns. Nevertheless, that was a ratio Jefferson Davis' government could live with. "About one in every four steamers is captured by the enemy," said a Confederate War Office clerk. "We can afford that."

Afford it they could. In just one month, from October 26, 1864 to December 6, 1864 – just two weeks before the first Union attempt to reduce Fort Fisher – the Confederate Secretary of the Treasury reported that blockade runners at Wilmington had brought in "3,632,000 pounds of meat, 1,507,000 pounds of lead, 1,933,000 pounds of saltpeter, 456,000 pairs of shoes, 316,000 blankets, 542,000 pounds of coffee, 69,000 rifles, 97 packages of revolvers, 2,639 packages of medicines, 43 cannon, with very large quantities of other articles." With the money to be made, not just high rollers were getting in on the act, either. Accounts say that pretty much everyone with a boat, raft or three logs they could lash together were attempting to smuggle in contraband. Even James Sprunt and a couple of buddies tried their hands, loading a small row boat with a bale of cotton and sneaking up the coast to the Cape Fear from Lockwood's Folly. The teenage boys were caught and threw their bale of cotton overboard in the attempt to get away from the pursuing federals.

At Smithville, the sixty or seventy river pilots there who could guide a ship through the treacherous maze of shoals and shifting Cape Fear riverbed suddenly became very wealthy men, as well. They and the crews of the blockade runners profited handsomely from the illicit trade. Just one trip from Nassau to the Cape Fear would earn a blockade running Captain 1000 pounds sterling, the Pilot 750, the Chief Engineer 500, the Chief Officer 250, the Second and Third Officers 150, and the crew and firemen 50 apiece. Half the money was paid up front, the rest when the trip was successfully completed. After as little as six months of running the blockade, many captains could afford to retire on their earnings. In fact, the British navy found itself having difficulty with its Jack Tars deserting to crew on blockade runners because of the wealth of money to be had.

Of course, the riches only followed if the journey was a successful one. While ship owners, captains and crews pocketed huge sums when things went right, when things went wrong the result was a total loss. When a ship was captured or sunk, the investors had no recourse but to write it off and start all over again. For blockade runner crews, capture usually meant a long hitch in a Union prison. Even if the ship managed to evade capture, there was still the risk of being maimed or killed in the hail of gunfire each blockade runner endured when discovered. For the Union, catching a blockade runner was a way to feather the crew's own bed. Captured

Spy Rose O'Neal Greenhow (left) and Captain Charles Hobart-Hampden (right)

steamers and their cargoes were sold as prizes, with many of the ships being converted into U.S. Navy hulls that were turned right around and put back into service catching their former cohorts. Sailors aboard a lucky Union ship could expect to see fifteen percent of the prize shares set aside for the captain, another twenty percent for the other officers, thirty percent for petty officers, and thirty-five percent for the rest of the crew. During the war the U.S. Treasury enriched its sailors by some $10,000,000 from the proceeds of captured blockade runner prizes.

The cat and mouse game played by both sides forced both the Union navy and the blockade runners to be creative in their efforts to beat each other. Among the many ploys used by inventive blockade runners was one that came as a direct result of the U.S. Navy's pressing captured steamers into service as blockaders. When a blockade runner approached the cordon of Union ships in the night, they would often hoist the Stars and Stripes from the stern and join the blockade line, impersonating a U.S. Navy ship. In as much as they looked just like captured ships that were now part of Admiral Porter's blockading fleet, the ruse often worked.

Blockade runners walked a fine line that had serious consequences if they deviated from it. A runner could try to evade capture and, if caught, be considered just a smuggler. But if even the slightest resistance was offered, then the ship and crew were considered pirates, subject to summary execution if the navy chose to take punishment to the extreme. Evading capture was something high on every blockade runner's list of priorities. At best, if caught they could look forward to an extended stay in a federal prison. At worst, they could lose their very lives. Then there was the question of protecting their investment. To try and salvage at least part of the profit, steamers being chased by federal forces would intentionally beach themselves to avoid capture. On the beach, runners were sent to the nearest Confederate military authority making them aware of the blockade runner's predicament. More than once, Col. William Lamb dispatched his flying batteries of Whitworth cannon from Fort Fisher to cover the unloading of a beached blockade runner, being menaced by shells fired from frustrated Yankee chasers not far offshore.

For the adventurous, it was a glorious life. Captain Hobart-Hampden, a British blockade runner who ferried Confederate spy Rose O'Neal Greenhow back to North

photo courtesy U.S. Coast Guard

Price's Creek Lighthouse, near Southport, was one of twelve range lights that guided successful blockade runners up the Cape Fear River to Wilmington.

Carolina from Europe, had a reputation as one of the most daring. He reveled in the risks of the run, and the money earned was in many respects a secondary motivation.

"Indeed, putting on one side the sordid motives which I dare say to a certain extent actuated us," he wrote in his memoirs, "there was a thrilling and glorious excitement about the work...One was always either running away or being deliberately pitched into by the broadsides of the American cruisers, the slightest resistance to which would have constituted piracy; whereas capture without resistance merely entailed confiscation of cargo and vessel."

Ships like the *Modern Greece*, the *Lynx*, *General Beauregard*, *Condor* and *Kate* all braved the steel net of Union warships to toss the dice on a gamble that had a big pay off if successful, and equally big losses if not. But mercenary motives aside, the fast ships that plied the waters of the Atlantic between Bermuda, Nassau and Wilmington brought the raw materials the South needed to fight the war and see its people through the darkest days of America's bloodiest conflict. When General Alfred Terry's Union soldiers accepted the surrender of Fort Fisher at Battery Buchanan, overlooking the same New Inlet where so many blockade runners had found safe shelter, it spelled the end of Wilmington as a Confederate port. And the fall of Wilmington's port guaranteed the failure of the South's bid for independence.

Beaufort residents were startled to see Redcoats coming ashore in 1782, even though the Revolutionary War was all but over.

Redcoats On The Waterfront:
The British Invasion of Beaufort

By Jack E. Fryar, Jr.

This is absurdly easy," thought Captain Duncan McLean, commander of His Majesty's Ship *Peacock*, as he watched the pilot boat pull out from the Beaufort shore. The sun shone a bright yellow-orange as it sank towards the horizon. The air was warm, although the slight sea breeze countered that warmth with a chill reminding the British naval officer it was still only April of 1782. The fourth day of April, to be exact, and so far it was turning out to be a good one for those laboring under the Union Jack.

The three ships of McLean's flotilla were strung out in line behind him, all of them flying flags that would obscure their true nationality. As the *Peacock* approached the bar, McLean ordered the anchors dropped, just as any merchantman would while waiting for the harbor pilot to come aboard and guide him in. The waters could be tricky at Beaufort, what with Shackleford and Bordens Banks funneling the entrance to the harbor in between two sets of shoals. It had been roughly a year since General Cornwallis had been bottled up on Yorktown Peninsula and forced to surrender. Talks were going on in Paris at that very moment over a treaty which would bring an end to the war that the colonials had begun calling the Revolution, and which would make the thirteen colonies a nation in their own right. The thought of it stuck in McLean's craw. That thirteen upstart colonies could defeat the world's greatest military power and wrest independence from the very country that had spawned them in the first place gnawed at him like a terrier with a rat. The audacity of the colonials was mind-boggling. But as far as McLean knew, the treaty was not signed yet. Perhaps it was time for a little audacity of his own.

✳✳✳✳

On the Beaufort waterfront, Dedrich Gibble and the militia's Major Dennis watched the anchor lines give way aboard the lead ship of the three strange sails in the harbor. They were of a size and design to be either warships or fast merchantmen, and locals flooded the waterfront to man small boats, rowing out to greet them. Boarding the ships, they seemed to disappear. Minutes passed, and still no sign that those aboard were working to lower a boat with an emissary for shore.

"Can't make out who she is," said Dennis, squinting into the failing light at the lead ship. "Reckon there's trouble aboard?"

"'Dunno," said Gibble, himself a captain of the militia. "Maybe there's illness aboard and no one can come to shore. Or perhaps they just aren't familiar with the way things are done here."

"Not likely." Dennis muttered an oath under his breath. "That ship's got British lines to her, Dedrich, flag or no. I don't like the looks of this. No one's made a signal yet, and no one from town has been seen since they boarded her."

The worry on Dennis' face was legitimate. Even though Cornwallis had surrendered and peace talks were going on in France, the war between Great Britain and its American colonies was still very much alive. Still, operations in the Carolinas had scaled way back in the face of the impending peace. Thoughts were turning back to plowing fields and shipping merchant cargoes, even though both armies were still in the field. Only a year before the British under James H. Craig had still been occupying Wilmington, to the south.

Gibble caught the look on his friend's face. "D'ye think it's the lobsterbacks? Surely they have to know it's all but over for them here."

"All I know is that there's not but a handful of men in all of Carteret County to stand against 'em if it is," said Dennis. "Between levies for the Continentals and militia call outs, the men who are left here to defend Beaufort are pretty much either blind, deaf, or too long in tooth to be much threat to the redcoats."

"So what do ye want to do, raise the alarm?"

"For what?" Dennis asked. "They haven't done anything wrong, they just haven't done what you'd expect of a strange ship just arriving at port. We can't raise a stink and call out the troops just for that!"

"I'll go out with a flag and see what's what," Gibble decided. "You stay here. If I don't come back, you'll know something's amiss."

Dennis nodded his agreement with the plan. Twenty minutes later he watched his friend pulling steadily out to the first ship in the line of newcomers, a white flag of parley prominently displayed at the bow of Gibble's rowboat. He watched as Gibble tied off and clamored up the entryway to the main deck. It was the last he saw of him.

✳✳✳✳

Dedrich Gibble hauled himself aboard with one final heave and immediately felt his arms grasped by strong hands calloused with years of shipboard life and work. He raised his head to see a British marine level a bayoneted musket at him, his red coat hidden by a blue cape. Other men from the town who had rowed out to the ship earlier were held under guard where they sat, their hands on their heads, below sight level on deck. From the quarterdeck a man dressed in buff breeches and plain cotton shirt greeted him.

"Welcome aboard, sir. Permit me the pleasure of introducing myself. I am Captain Duncan McLean, master of this, His Majesty's Ship *Peacock*. And to whom do I have the pleasure of addressing?"

"Bloody hell," Gibble swore before turning to answer McLean. "My name's Gibble, and I live here in Beaufort. What are yer intentions here, sir?"

"Why, to deprive His Majesty's enemies of anything that might provide them with comfort and support, as well as strike at what rebel military forces might exist in your lovely little town. In short, this is a raid, Mr. Gibble!"

"There's nothing much to take here, sir," Gibble argued, trying to buy time for Dennis to realize something was wrong and raise the alarm. "Besides, the war's all but over. Surely you must know that."

"Yes, my dear colonial friend, I am aware of the negotiations between your government and mine. As repulsive as I find those talks to be, I will of course heed the promises of my government. But you see, that treaty does not yet exist. The war is still on, sir, and as an officer of the Royal Navy I am obliged to pursue it until that changes. As for what there might be to pillage, well, your neighbors have already spilled the beans, so to speak. We know about your warehouses of food and your salt works. I cannot wait to see the bounty of your fields! Now, could you kindly guide us into your fine little harbor? If you cooperate, it will go much better for your charming town, as I might not have to shell it."

Gibble reluctantly made his way up to the quarterdeck, where the *Peacock's* helmsman awaited his knowledge of local waters. He hoped Dennis was on top of things ashore.

The pounding on the door startled Colonel John Easton, who had just settled down for an after dinner pipe and a little reading. The sound of bullfrogs singing outside his window in Russell's Creek was a soothing harbinger of spring, and Easton was looking forward to sowing the fields of his plantation home once again, after nearly seven years of war worries. But the insistent beating upon his door could not be good news. He set his book aside and went to see who his late caller might be.

"It's the British, sir," Major Dennis said without preamble once the door was open. Three ships appeared at the bar this afternoon, and were joined a little later by a sloop and a smaller boat. They were flying false flags, so when everyone went out to meet them, they were all captured without a shot. Captain Gibble and I had our suspicions, so he went out under a flag of parley. They took him, too, and forced the pilots among the townsfolk to guide them into Beaufort harbor."

Easton was a resolute man, and it didn't take him long to switch from relaxation to command mode.

"Send out riders, warn the rest of the county that British raiders are here," he said to Dennis. Then he turned to the servant waiting on the porch. "Ezekiel, take a message to Harkers Island telling them what is going on. The militia on the island is to stay put. We'll need them to repel any redcoats who try to land there and take the naval stores warehouse. Before you do that, though, saddle my horse. I need to have a look at what our English visitors are up to. Dennis, what about the granary?"

"Taken care of, sir. I took the liberty of stationing a few men on the west end of town for the express purpose of protecting it."

"Good man. Well then, let's be about it!"

Easton reasoned that the most likely landing place for any incursion by the British would be via the east channel near Carrot Island. The most immediate trouble he faced was where to find the men he would need to repel any such landing. Most able-bodied men were already serving either in the militia or regular army someplace else. What was left didn't inspire the militia colonel with a lot of confidence. Still, a soldier makes due with what he has.

"Dennis, ride ahead and see what men are available to stand to. Have them meet me at the town fort." The two split up at the Beaufort town boundary, Dennis headed for the watering holes near the docks, and Easton to set up his command post at the small installation built to protect the town.

Major Dennis' heart sank when he threw back the door to the town pub and spied only five men slaking their thirst. Not only were they few in number, but they were also something a great deal less than perfect military specimens due to age or infirmity. Not to mention that they had also been quaffing ale for a considerable period, too.

"The British have anchored in the harbor, lads," Dennis declared to the tavern's patrons. "I need men to help fend them off until help can arrive. Who's with me?"

The startled drinkers exchanged a glance, and then one of them spoke up. "Well, sir, I reckon if'n ye think we can help, we'll stand with ye."

Dennis breathed an inner sigh of relief, then sent several of the men out to warn others. The rest he led to his home. Trampling down the stairs to his cellar, Dennis fumbled with the key ring that would open its door. As militia units came home and disbanded in the wake of Cornwallis' surrender, their arms and ammunition had been temporarily stored at Dennis' home when they mustered out of active service. He lit a lantern and began handing out muskets to the waiting volunteers. "Get these to the fort. The Colonel will need them if he finds more help."

Aboard the *Peacock*, McLean and his officers enjoyed a leisurely meal. From the townspeople taken hostage, the British knew there were precious few men to stop them from doing as they pleased in Beaufort. A local man with secret loyalist leanings had pointed out on a map where the strategic points of the town were. Sipping from a glass of claret in the officer's mess, McLean studied the plan of the town.

"I rather think the granary should be worth a visit," he observed. "Too, the naval stores on Harkers Island should fetch a nice purse."

"Let's not forget whatever valuables might be found among the homes," Major Stuart, the officer of *Peacock's* marines, interjected. "Some of the houses here are quite nice. They're bound to have prize-worthy materials in them."

"Very well, then. Let's ready an away party to see just what we might find in fair Beaufort, shall we?" McLean stood and pointed a finger at Stuart. "Send a detachment of your fellows ashore here, at Taylors Creek. From there we'll work street by street to the bridge on the town's western boundary. Let's be ready to go in a half hour, if you please, Major."

It was a sad thing, thought the sentry near the mouth of Taylors Creek, when a man his age had to be out at night all alone, looking for boatloads of enemies less than half his age. Sixty-five Aprils had past since he first came into this world. He thought he was at a time in his life where he had outlived most of the dangerous things. Not that he minded doing his part, of course. If he did, he wouldn't have volunteered to go with Major Dennis in the first place. He had marched against the Regulators back in '66, but even ten years ago he had been a much spryer man.

The least Dennis could have done was put someone with him who had decent eyesight. This last thought came as he squinted into the blackness where the water met the land, trying to identify the sounds coming from the darkness towards the harbor. The muffled sound was familiar to someone who had lived their whole life by the sea, as the sentry had. It was oars slicing into the water, the boat's oarlocks muffled for stealth.

"Who goes there?" the old sentry croaked. His throat was suddenly very dry.

"Ahoy the shore," came the hushed reply. "Don't shoot! We're coming to answer the call-out, men from up the coast a ways."

"Bugger me for a fool, will you?" The tension in the old man's voice went up a notch. "I reckon I know a British accent when I hears it!"

"No, you old goat, we're here to help defend the town!"

"Then you'd best do a better job of identifying yerselves!"

The voice from the water swore an oath, and the sentry heard the unmistakable sound of a musket hammer being cocked. He raised his own musket to his shoulder and braced for whatever came next.

It was the best he could do with the pitifully small number of men at his disposal. Col. Easton had placed a single man at intervals along the length of Beaufort's waterfront, eight men only to guard a waterfront that stretched for nearly a mile, from the Newport River to Taylors Creek. At best they could only act as tripwires, sounding the alarm and letting Easton know where the enemy was making their landing. At worst, they would be either caught unawares or overwhelmed, and their deaths would weigh heavily on the militia colonel's conscience. But it was all he could do.

Easton plodded down the beach with the four men he laughingly called his reserve, moving from sentry post to sentry post, keeping a weather eye out for boats approaching from the harbor. Not three hundred yards away sat the *Peacock* and her cohorts, lights shining on their decks, sitting as tranquil as if they were at anchor off Dover. Easton knew that looks could deceive, and that the apparent peacefulness could well be a ruse.

As they approached Taylors Creek, the colonel held up a hand. His men froze where they were, senses on high alert with the gesture from Easton. In the dark, they heard the old man placed there as a sentry shouting out a challenge to something on the water. The militiamen heard someone offshore say they were here to join in the defense of Beaufort, but something smelled fishy to their ears, just as it did to the grizzled veteran guarding the creek. The Colonel must have thought so as well, for he suddenly called for the old man to back away from the beach and join their ranks. Moments later, following their officer's lead, the men raised their muskets and fired a ragged volley in the direction of the voice on the water. Then the dance was on in earnest.

Stuart's marines immediately returned fire in a more coordinated volley, though still far more ragged than the officer would have liked. On the beach, Easton and his men hurriedly rammed powder and ball down smoking barrels and primed pans to ready a second shot. British balls buzzed angrily past their heads, urging them on to greater speed. This time Easton and his men took the time to be a bit more organized in their firing, and by the cry of pain from the boat full of redcoats, at least one of the rounds struck home. Stuart's men began pulling back out to deeper water, putting distance between themselves and Easton's determined band. Stuart's party came to rest at Carrot Island, a half mile distant.

By sunrise things had quieted down again. Easton's men kept up their patrols of the waterfront, and the British seemed content to wait. Then a shot was heard from the direction of Carrot Island, and the colonel rushed to the north end of town. They got there in time to see the sentry squeeze off one more shot before falling back, the round aimed at the British sailors and marines fording the creek. Col. Easton and his men let fly with a volley, which was quickly answered in kind by the British, who outnumbered the Beaufort men significantly. Easton began falling back, trying to execute an orderly withdrawal back to the town's battery.

At the fort, Easton found Major Dennis and three more willing, if unarmed, men. Moments later two more men darted into the fort with disturbing news.

"The lobsterbacks are clustering behind Cap'n Gibble's house, sir!"

Easton whipped open a spyglass to see the Gibble home and what might be going on there. Instead, he saw Captain Singletry strolling along the beach as if he didn't have a care in the world. The colonel snapped the glass shut when the British suddenly surrounded Singletry and took him prisoner. Shouts from the harbor drew Easton's attention, and he saw the captured boats of the townsmen taken prisoner the day before being filled with British sailors, pushing off from the *Peacock* and the other ships and pulling for shore. The raiders poured into every part of Beaufort, and Easton realized his position was now untenable. The town fort was a meager installation at best, and now was even more lacking as it was not provisioned for a long fight. He decided to cede the position to the enemy.

The militiamen grabbed what powder and ammunition they could and pulled back to the bridge on the western boundary of Beaufort. Here Easton at least hoped he could stop the British from mounting any expedition into the interior of Carteret County. It would also be a convenient rally point for the reinforcements he hoped would be coming from other militia units in the surrounding countryside. He set up a post to provide advance warning three quarters of a mile between the British and the bridge.

On the way, the militia captured two British Jack Tars loaded down with plunder from a nearby home. Prisoners were not something Easton wanted, as he didn't have the manpower to look after them and defend the town, too. So he was happily surprised when he got to the bridge and found twenty men under Colonel Ward waiting to join him.

Easton breathed a little easier when he set up his headquarters at the bridge. It was a natural choke point, the only way to leave Beaufort except by water. The west end of the bridge rested firmly on the land side of the county, making it easy for reinforcements and supplies to reach him. That food would come in handy, because even now refugees were filing out of the town, seeking shelter among Easton's militiamen.

Meanwhile the looting continued. Rampaging British sailors grabbed up anything they could find that might be worth a penny, up to and including the very clothing off some women's backs. The refugees all reported great indignities and losses at the hands of McLean's forces. Easton tried to be sympathetic, but he had more pressing issues on his mind, such as how to drive out the invaders. He delegated some of the more levelheaded among them to find food and places to sleep for the displaced Beaufort citizens.

McLean sank his teeth into a sweet potato and chewed delicately. "My word, this is quite remarkable!" He nodded to his cook to place the orange tuber on his plate. "I've heard tell of these, but you know it's the first time I've actually tasted one."

"Just one of the many items the good people of Beaufort have shared with us from their larders, albeit rather reluctantly," his lieutenant reported. "A rough tally shows this to be a most profitable trip, sir. The exceptions being, of course, the wound Major Stuart suffered to his hand in the action at Taylors Creek, and a marine who I fear has been mortally wounded in town. We also have lost two men taken as prisoners by the Americans."

"Yes, that is unfortunate. Just what are our American brothers up to now?"

"It seems they are reinforcing their position at the town bridge, sir. Skirmishers report that at least eight light cavalry arrived this morning and have begun reconnoitering our lines around town. Also, we believe it safe to assume other reinforcements will be coming in from other precincts around Beaufort."

"Hmm, shame, that," McLean mused. "Would've been nice to poke around the countryside a bit, see what mischief might be had there. Well, even without that, the Beaufort loot alone will make for a nice prize."

"What shall we do about our prisoners, sir?"

"Let's send a message to the colonials, Lieutenant. Arrange a prisoner exchange. See if we can get our boys back. Damned Americans eat too much, anyway!"

The wife of Beaufort's Colonel Thompson, away from home serving in the north with the Continental Army, gently wiped sweat from the brow of the wounded and dying British marine laid out on her couch. The boy wasn't more than eighteen, and would not live to see nineteen. The large hole in his chest from a militia musket ball was bubbling blood, a sure sign that the boy had suffered a lung wound. There was little Mrs. Thompson could do beyond offer him what solace she could out of Christian charity. Hopefully if the tables were turned, and her husband should find himself dying in a strange place, someone would do the same for him.

"Please, ma'am," the boy begged through lips tinged red with coughed blood, "make them bury me in uniform, standin' up to salute King George. I'm a Marine, ma'am. Let them know I did my duty."

Mrs. Thompson made shushing noises to quiet the boy. The boy was quite brave by most standards, she thought, but it was always a shame to see life cut short. Her thoughts were interrupted by a sergeant who handed her a note.

"Cap'n's regards, ma'am," he said. "He wants you should deliver this note to your fellows at the bridge. Be kind enough to wait for a reply, if ye please. Captain McLean wants to discuss a prisoner exchange."

Thompson took the note and rose, wiping her bloodstained hands on her apron.

"One other thing, ma'am," the sergeant said. He nodded at the boy whose eyes were beginning to glaze over in death. "I appreciates what ye did for the lad. It's a hard road to travel alone, dyin' is, but it's nice that he felt a gentle touch at the end."

Mrs. Thompson gave a last look at the dead marine, and then left for the bridge.

Easton's face flushed crimson as he read the note. "Fat lot of good it is to exchange prisoners *after* he's looted the town!"

He read the note aloud for Dennis and Ward. "It's written by William Bull. He's one of the hostages aboard the *Peacock*. It says this McLean fellow doesn't intend to destroy the town, and would we kindly not shoot at his men anymore! He only wants to exchange prisoners, he says."

"That's cheeky," Ward exclaimed. "He's already carted off half the town, and he expects us to just wave goodbye while he does it?"

"So what do we do?" asked Dennis.

Easton thought for a moment, then wrote a reply. "Tell the good Captain that we'll parley," he said to Mrs. Thompson, handing her the note. "Let's see just what he does have in mind."

Mrs. Thompson returned the note to the British, who in turn accepted the offer. At two o'clock the next day the two sides would meet.

"No, I rather think not," Major Stuart said as he held his bandaged hand to his chest. His response came to a note from Easton asking that Dedrich Gibble be released in exchange for Easton's sending two officers to meet at the town schoolhouse to negotiate further. "We'll be keeping Mr. Gibble and company. Furthermore, we demand the release of our deserters taken prisoner by the Americans."

"Deserters my foot," spat the Beaufort messenger. "The dogs were looting the town and taken as legitimate prisoners of war."

"Well, that's not how we see it. Tell your colonel that those are our terms."

To punctuate their position, the British fired a cannonball from one of the guns at the town fort, now manned by Major Stuart's men. It came screaming into Camp Town Bridge, the name given to Easton's position, and though it caused everyone to duck, no real harm was caused. But it made it clear to all concerned that the affair was far from over.

At the bridge, Easton was gratified to see more reinforcements rolling in. Among them, Major Mountflorence brought word that the British were working like busy bees to shuttle plunder from the town to their ships. The militia leader sent a squad to commandeer some boats and intercept the British boats if possible. As the dozen men ran to carry out the order, militia Captain Nixon arrived with thirty horsemen. At roughly the same time, a six-pounder ball fired from the fort slammed into a camp cauldron, scalding the cook.

"Whoa there, Ward!" Nixon exclaimed. "Looks like it's been hot here right enough."

"Not so bad, Nixon," the militia officer replied. "You just got here when the lobsterbacks gave us a little nudge to make sure we're awake. We're sure glad to see you boys. Any news?"

"The Brits tried to raid Harkers Island, but our lads beat 'em back. Looks like they were after the naval stores."

"Good for them," Easton said, coming up to greet the newcomers. "Maybe that'll give them pause long enough for us to mount a counterattack. The townspeople are eager to get back to their homes."

"Can we attack?" Ward asked.

Easton shrugged. "We could. I've enough men and guns now. But the hostages aboard the ships leave me shackled still. I can't do anything but negotiate while the British have them. I've been advised by the good Captain McLean, through notes from Gibble and Captain Bull, that it would go badly for them if we do anything rash. I maintain that these prisoners of ours are prisoners of war, not deserters. That Major Stuart of the marines finally allowed that the officers at the parley can make that decision."

Throughout the day shots were heard, and reports of looting and destruction came in. William Borden's plantation on the Newport River was in flames after a British raid, his storehouse and mill torched and slaves herded back to the British ships as plunder. At a man called Lewis' home near Lennox Point, redcoats were surprised by a party of militiamen who opened fire on the unsuspecting British. Several of the English were wounded, and three taken prisoner. Easton tried hard to keep it all pictured in his head, to stay abreast of the big picture as it developed. The British tried a major push during the day that was met by an equally determined force under the command of Colonel Ward. The redcoat attack was repulsed, but rather than pursuing the fleeing British, Ward led his men back to camp to prevent retaliation against the hostages aboard ship. When the men complained, Col. Easton backed him up, emphasizing the handicap of having to look to their neighbors' welfare while they were in British custody.

Mrs. Thompson was again in camp. Again she carried a message from McLean. The tone of the note was short and angry. The British captain wanted to know why he should not destroy the town. Beaufort's defenders could only relent. The guns of the *Peacock* and her sister ships could turn the town into so much kindling without ever landing a single man, and the few guns available to Easton could do little to stop it. The British had already burned the town's schoolhouse after the skirmish with Ward's men earlier. Easton agreed to the exchange.

Beaufort was deserted the next morning when Easton and his men went to keep their rendezvous with McLean. The British had pulled back to their ships during the night. At the charred remains of the school the Americans met their English counterparts and prisoners were exchanged. Later, as townspeople ventured back to their homes to assess the damage, Easton found the British had not complied fully with the exchange. There were still four hostages missing, plus the slaves from Borden's plantation and the pilots they would need to find their way back to open sea. At the fort, Easton found the guns spiked or otherwise disabled. Militiamen were able to get one of the guns back in working order by nightfall, but it was a weak response in the face of the firepower represented by the British ships.

By morning another gun was ready and Easton felt comfortable enough now to prod the British on their way. The ships were still anchored in Beaufort harbor, and the colonel felt it was time to let them know they had overstayed their welcome. A shot was fired at a sloop making preparations for sailing. The rude gesture was immediately answered by British guns that commenced shelling the town and damaging two homes.

Nine o'clock the next morning found the ships still at anchor like houseguests you just can't get rid of. Twelve hours later the British inexplicably set fire to one of the sloops loaded with captured naval stores. It burned like a Viking funeral pyre, lighting the whole of the waterfront and frightening townspeople with what it might mean for their safety and well-being.

Easton knew that fresh water is always at a premium aboard a ship, and rightly suspected that the British would want to reprovision themselves with potable water before leaving. The colonel dispatched a party of men under Captains Fulford and Foot to make sure the redcoats stayed thirsty. On Shackleford Banks, the move paid off. The militia met and engaged a landing party trying to get fresh water. Fulford and Foot managed to wound or kill several of the British, and destroyed their water casks, forcing the two small ships to withdraw back to the main British force in the harbor. When the enemy withdrew to a new position the next day, townsfolk were able to salvage a three-pound cannon from the wreck of the burned sloop and transport it to the town fort, where it was added to Easton's small but growing artillery train. On Sunday things were quiet, but Easton's men busied themselves preparing for the fight that might still be coming.

As preparations were being made, a lookout sighted a sail making for Beaufort harbor. The sloop was coming in under full sail as if oblivious to the enemy fleet anchored off Borden Banks. The militiamen hollered and fired guns in the air to warn off the unwary merchantman, but were too far off to be understood even if they had been spotted. When McLean opened *Peacock's* gun ports and ran out her starboard battery, the sloop struck her colors and docilely submitted to being taken. The capture dismayed the townsmen in the fort.

Still thirsty for water, the British tried again. If Shackleford Banks had proved inhospitable, perhaps Borden Banks might be more amenable. McLean sent a water party ashore on the banks the next day under the protection of some of Stuart's marines. Word of the move reached Easton, who sent troops to stop them. The appearance of the militiamen sent the British scurrying back for their boats, their casks still empty. But empty or not, McLean's force still controlled Beaufort, and that was a condition which Easton and his men could not let stand.

****

The plan was simple. Build large rafts, load them with tinder, put a match to it, and set the raft adrift to float on the current into the British ships. Easton's men labored out of sight of the British lookouts as they built their rafts behind buildings and fences near the waterfront. Low tide came just after dark, and in the gloaming the militia quietly carried their constructs down to the water. Pine knots were lit and the orange flames grew quickly when fed the turpentine covered lighter wood. From the fort Easton and his men watched the current grab the rafts and take them out into deeper water, closer and closer to where McLean's ships lay at anchor. Aboard the British warships, men could be seen scampering back and forth, some with long spars to fend off the threatening fire rafts. Others were hauling at capstans to raise anchors in a futile attempt to move the ships out of the way. At gun ports, crews tried to depress the muzzles of their cannons enough to possibly blow the rafts out of the water, but without success.

For the first time in days, Easton felt something that vaguely resembled hope flare in his chest. By the artificial light of the rafts, he could see the looks on the faces of the British sailors. Fire aboard a sailing ship, whose every inch was coated in flammable tar and pitch and whose very body was made of wood and canvas, was the most terrifying thing a sailor could face. The militia colonel imagined an almost palpable smell of fear in the air. He stood watching the tide do its work, and then the first touch of breeze caressed his cheek. It took him a moment to realize what it meant, but when he did his heart sank. The breeze was coming in from offshore. Moments ago the men around Easton had been jubilant in anticipation of the havoc the fire rafts would wreak. As the wind picked up and began to turn the first raft back towards shore, the cheers and taunts died down to dismayed silence. In what seemed like moments the rafts were burning themselves out on the Beaufort beach.

Now it was the British sailors' turn to cheer, and they did so with a gusto that was like a knife in the craw of Easton and his men. It seemed not even Nature would come to their aid. The crowd trod wearily back to their homes, hoping that the new day would bring better news.

Easton wiped the sleep from his bloodshot eyes on the morning of April 17, 1782, and rinsed the foul taste of smoke out of his mouth with a cup of water. Spitting the liquid into the fireplace, he pulled back the drape covering the window of the house he had slept in near the waterfront. At first glance he thought he must still be partially asleep. He rubbed his eyes and confirmed what his initial look had told him. The British ships were no longer in the Beaufort harbor. He could see their sails making for the bar. He hurried to the town battery and found his men already manning their weapons. The colonel ordered a shot fired as a parting sentiment, and McLean's gunners answered in kind.

At the bar a boat was put out carrying Dedrich Gibble and the other hostages from town, except the slaves taken from the Borden plantation. Once ashore, townspeople greeted the last of the Beaufort captives with hugs and cheers, Gibble delivered a final message from Captain McLean, advising that if there was any retaliation against the pilots for aiding the British, the fleet would return and pound Beaufort to splinters.

Easton gave the British ships once last look as they began to fade over the horizon on their way south to Charleston. He considered that things hadn't turned out too badly. True, the town had been looted and Borden had lost a number of valuable slaves. Also, Beaufort would need a new schoolhouse after the British had burned the old one. Nevertheless, given how woefully under strengthed he was, the local men hadn't done too badly. The damage was confined to Beaufort. Easton and his patched-together force had stopped the enemy from getting into Carteret County proper, and most important sites like the salt work and granary were still intact. Not a bad outcome at all, considering what might have happened, for one of the last battles of the American Revolution.

J. Lewis Warlick would have been a young man similar to this Confederate soldier when he was stationed in Wilmington.

"My Dearest Friend...":
A Long Distance Civil War Love Story

By Mike Lawing

When J. Lewis Warlick came to Wilmington in May of 1862, he was already a veteran of both the War Between the States and an unsteady courtship. His regiment, The First North Carolina Volunteers, had been at Bethel Church on Virginia's York Peninsula in June of 1861 when Union and Confederate forces engaged in battle for the first time. This first Confederate victory against a superior Union force seemed proof that a six month enlistment would be enough time to whip the Yankees and restore peace.

In November of 1861, Lewis mustered out of his regiment at the end of his six month enlistment, returned to Burke County, N.C. and the woman he called "My Sweetheart" and "My Dearest Friend." Her name was Cornelia McGimsey. Lewis and Cornelia had written to each other every week while he was in Yorktown and Bethel, and Lewis obviously anticipated a marriage when he returned home. His next correspondence was from Wilmington in May of 1862 and he was not married.

"...I have got down to the turpentine country and sand where the staple production is peanuts," Warlick wrote. " ...I have not joined any company yet...I wish you were here to advise me, but that wouldn't do for I adhered to your council last winter when I could have got a position and now am about to go in the service as a high private...If it was not for my darling sweetheart at home these troublesome times would pass more swiftly but my mind is always upon her and the time drags heavily." (*Lewis Warlick, Camp Davis near Wilmington, May 21ˢᵗ 1862.*)

Warlick's decision to reenlist was a major stumbling block in his relationship with Cornelia. Her attitude was, "You've done your part, now let someone else fight". Lewis felt otherwise, as he explained in his next letter.

"You say I ought to go home and hire a substitute, that I guess would be a hard job for men are so scarce at home I would not know where to get one that would be received in my place, and furthermore would not get one if I could from the fact that it shall not be thrown up to my relations in future years that you had an uncle, brother, or that your father or perhaps grandfather would not go into service when he was called on to assist his country in this great struggle for independence—was too cowardly, afraid of the Yankees..." *(Pvt. Lewis Warlick, Camp Davis near Wilmington, N.C. June 3, 1862.)*

Lewis enlisted in Company B, 11ᵗʰ Regiment N.C. Troops with two brothers and many friends and neighbors. The 11ᵗʰ Regiment was the successor regiment to the First N.C. Volunteers and was called "The Bethel Regiment" for the duration of the war. As the summer of 1862 wore on, Lewis and Cornelia established a steady correspondence and each of his letters carried some news of the Cape Fear Region.

"Last week the blockading squadron captured the steamer *Gordon* off Ft. Caswell from Bermuda bound for Wilmington...three of the squadron engaged the batteries at Fort Fisher. After firing over a hundred shots they withdrew..."*(June 3, 1862)*.

Lewis' appraisal of the Wilmington area beaches would have pleased any local chamber of commerce. "I was over on the beach a day or two ago and could plainly see six blockading steamers...after looking at them awhile I walked down the beach to Fort Fisher, and by the way it is the most beautiful beach I ever saw, the sand where the tide has receded is as hard almost as a floor which makes it first rate walking." In another part of the same letter, Lewis passed along a rumor. "...France has acknowledged the independence of the Confederate States; all of which is very good if true but I will not vouch for the certainty of it." *(Pvt. Lewis Warlick, Camp Wyatt near Ft. Fisher N.C. June 17, 1862.)*

"Our company left here last night at 10 for Masonboro sound eight miles distant to unload a schooner that run the blockade and is now safe in port," he continued in another letter. "...Two companies of our regiment have been for the last week unloading a valuable cargo near Fort Fisher, the vessel was the *Modern Greece* from England, in attempting to run in the port the blockaders cut her off and also got in her rear. The only chance for her to keep from falling as a prize into the hands of the Yankees was to beach her which was done in three fourths of a mile of Fort Fisher. The steamer is a total wreck and only about two thirds of the cargo (900 tons) was saved..." *(Pvt. Lewis Warlick, Wilmington N.C. July 5ᵗʰ 1862.)*

Eastern North Carolina is nothing like the area Lewis and Cornelia called home. Burke County has well defined peaks called Hawksbill, Table Rock, Short Off,

ınd Winding Stairs Knob which are a sharp contrast to sand, flat land and ocean.
As the war progressed, Lewis began to write of seeing his native hills again.

The major eastern theaters of war during the summer of 1862 were in Virginia ınd Maryland. As news of the Seven Days Campaign, Second Manassas, Harpers Ferry and Sharpsburg came into camps through dispatches and newspapers, the men in the 11th Regiment hoped for a chance to be sent north to share in the victories.

"It is not known how long we will stay here or where we will go when we leave, my opinion is that we will be ordered to Va. before long; there has been two regiments gone since we came up here...Gen. Beauregard and staff passed through two nights since and a week or two previous Gen. Price and staff also bound for Richmond, and by the papers I learn that a portion of their army is now on their way. It seems Richmond is to be held at all hazards; there will be one of the most bloody battles before long you ever heard of in modern times. I think the whipping we are going to give them there will be the means of effecting a peace." *(Pvt. Lewis Warlick, Wilmington, N.C. June 24, 1862.)* The Seven Days Campaign lasted from June 25 to July 1, 1862. All of the fighting was around Richmond and by the end of the campaign General George B.McClellan's threat to Richmond was in retreat.

The company Colonel kept the men busy drilling and preparing for a fight no matter where it came. Col. Collette Leventhorpe had been a Captain in the British Army before emigrating to Rutherford county N.C. to marry.   Leventhorpe was a Confederate by marriage but he was one of the best and most efficient Colonels in the country. While his men complained about unloading ships instead of fighting, the colonel drilled and marched his men around the Wilmington area every day. Leventhorpe had an English standard of perfection that was unknown in either the North or South. Eventually the 11th Regiment became the best drilled regiment in the state. Troops were needed in Wilmington because federal forces occupied most of northeastern N.C., including New Bern, Washington, Plymouth, Hatteras, and Fort Macon. An attack on Wilmington or the Wilmington and Weldon Rail Road was not just possible, but also likely. The men in the Eleventh may have thought their post was a backwater, but the state and the Confederacy considered the protection of Wilmington vital.

The most dangerous cargo to enter Wilmington during the summer of 1862 was the yellow fever epidemic. It all started simply.

"I suppose ere this you have heard of the arrival of the steamer 'Kate' from Nassau to this port with a valuable cargo of arms, ammunition etc. I was orderly for the General Court Martial and was in the third story of the Post Office, which is near the wharf, looked out of the window and saw her coming most beautifully up the river, went down stairs immediately and proceeded to the wharf and went on board to hear the news and to have it said that I was on board of a vessel that had been so fortunate as to get in by the blockading squadron without a single shot being fired; the previous day to her arrival she was chased by a Yankee cruiser six hours, but the swiftness of the *Kate* left her on the briny deep without a prize." (*Pvt. Lewis Warlick, Camp Lamb, Wilmington, N.C. Aug 17ᵗʰ 1862.*)

This simple announcement had unknown consequences. "I dislike for the yellow fever to be in Wilmington; on yesterday morning there were 50 new cases reported and five deaths the night previous. It has been there six weeks and the doctors did not ascertain that it was yellow fever until a few days since. It was brought in by the steamer *Kate*, one case was taken to the hospital and there it began to spread till it has gotten extensively circulated in the town; all business is closed and everything doing to prevent it from getting any wider hold in the streets. They are burning turpentine and rosin—the trains not allowed to come into the depot, they stop outside not far distant. I fear we will get it into the Regiment as there was a good many of the boys in town Saturday night. It is said to be very contagious and fatal. I wish we could get to go to Maryland." *(Cpl. Lewis Warlick, Camp Davis N.C. Sept. 16ᵗʰ 1862.)*

General Robert E. Lee crossed the Potomac into Maryland on September 5, 1862. The Battle of Sharpsburg on September 17, 1862 was not a good day for either the North or the South. 23,000 men were casualties on the 17ᵗʰ and at the end of the fighting and very little advantage had been gained by either army.

The 11ᵗʰ Regiment was ordered to Franklin Va. for defensive operations in the Blackwater River area in early October 1862. Whether or not the yellow fever epidemic played a part in the change is unclear. A change in the weather in November 1862 finally stopped the yellow fever. An estimated 650 people died during the epidemic and many residents were forced to evacuate the city. While the 11ᵗʰ Regiment was in Franklin, they had two small battles with Yankees outside the city.

Events between Goldsboro and Kinston caused the 11ᵗʰ Regiment to be recalled to North Carolina. Union General John B. Foster sent federal troops from New Bern toward Goldsboro and Kinston on December 11, 1862, as part of an overall plan to destroy the Wilmington and Weldon Railroad and possibly attack Wilmington.

"...we left Franklin on Sunday morning and before daylight, Monday we were at camp Campbell a few miles above Kinston. There we remained a few hours & then marched to White Hall Bridge on the Neuse River 18 miles from Kinston and 16 from this place. There we took a light shelling on Monday night. The next morning the enemy appeared on the opposite side of the river and began to fire, we returning the fire as briskly as possible with our small force having only Cos. B& H who were on picket and we held the enemy in check for two hours or more before the remaining part of the Regiment was ordered down. We finally repulsed them after seven hours of the severest fighting I ever experienced...Our Regiment did nearly all the fighting with the assistance of two pieces of artillery...Our Regiment had 40 or 50 killed and wounded, 2 in our company killed, Orderly Bristol and Walt Duckworth...A man from Co. I was severely wounded by my right side in the shoulder. I tell you it made me feel bad to see the poor fellow bleed the way he did. When Walter Duckworth was killed he fell over on Pink's leg and bled a considerable amount before he knew he was shot." *(Cpl. Lewis Warlick Goldsboro, N.C. December 17, 1862.)*

After Whitehall Bridge, Lewis was promoted to 3rd Sergeant and the 11th Regiment was placed in Brigadier General James Johnston Pettigrew's Brigade. A Department of North Carolina was created under Major General Daniel Harvey Hill and Pettigrew was placed under Hill's command. Other Regiments in Pettigrew's Brigade included the 26th, 44th, 47th and 52nd. Of these Regiments, Pettigrew considered the 11th to be his best because of experience and Col. Leventhorpe's training. Governor Zeb Vance had been the Colonel of the 26th before he moved into the Governor's Mansion, so the chief executive of the state had an interest in the Brigade.

Pettigrew bivouacked the entire brigade at Magnolia, N.C. in January of 1863. While in Magnolia, a soldier trying to desert was sentenced to be shot.

"Tomorrow our brigade (Pettigrew's) will be ordered out to witness the execution by shooting of a member of the 26th N.C. for desertion. I understand there has been about fifty desertions in that regiment, perhaps by shooting one now and then it will put a stop to their leaving...Tuesday morning: The Brigade was called out yesterday to witness the execution of private Wyatt of Co. B, 26th N.C.T but to the satisfaction of the assembly he was reprieved by the commanding general." *(Sgt. Lewis Warlick, Camp near Magnolia, Duplin Co. N.C., Sunday, Jan. 25th 1863.)*

Private Andrew Wyatt, 26th Reg. N.C. Troops from Wilkes County was killed July 1, 1863 at Gettysburg, "bravely doing his duty".

Lewis continued to write proposals of marriage but described little military activity during the winter of 1863. General D.H. Hill began a siege of Washington, N.C. March 30, 1863. The town was a Union stronghold under the command of General John Foster, the same General Foster who attacked Whitehall Bridge. During the next two weeks Pettigrew's brigade, in conjunction with two other brigades, drove off Union gunboats and repelled an attempt to reinforce the city. On April 15, 1863, several boats managed to get through the blockade on the Pamlico River with reinforcements and supplies. General Hill's decision to withdraw from the blockade was very unpopular with the common soldiers.

"We were all disappointed at leaving Washington in the hands of the enemy when we were confident that Washington would be ours with all its contents but not so...our battery at Fort Hill below the town could not successfully blockade the river..." *(Sgt. Lewis Warlick, Head Qtrs. Pettigrews Brigade, Camp near Hookerton, N.C., April 26th 1863.)*

Union General Joseph Hooker's Army of the Potomac moved south across the Rappahannock River in late April of 1863 and the Chancellorsville campaign began. On May 1st and 2nd, Pettigrew's brigade boarded trains in Kinston N.C. for Petersburg, Va. At this time, the brigade was transferred out of the Department of

N.C. The 11th Regiment played a crucial role in protecting Richmond from a Union cavalry attack while General Stonewall Jackson and General Robert E. Lee were defeating a much larger federal force at Chancellorsville. On June 1, 1863, the brigade was officially incorporated into the Army of Northern Virginia. Major General Henry "Harry" Heth was the Division commander. Lt. General Ambrose Powell Hill was the Corps commander. After waiting for over two years to take part in a major victory, Gettysburg was just 30 days away. All of Col. Leventhorp's training was called upon to survive the ordeal. Lewis was wounded and captured at Gettysburg, imprisoned at Davids Island, New York, then exchanged and hospitalized in Petersburg and Raleigh.

Lewis and Cornelia were finally married on February 17, 1864, less than a month before his return to duty as a Second Lieutenant. Lewis spent the last year of the war describing the Wilderness, Grant's tenacity, and the Petersburg siege as he saw them. Along the way, Lewis reported the deaths of four brothers who served in the same company with him during the last two years of the war. General Lee surrendered the Army of Northern Virginia on April 9, 1865 and Lewis Warlick surrendered in a hospital in Farmville, Virginia a few days later.

(Editor's Note: Lewis Warlick's letters are in The McGimsey Papers, The Southern Historical Collection, Wilson Library, The University of North Carolina-Chapel

Lewis Warlick was spared the fate of this Confederate soldier killed at Gettysburg, but he did suffer as a prisoner of war after being captured during that Pennsylvania fight.

Hill. Mike Lawing and his wife, Carolyn, are the editors of **My Dearest Friend, The Civil War Correspondence of Cornelia McGimsey and Lewis Warlick** *.)*

Need More History?

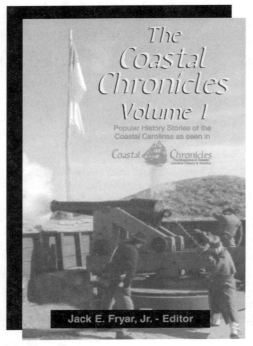

The
Coastal
Chronicles
Volume 1

Popular History Stories of the
Coastal Carolinas as seen in

Coastal Chronicles
The Magazine of Coastal
Carolina History & Tourism

Jack E. Fryar, Jr. - Editor

Pirates...
Patriots...
Redcoats...
Johnny Rebs...
Billy Yanks...
Yellow Death...
Stamp Resistance...
Stately Plantations...
A Lady Spy...
Spanish Raiders...
A Confederate Goliath...
Rice Fields & Rosin...

...plus much, much more! *The Coastal Chronicles Volume I* is a great gift idea for locals wanting to know more about the place they call home, for tourists fascinated by the over four centuries of colorful history stories we have to tell, or for teachers looking for something to supplement their local history lesson plans! Get your extra copies at your local bookstore, gift shop, museum or tourist attraction. Or, order directly from the publisher by sending your check or money order! *(Volume & educational discounts available - email to JEFPUBS1@aol.com for details.)*

"There is great history in these books."
- N.C. Governor Michael Easley
"...fascinating stories from the past of North Carolina's coastal region...an outstanding offering..."
- Our State *magazine*

Send a check or money order for $17.95 plus $3.50
shipping & handling to:
The Coastal Chronicles Vol. I
Dram Tree Books • 2801 Lyndon Ave. • Wilmington, NC 28405
(910) 845-2680

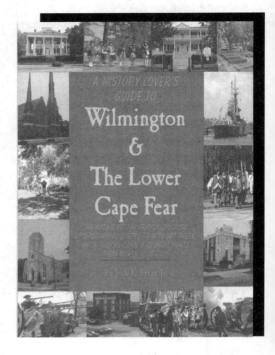

About Jack E. Fryar, Jr. ...

Jack E. Fryar, Jr. at St. Philip's Church at
Brunswick Town/Ft. Anderson State Historic Site.

Jack E. Fryar, Jr. is a life-long resident of southeastern North Carolina, having been born and raised in Wilmington. He has been a professional writer and publisher since 1994. In 2000, he founded Dram Tree Books, a small publishing house whose titles tell the story of coastal North Carolina's vivid and exciting history. Jack has been a professional sports announcer and a radio announcer, and founded The Writer's Roundtable writer's conference at the University of North Carolina at Wilmington. He is also the author of *The Coastal Chronicles Volume I* (Dram Tree Books, ISBN 0-9723240-0-3), and *A History Lover's Guide to Wilmington & The Lower Cape Fear* (Dram Tree Books, ISBN 0-9723240-1-1). The real reason he started his company is so that he can indulge his passion for North Carolina history by going to reenactments, historic sites, archives and libraries and take it all off his taxes.